THE
LITHUANIANS

THE LITHUANIANS

A Story of Love and Betrayal

AUDREY ADAMS HILL

authorHOUSE®

AuthorHouse™ LLC
1663 Liberty Drive
Bloomington, IN 47403
www.authorhouse.com
Phone: 1-800-839-8640

Published by AuthorHouse 11/09/2013

ISBN: 978-1-4918-0375-2 (sc)
ISBN: 978-1-4918-0376-9 (e)

Library of Congress Control Number: 2013913525

In loving memory, this book is dedicated to Janet Adella (Azcherovitch) Asbury, best friend, who inspired and supported me on this journey, one that really began in our 9th grade journalism class. And to Laurie and Jann whose great grandparents, Mikael and Agnes, immigrated from Lithuania a half century before they were born.

The Lithuanians is a story of two brothers, Mikael a Roman Catholic priest, and Erik an officer for the Third Reich, and the extraordinary journey to find each other after three decades. It is also a love story between the priest and Sophie a beautiful resistance fighter and Erik and Sara finding love on Half Way Island during the days of World War II, and his commitment to find Sara after the war ended.

PREFACE

Though based in part on historical events and actual locations this is a work of fiction. Except for certain recognizable historical characters, any similarity to persons living or dead is purely coincidental.

Any error or inaccuracies are the author's own.

TABLE OF CONTENTS

Prologue..xi
Chapter 1 1
Chapter 2 4
Chapter 3 6
Chapter 4 11
Chapter 5 14
Chapter 6 17
Chapter 7 20
Chapter 8 25
Chapter 9 27
Chapter 10 29
Chapter 11 30
Chapter 12 32
Chapter 13 44
Chapter 14 45
Chapter 15 49
Chapter 16 51
Chapter 17 57
Chapter 18 64
Chapter 19 75
Chapter 20 78
Chapter 21 80
Chapter 22 82
Chapter 23 84
Chapter 24 89
Chapter 25 90
Chapter 26 92
Chapter 27 96
Chapter 28 100
Chapter 29 101
Chapter 30 105
Chapter 31 107

Chapter 32 110
Chapter 33 116
Chapter 34 118
Chapter 35 120
Chapter 36 127
Chapter 37 131
Chapter 38 133
Chapter 39 136
Chapter 40 142
Chapter 41 146
Chapter 42 147
Chapter 43 150
Chapter 44 152
Chapter 45 158
Chapter 46 164
Chapter 47 168
Chapter 48 173
Chapter 49 179
Chapter 50 185
Chapter 51 191
Chapter 52 192
Chapter 53 197
Chapter 54 199
Chapter 55 201
Chapter 56 209
Chapter 57 212
Chapter 58 215
Chapter 59 227
Chapter 60 232
Chapter 61 238
Chapter 62 243
Chapter 63 249
Chapter 64 254
Chapter 65 258

PROLOGUE

November, 1915

The old priest shuffled across the floor. He had been summoned during the night to administer Extreme Unction, the last rites of the Roman Catholic Church. It was dawn, and the sunlight had begun to filter through the shutters. The priest had difficulty finding his way in the darkened room.

The young woman was barely alive. Father Kapocius wondered how the young woman had found her way to this place. He knew she was not of this parish as he would know her name.

He reached out to touch her hand. It was ice cold. He removed the old quilt from the foot of the bed and placed it gently over her. The priest would guess she was barely twenty years old. She lay in the shadow of death, but he would not leave her. He would stay with her until the end.

It would be a long day, he thought as he lowered himself into the over stuffed chair which had been arranged next to the wood stove. He would heat some soup a little later. At this point he was more tired than hungry.

The hours moved slowly and night followed the long day. Miraculously, the young woman clung to life. She was determined to prolong life for another hour, another day, as long as it would take for her beloved, Darius, to come to her.

Darius would not leave her alone in this strange place. Certainly he would join her soon. He would come to her and hold her, and she would not be afraid.

Night passed and dawn appeared once again. In the distance a rooster crowed, welcoming the new day. The young woman opened her eyes for a brief moment. The rooster crowed again. This time he crowed three times. Her time was drawing near. Darius would have to hurry!

The sun disappeared behind the horizon and once again the sky, a kaleidoscope of blues and pinks, turned into darkness. The priest lifted himself out of the chair and moved closer to the old stove. It was angled in the corner next to a box of firewood. He needed a small miracle about now. The room remained cold and damp so he stoked the fire. The embers turned a brilliant orange. That, he felt, was a promising sign, but he would add more wood and pray for that miracle.

The young woman who had been lying motionless for so long turned herself slowly toward the window. At first she thought she was in a dream; but no, her beloved Darius was finally here in the room with her. He was so handsome! She reached out to him, but he slipped farther away from her. She called his name, but he did not answer. He surely would not leave her now.

The priest watched as the woman raised her head from the pillows. He thought he saw a faint smile.

In the last few minutes of her life another figure appeared to her to bid her farewell. It was her mother! She was lighting the candles and praying over the Seder table. The two people she loved the very most had come to say goodbye. She could leave now. She closed her eyes and went peacefully forth on her final journey.

The old priest made arrangements for the young woman to be buried behind the church in the old cemetery. On her grave was a simple wood cross with a single date '12-01-18, Known Only To God'. It would be three decades before her twin sons, born two days before the angels came for her, would be reunited and find their mother here in her final resting place.,

The next morning Father Kapocius went to the grave and planted a dozen tulip bulbs. The flowers would bloom in the spring, pinks and white. The young woman would be pleased, he thought as he dropped the bulbs into the shallow holes he had dug with a trowel in front of her grave. He spent a few minutes praying before he returned to the church. Mass would begin in fifteen minutes.

CHAPTER 1

Vilnius, Lithuania, October, 1939

It was almost time to make the journey to Trakai. Mikael hung his cassock in the linen press, lingering a moment. He felt he was bidding goodbye to an old friend, hoping their separation would be brief. He crossed the room, removed the crucifix that hung over his bed, and placed it in his suitcase on top of the few possessions he would be bringing with him. His rosary beads, a gift from his pastor, Father Ricikas, he placed in his pocket.

Father Ricikas was the pastor of St. Casmir and yesterday he had summoned Mikael and Justas, who, like Mikael, had come here directly from the seminary, and requested that they join him after Mass. Mikael sensed that the old priest would be announcing something extremely important; however, nothing prepared him for the events that would follow.

Father Ricikas had suggested that the two priests meet in the parlor, and he soon joined them there. The old priest appeared exceptionally quiet, tired and weary, fatigue visibly lining his face.

He paced the floor as if garnering some extra strength, divine perhaps. He placed both hands inside the pockets of his cassock. Several minutes slowly passed before he began to speak.

"My sons, this is one of the most difficult tasks God has ever assigned to me. Mikael, Justas, I am the bearer of very sad news. As you, along with the rest of Lithuania, have become aware, Germany has invaded Poland. The Polish population has suffered great losses, the city of Warsaw is in ruins and people trying to escape are being gunned down by the German Luftwaffe. It is beyond comprehension. The Germans, as they did in the Great War, will eventually invade our country. Our country will be the next casualty. There will be no preventing it. Because of our proximity to Germany, it is inevitable. There will be an invasion of Lithuania in just a matter of time, I'm afraid. However, we have one small advantage that has been granted to us; and that is time, not a great deal of time, but a small window of opportunity to make some critical decisions."

He hesitated briefly and continued.

"Our Bishop has issued an order to send young priests and nuns to Trakai. It is certainly not a guarantee that his plan will have the results we are hoping for but there is little alternative for us, for our country, for our Church. Our future, if there is to be one, depends on planning our direction now, before time expires and it is too late. We must employ every means available for this endeavor now."

The young priests sat attentively listening not sure if they were grasping everything being presented to them, the seriousness of it.

The old priest continued.

"Tomorrow you will take the afternoon train to Trakai which will leave from the station at 2:20 p.m. The Bishop feels, and I agree, that there is no way to predict how much longer the trains can continue to operate so your departure should be as soon as possible.

Arrangements are complete. You will be greeted in Trakai by either Mrs. Massud or by a member of her family, and they will provide you with the details for your stay there. There will be other nuns, priests, students from the universities, possibly two hundred in all."

And as if Father Ricikas had read their minds, he asked them, "Do you understand the importance, the serious of the situation, my sons?"

Yes, they nodded, not saying a word. It would take Mikael some time to completely absorb what the priest had just relayed to them. He found it difficult to comprehend the full scope of it. Father Ricikas appeared even more fatigued but went on to finish, "Please be prepared to leave tomorrow."

Without a glance toward them he turned and left the room. The old priest was sixty-eight years old and had been pastor of St. Casmir for most of the century. Three years ago he had been hospitalized for several days after complaining of chest pains. After completion of tests, all returned negative, it was determined that he could return to his religious duties and the advice from his doctor was to avoid stress, to restrict strenuous exercise and to give up his two pack-a-day cigarette habit. The advice fell on deaf ears and the stubborn old man continued on pretty much the same with little or no change in his daily routine and seemed no better or worse than before the episode. He knew there would be little hope of giving up his cigarette habit; that there would be no way for him to quit, except of course if the Saints intervened. In fact, each time the subject of his health was discussed, he would shrug his shoulders, turn his eyes toward heaven, and assert that he had placed the matter of his health in Gods hands, assuming that He had the time. So in the months that followed, this subject was rarely mentioned.

Being in the garden would be a diversion from the unpleasant events of the morning so Father Ricikas decided to go outside and do his gardening, a pleasure he enjoyed daily, weather permitting. It was a task he had gladly assumed responsibility for since arriving here so many years ago, finding it a source of great relaxation. Today it would serve as a welcome distraction.

He removed the wire basket from its hook, headed down the hall and stepped through the doorway into the back yard. One of these days, he thought as the screen door slammed shut behind him, he would find a few minutes to mend the screen. He also promised to dust the grandfather clock he had just passed in the hallway. The old clock kept perfect time, dust or no dust.

Father Ricikas took pride in his garden. The firethorns leaned on the picket fence, their bright orange berries still in full clusters on this warm October afternoon. His beloved roses were grouped in three areas, clinging tenaciously to the stone walls. Their petals were faded but the leaves appeared as fresh and vibrant as ever.

The rest of the garden was devoted to his prize vegetables. There were a few winter squash still on their vines and the priest gathered them and placed them in the wire basket. He would offer a few to Mikael and Justas to take with them tomorrow.

The old priest knew tomorrow would be a difficult day and he dreaded its arrival.

Mikael glanced out the window and watched Father Ricikas for a few minutes before he returned to his room. He had come to love this dear and wise man and he knew he would truly miss him while he was in Trakai. Mikael couldn't have known that there would be no reunion, that the Einsatzgruppen had a different plan for him.

3

CHAPTER 2

T he next morning, Father Ricikas bade Mikael and Justas farewell. "Remember you are our future, the future of our church, our country. You must return safe and sound. So take care, pray to God to watch over you. I will miss you more than words allow and I will pray for you every single day. God willing, we will meet again."

But they would not meet again, not in this life anyway. No one could have predicted the horror the Germans would instill on this small Baltic nation. The Germans marched onto Lithuanian soil, their Einsatzgruppen along with them. In less then two years after the young priests were sent to Trakai, the Nazi's entered Vilnius, rounded up priests, nuns, students and the professors from the University and, at gunpoint, herded them like animals into the trucks that would take them on their final journey. The Church of St. Casmir was on their list. Father Ricikas, the gentle gardener, mentor, teacher of Christ, would die before this infamous firing squad, Hitler's solution to the enemies of the Third Reich. The Einsatzgruppen, after ordering their prisoners to dig their own graves, executed them.

In the last minutes, just before the bullets ripped open his skull, Father Ricikas did not pray or seek forgiveness for his sins. Instead he remembered the precious days he had spent as a young boy with his grandmother. Her hair, a sprinkle of gray close to the temples, was pulled back in a bun, a few hairpins holding her hair in place. She wore the same apron, the one she cut and sewed from an old chicken feed bag. He remembered the many uses of her apron. In the summer months, she would carry all sorts of vegetables in that apron. In the winter, she would cradle firewood in it, making several trips back and forth from the woodpile to the house; but most of all he remembered her drying the tears from his eyes with the corner of the old apron, always able to soothe his pain. At the end of each day, the apron would be returned to a hook in back of the pantry door. When tomorrow arrived, she would remove it and place it back on again for another day of gathering vegetables, hauling firewood or drying his tears.

This tiny woman had given him a special gift, a gift he would enjoy the rest of his life. Each summer for as long as he remembered he would take the wire basket off the hook, fill it with vegetables from the garden and offer them to his parishioners. Many were amazed, some even a little envious, at his talent for growing the best vegetables in Vilnius, possibly the entire country. Some even suspected intervention of a higher power.

"Father has divine help!" his parishioners would tease, not hiding the pride in their tones. "No," the modest pastor would repeat, "the credit goes to my grandmother. She passed her gift of gardening to me."

If the truth were to be known, the chickens would have to receive most of the credit and maybe a little to divine intervention. After all, God made the chickens. Now, as he stood before the Einsatzgruppen, he thought his grandmother would be proud. He had a feeling she would be there, beyond the clouds, waiting for him. And he would guess she would show off her garden to him and he would bet she would be wearing one of her aprons.

At the end of the war the two young priests would come to this place, a short distance from Vilnius, called the Panerial Woods. Their efforts and determination would finally lead them to this mass grave where their beloved pastor and friend had been buried. They would kneel beside the grave, share prayers, shed tears, and know that one day all three would have the reunion that had been denied them here on earth. And the two priests that survived the war were hoping that the Angels were present and that they were listening to their prayers for the man who had taught them so much, the man whom they missed so very much.

The rain that had fallen most of the day suddenly stopped and the sun appeared miraculously on the horizon slowly drifting toward the west, revealing a purple and pink sky. Mikael and Justas smiled at each other, both thinking the same thought. They would soon return to this place. Father Ricikas would probably be pleased. They turned to each other as they were leaving, neither of them able to say a word. It would be less then a year before the Soviets would come for Justas, and once again he would not have the opportunity to say good-bye. Somehow, through all of it, Mikael never questioned God as he knew God had no part in it.

CHAPTER 3

The trip from Vilnius would take just under two hours despite the fact that Trakai was only forty miles from the capital city. They would make several stops on the way there. This would be the last train scheduled for the day and chances were the coaches would be crowded. Mikael and Justas waited on the platform and watched as the train, heavy black smoke billowing towards the sky, slowly pulled into the station and came to a stop. They wasted little time in climbing aboard and getting settled. Placing their bags on the rack over the seats they sat down and waited for the train to continue on to their final destination.

"Excuse me, gentlemen, is this seat taken?" a young girl, luggage in hand, directed her question to the two young men.

"No, no it's not taken." Mikael was the first to speak. "May I help you with your suitcase?"

"Yes, thank you. This will be my first trip to Trakai, and I understand it is quite beautiful," the pretty girl with the blond hair and blue eyes replied. "And I am told that the town is on a lake. Will you be going there?"

"Yes, replied Justas. It is a special place. My family rented a cottage there one summer. And even though it was a long time ago, I think I was seven or eight years old, I can still remember the lake with boats in every size and shape on the water."

"May I introduce myself? My name is Justas and this is Mikael. Please feel free to sit on either side, beside the window if you wish."

"Thank you again! I think I will. And my name is Sophie," she said as she moved to take the window seat facing Mikael. "I was a student at the University before being selected for this project, and I must admit I have some trepidation about it. I'm not sure what to expect. Even though we were given some information, everything appears so secretive. Was I right to assume you have been selected for the resistance?"

"Yes, we too weren't given much information, and we only had two days to get our affairs in order. I admit it is a turbulent time. At some point, and shortly I'm afraid, everyone in Lithuania will have their lives disrupted. Ours just came a bit sooner."

The three seemed to take an instant liking to each other and continued to converse for a short time. Each then settled into their own thoughts. And this was the beginning of what would become a friendship and love that would endure a lifetime for the young student and the priest, Mikael. Justas, sadly, would be sentenced and shipped to a labor camp shortly after the war when the Red Army invaded Lithuania. The swastika would be replaced by the hammer and sickle, and once again in such a short period of time the people of this small country, having no time to recover from the war, would again suffer under a tyrannical, oppressive leader named Josef Stalin.

Mikael, watched the countryside roll past. There were farmers walking behind their horses plowing the fields, taking time to wave as the train sped by them, a ritual Mikael imagined was probably a daily one. Women, sickles in hand harvesting the wheat, also paused for a moment to wave as the train roared down the tracks. It appeared to be a small diversion from the tedious tasks of the day. He wondered, once Hitler's army overran the country, to what degree and manner it would affect the farmers, the growers and suppliers of the food source. No doubt food would become rationed and the most arrogant race on the planet would feel an entitlement to gather up or cast away whatever they desired.

Mikael had awakened in the morning with a headache and even the powder that Father Ricikas had suggested he take, brought only a slight relief. He was feeling little emotion as he wondered what the future had in store but felt a lassitude that was completely foreign to him.

He glanced at the young girl sitting across from him, the sun shining through the glass on to her hair which was like spun gold hanging almost to her waist. She, too, like the rest of Europe would have her life interrupted by this lunatic of the Third Reich, the present leader of Germany. It was so difficult for any sane person to comprehend why he was admired and respected by the citizens of Germany.

Mikael knew in his heart the times ahead would become much worse before they could ever get better. Not in his wildest dreams would he have predicted it would take six long years before the collapse of the Third Reich and the end of the war in Europe. In August 1945, less than 3 months after the surrender of Germany, Japan would surrender marking the end of World War II. Fifty million people had perished form the planet called Earth before it all came to an end.

Sophie, too, was tired. Anger smoldered within her. It wasn't fair. Because of some madman in Berlin or Munich, or wherever he made his headquarters these days, all her dreams and ambitions, her graduation from the University, were being interrupted for God only knows how long! But no one, not even this evil warmonger, would steal her future. No matter what price, what sacrifices she would have to endure, she would survive these trying times. She believed it with every ounce of her being, and her prediction would eventually come true. But her life would never be the same. Now her whole world had collapsed, and she like thousands of others would have no control over it nor prevent it from spiraling out of control. Everything seemed so bleak. It felt as if she was in a room without any windows or doors and she couldn't find a way out of it. She had devoted her young life to preparing for the university and to studying, thinking there would be ample time for romance. Now that, too, would have to be put on hold; but she made a promise, a silent one, that not even Hitler and his quest to conquer Europe would put her in the grave still a virgin.

Justas, too, felt tired. He was twenty-four years old, a year older than Mikael. Both had attended the same seminary and shortly after their ordination they were appointed to St. Casmir. There was one detour on his journey to the priesthood, when he took a class at the University and met a young girl named Anna. Their friendship eventually evolved into a romance and the priesthood was put on hold; but God had other plans for him and after seven months the romance with Anna ended. His younger sister, only fourteen years old at the time, was diagnosed with tuberculosis. He went home to give comfort and support to his parents who had been given little hope for the recovery for their youngest child and only daughter. He attended Mass everyday in the village church and prayed for a miracle. His sister survived and he was certain that God had something to do with it. And his parents, too, had prayed for their daughter but they prayed, too, that their son would return to the seminary. Both of their prayers were answered!

Sophie had been selected along with fifty or so other students at the University of Vilnius to be considered for training for the formation of a resistance force in Trakai. She had absolutely no idea how or why her name appeared on the list. She had found a typewritten note that had been placed under her door requesting that she attend a meeting scheduled for the next morning. There was no explanation of what the meeting would be about but it was mandatory that she attend. The next morning at the meeting the first thing she noticed was that only a few women were in attendance and could not decipher what the common denominator among them might be, but later an explanation would be given to those in the room. She reasoned that the group that was gathered that morning must have a combination of qualifications that fit into some sort of a profile deemed necessary for the project in Trakai, but it still remained a bit of a mystery to her.

A tall thin man addressed the group "Good morning ladies and gentleman. Thank you for being prompt. I know you have some curiosity as to why this meeting has been called on such short notice so I plan to present a brief description and then we will hold a question and answer period. Let me begin by saying that this will be a completely voluntary decision on your part. There is no obligation whatsoever for any of you to participate. You may decide for any reason that you are unable to contribute to this undertaking."

Unfortunately, we have nothing to compare this project to and we can not promise that all danger can be eliminated. In fact, this will probably be a dangerous assignment. After all, we will soon be part of the war now raging in Poland, our neighbor. My name is Vidas and to those of you who make the decision to remain here for more information, I will introduce my other family members. We are currently developing a survival course in the town of Trakai which is approximately forty miles southwest of here. There is now a class from Kaunas, the first class to date, whose courses will be completed in a little less than one week if all goes as scheduled. For those of you who decide to join us, this will be the start of our second class, a program that runs for six weeks. Let me take a few minutes to tell you that it is a concentrated six weeks and requires a great deal of persistence, tenacity, dedication, and loyalty to Lithuania. The names submitted to me have been selected because of a unique combination of talents but at the top of the requirements are tenacity, patriotism and the ability to adapt and step outside of your comfort zone.

The University realizes that it is just a matter of time before the Germans will be here and eventually all classes will be cancelled indefinitely. We have to be somewhat prepared for our future. No one here today, I believe, is unwilling to take some risk and some control over the direction of their lives. Let me say in closing before we begin our question and answer period that for those of you who decide to become a part of this, to join forces with our group, there is only one week before you will depart. There are two trains to Trakai each day, and we have reserved seats on each. The first that sign up will have a choice of morning or afternoon departures. Once you arrive in Trakai your training period will commence. I assume that most of you don't have any knowledge of weapons with the exception of perhaps a few hunters, but I assure you, this experience will be very unlike a hunting expedition.

As you are well aware Poland has already suffered from the invasion there. There had been no warning and the casualties now number in the thousands. The devastation is beyond belief. Our small country has been given an extra gift, a gift of time to make preparations though it would be ludicrous to hope that we have even a slight chance of any major victories. But we can use the time allotted to prepare resistance tactics. I am convinced that we can be successful in many circumstances, absolutely, but it will not be an easy task. There are many risks involved. Remember however, that staying here in Vilnius does not necessarily mean you will escape the pain of war. It may all seem a little surreal at the moment, but we are in a real war. Seven days is a short notice but I cannot change that."

So on this last Friday of October, 1939, sixteen women and thirty-three men were handed a train ticket and a sheet of instructions which included a map of Trakai, a place that would become their home for the next six years. They would train to be a team of Lithuanian resistant fighters instrumental in carrying out hundreds of missions, and successful ones at that. By the grace of God and the tutelage of Mrs. Massud most would walk away at the end of the war, and the majority of these patriots would live for many years after the war had ended. But they would not gain the freedom they had hoped for.

CHAPTER 4

One of the few things that Erik and Herr Richter had in common was their love for Claudia and a strong admiration for their Fuehrer, Adolph Hitler, Chancellor of Germany. The two would spend hours discussing the Third Reich, born in January, 1933, and predicted to endure for a thousand years. They were in total agreement on the subject of the Jews. The Jews certainly were responsible for the sad state and decline of Germany's economy but hopefully all future generations would not have to deal with the problems the Jews had created, as was the concurrence of the German people. In the near future, Hitler would enforce laws to prevent all Jews from entering universities and deny them the right to own or establish any type of business. But as history would soon discover this demonic man would later take his own life, and the Third Reich would be diminished to ashes along with the evil Devil named Adolph Hitler.

Claudia grew weary of all the Hitler talk. She was not and never had been remotely interested in politics and wished that her father and Erik would let it rest. She couldn't fathom what all the fuss was about. This funny looking man, not even a German, was predicted to return their country to a world prominence. She remained a skeptic but she kept her opinion to herself. The only thing Hitler did for her was to postpone her marriage to Erik, for perhaps months or worse, years. It was so unfair, and unlike her father and the man she loved, she did not blame the Jews for anything but this too she kept to herself.

Claudia knew only too well that it was only a matter of time before Erik would receive his dreaded papers, his orders to report to Berlin. The thought of their separation was unbearable. Insomnia became a constant companion and anxiety reared its ugly head.

And the dreaded news finally did arrive. Erik didn't hear the knock on the door at first and when he became aware that someone was at the front door, they had already gone on their way, leaving an envelope under the door. Erik knew exactly what the envelope contained as he had seen identical ones on different occasions. He experienced mixed emotions. He wanted to be part of the battle. There was no doubt he wanted to participate in the struggle to win this war, to elevate Hitler to a world-class leader and provide the next generations of Germans with a brighter more optimistic future. The regret, of course, was in having to leave Claudia, and there were times recently that he questioned whether he would be able to return to her unharmed. He was well aware of the danger of war and there was no guarantee that he would not become another victim and lose his life in a place far away from her. He did not dwell on the subject of dying in the war, but he knew there was that very real possibility.

Erik decided he would wait until tomorrow to bring the news to Claudia. He knew it wasn't going to be easy. In fact he was dreading it and was surprised when he slept soundly through the entire night and rose at the crack of dawn. Max, his beloved German Shepherd, slept at the foot of his master's bed waking as soon as he heard Erik arise and followed him downstairs to the kitchen. He pushed his dish over to the sink where his master stood, a daily ritual the dog had perfected since he was a young puppy.

"Max, hurry and finish your food, and we will go for a walk."

Max knew the routine well. He was intelligent—and he was spoiled! In addition to missing Claudia, Erik would miss his old faithful companion. Max had been part of the family since he was a puppy, a gift to Erik from his favorite aunt and uncle.

Erik wished that time would stand still just for the day so he could have a few more hours before delivering the news to Claudia even though they had both been anticipating it for some time now. He had rehearsed it a bit, but he knew in the end, it would measure up to be exactly the same.

The moment Erik entered the room, Claudia knew. She ran over to him, tears streaming down her face, saying nothing but clinging to him like a frighten child.

"Claudia, I love you so very much. If I were capable of making these terrible times disappear, to free you from being so sad, I would not hesitate for one second. Our generation it seems has been appointed to reclaim our country to its rightful place. Hitler hates the communists even more than the Jews, and he feels they are a real threat to Germany.

And, of course as you know, there is the humiliation we have endured since the end of the last war. We have the right to reclaim that portion of our country that has been confiscated from us. There are no other choices. Maybe God will intervene and give us the rest of our lives to grow old together and boast to all our friends and neighbors about how smart and beautiful our grandchildren turned out! So my darling, do not assume that our lives are over!"

"I hate him! I hate him! I hate him for taking you away from me." The reference was, of course, to Hitler, and Erik was wise enough to know that there was nothing that he could say that would make a difference. He just continued to hold her close to him.

CHAPTER 5

"Claudia, listen to me for a moment. Please, just for a few minutes! You and I have two weeks together before I report to Berlin. I have an idea. But the decision will be yours. Would you be willing to exchange a huge Church wedding for a small civil ceremony before I have to leave? There would be enough time, a few days for a honeymoon. I am deeply in love with you and I want you to be my wife, but I will understand if you want to wait for the wedding of your dreams, you know, the one with all of the bridesmaids, a Church wedding."

And so it came to pass. With the approval of the bride's father, the civil ceremony took place at the small courthouse on the corner of Barnhofstrasser on the last Saturday of October in the year of 1939. Claudia, dressing for her wedding, detected what she thought was a rumble of thunder in the distance, an unfamiliar sound so late in the season. With rare exception during this time of year, the rain fell during the morning hours and eventually drifted farther south close to noon time. But on this day, her wedding day, she was absolutely convinced that the sun would make an appearance because, she had remembered to hang her rosary beads on one of the old oak trees that bordered the yard. The ritual was rumored to be foolproof.

So on this sunny afternoon in late autumn, Claudia and Erik exchanged their wedding vows to "honor and cherish until death do us part" not possibly knowing how prophetic it would become, and they were pronounced man and wife. There were no bridesmaid's taffeta gowns rustling down the aisle, no relatives and friends crowded into church pews with handkerchiefs dabbing at moist eyes. But these two young people, so much in love with each other, were full of joy and happiness.

Herr and Frau Mueller . . . Yes, Claudia liked the sound of it! She was remembering how, years ago as a schoolgirl, she would practice writing her new name in her note book during class: Claudia Mueller! She always knew in her heart that her wish would come true, that she would someday become Erik's wife. She didn't have the gala wedding celebration in church with flowers overflowing from the altar, escorted down the aisle on her father's arm as he gave her away to the man she loved. All of her family and friends weren't able to join and celebrate the most important day of her life. But she was now married to the man who was in love with her and wanted to spend the rest of his life with her.

Unbeknownst to them, their time together would be short-lived as Fate would have other plans for them.

Frau Richter had dabbed at her eyes throughout the entire ceremony and Frau Mueller had beamed and smiled. They were so proud of their children—such a handsome couple. They both were thinking of the beautiful grandchildren the couple would give them to love and spoil, God willing. They wanted to believe that the war would be short and life would soon return to some semblance of normality.

Following the civil ceremony, the bride's parents gave a small reception in the garden on the edge of their property. The trees were dressed in their autumn colors and wildflowers in every shape and color dotted the woods just behind the old picket fence. One of the few guests that had been invited, as the reception was limited to close family and the two witnesses, Heidi and Otto, best friends of the couple, was Erik's favorite aunt, Ingrid and her husband. This was his aunt's second marriage. They had been married for twenty-three years and he was the only uncle Erik ever had. Ingrid had held a secret for over two decades that she promised her sister, Erik's mother, that she would never reveal, a secret that she would take to her grave. But it would not play out exactly as she had planned and it would change her nephew's life forever.

Claudia's grandmother, who had just celebrated her ninety-second birthday, joined the small party of guests and appeared to be truly enjoying this special day. She sought out her granddaughter, hugged her, and whispered to her how beautiful she looked and what a handsome man she had chosen to spend the rest of her life with. And, likewise, she approached her new grandson-in-law and reminded him of how lucky he was to have such a beautiful wife!

Everyone appeared to be having a wonderful time, especially the new bride, and as the day passed, she had completely forgotten her slight disappointment in forfeiting the big wedding she had dreamed about most of her life.

Erik found it difficult to keep his eyes off his new bride. He could not remember when she had ever looked more beautiful, and he was feeling like a very lucky man. This war would sever and deny them the happiness they deserved and were entitled but on this day, their wedding day, Erik and Claudia could not be happier!

CHAPTER 6

Erik would have to report to army headquarters in less than two weeks so the honeymoon would be spent at the lake cabin that had been in the Richter family for as long as anyone could remember.

For generations, the Richter men would spend hours there hiking, fishing, hunting, and drinking good German ale. They would bring their catch, fish and game, back to the cabin where the German wives would filet the fish, prepare the game and cook it, at times reluctantly.

It was late afternoon when they finally arrived. Erik brought in some small logs and kindling that had been stored and stacked in the back of the cabin and proceeded to light the fireplace. Shortly the heat would engulf the small space. Later he would throw more logs on the fire to ensure that it would continue through the evening and possibly until morning. The weather remained unseasonably warm for this time of year but was cooler at the lake in the shadow of the mountains that surrounded it. The trees were almost completely stripped of leaves that piled into heaps on the ground, only a few left clinging to their branches possibly in an effort to postpone the impending cold months ahead. Birch trees dotted the empty spaces competing for a place with the pines and maples. It was a peaceful and beautiful setting and a world away from the dark clouds that erupted over Europe. In these idyllic surroundings, no one could have predicted the demonic events occurring in Poland, a Hell beyond anything in modern history and just a preview of events to come.

"Erik, before you carry our luggage in, could you please bring in the small chest with the groceries? I will start dinner."

He pretended not to hear, walked over to her, and whispered, "I love you, Frau Mueller. I will always love you!"

"Erik, darling, and I love Herr Mueller. I have been in love with him my whole life!" She refused to refer to her new husband by the title he had recently acquired, Captain Mueller. It was too painful a reminder that she would lose him in the weeks ahead.

"How will I bear it when you have to leave me? And worst of all, I will worry about you. How will I possibly know if you have been hurt or are missing in some faraway place? You know I could not bear it if I lost you, if anything were to happen to you!"

He reached to her and held her close. He kissed her on her cheek, on her forehead, on her lips, and stepped back and looked at her trying to think of something to say that would comfort her but he knew there would be no words that could comfort for her. But he knew he wanted to make love to her, and he wanted it to be soon.

"I am going to make love to you. I've wanted you for so long! I'm madly in love with you, madly passionately in love with you, my wife, you know!"

And on this first night of their honeymoon, Erik made good on his promise and the lovemaking was just getting started. The days and nights had been filled listening to Mozart, sipping wine, taking long walks around the lake, hikes into the mountains, and true to his promise, lovemaking wild and passionate.

The days slipped away, and it soon became time to think about packing up to go home and face the dreaded task of seeing Erik depart for Berlin.

On the last evening at the cabin, having made love, uncharacteristically, neither could sleep. The embers that remained were slowly burning themselves out, and the room started to feel chilly. Erik placed several logs on the fire hoping it would be enough to make it until the morning.

They lay there under the blankets holding each other and staring into the last of the dwindling flames well aware that their time together was limited, and God only knew how long the separation would be.

"You must promise me, Erik, that you will write to me as often as possible. I need to know you are alive and well!"

"You know I will, and I promise!" he answered knowing there would be only a small chance of his mail reaching its destination during war time. But he choose not to share these thoughts, he knew it would only upset her.

"I will call you from Berlin as soon as my indoctrination is complete, and maybe you can meet me there even if only for a few days before my deployment. I doubt they will be calling me up immediately, but it's too early to predict. Your husband will be just fine and before you know it I'll be home. We have the rest of our lives. We will make babies, vacation in the Alps, and grow old together. And we can look forward to a second honeymoon!"

They held each other close, into the night. Neither of them spoke of the war or of Erik's deployment and they finally drifted off to sleep.

CHAPTER 7

The young woman, they would later discover, bore a strong resemblance to her mother, the older woman who would become teacher, instructor, and their leader for the next few weeks. Their black eyes and jet black hair were typical of the Karaim originally from a region in Turkey. The Karaims had settled in and around Trakai since the end of the 14th century. They were brought to Lithuania by the grandduke Vyautus.

"May I welcome all of you to Trakai", the young woman walked up and down on the platform directing each group to a specific place just a few steps from the platform. The area, in the shape of a small circle, had several benches. In the center there stood a crucifix carved from birch wood stretching to the sky above, a flower arrangement placed at the base of the cross.

"Please have a seat if you wish, but I'm going to request that you stay here in this area. Take a minute, introduce yourself."

When the train pulled away from the station she turned toward the group that had assembled. Most took the young woman's advice and found a place to sit on the benches. She would estimate twenty-five to thirty young Lithuanians, luggage in hand and close by, they appeared remarkably calm and ready to move on to their next destination.

"Hello, my name is Dalia."

"We have a fifteen minute walk to our quarters from here at the depot. Please take an extra minute and be sure that everyone in your group is accounted for so no one gets left behind."

She waited a few minutes, assumed all were present, and signaled the group to follow her. The weather was overcast; but for now at least, men, women, and luggage would remain dry. The rain, no stranger this time of year, would arrive later in the day usually before sundown.

The dashas were halfway between the town and the lake and built in clusters around the turn of the century by Russians that had immigrated to Trakai from Russia. They were built and painted in the typical Russian style. Each was painted in a palette of colors, deep red, some darker blues toward navy, yellow, and greens. Over the years when a fresh coat of paint was needed, the dashas were always painted in the original color. It became an unwritten code of sorts. This complex would become home for the next six weeks the length of time to complete the survival courses. Most would transfer to locations in other areas of the country and those remaining would move to cabins on and near the lake. Eventually five hundred in all would master these courses and over the next several months approximately one hundred ninety would make the transition here to the cabins in the woods.

This new group entering the program was divided into five groups, with eight each being assigned to a dasha. The group was divided by gender. During the day for the training sessions the entire group would remain together.

Mrs. Massud was in charge of the survival courses assisted by her daughter and two sons, focusing on the tools and instruments preparing them to outsmart the enemy and to remain alive. It was not a question of what if but when the Germans would invade their country. And the Germans eventually did arrive, and this training would prove the major factor in keeping these young people safe. These young students, nuns, priests would become an important part of Lithuania's underground. The women would show as much courage as the men. They, too, would join the gorilla detachments; and in all, these young men and women would be part of a larger group that would be responsible for derailing trains, over fifty-five total, destruction of bridges and responsible for the deaths of 14,000 Germans. Sadly, before the war ended, 770,000 Lithuanians would loose their lives and only a small number of priests and nuns would survive. Mikael and Justas, by the grace of God, would be spared, but their lives would never be the same.

Each morning the group would gather for what their instructor called the most important course, the mastering of the crossbow. These people who came here from Turkey to Trakai so many generations ago were experts with this weapon, a skill handed down from one generation to the next.

"The crossbow will become your secret weapon. It is a silent weapon and a deadly one." Mrs. Massud stared out into the small crowd.

"I'm hoping to remember your names before the end of the day. Believe it or not, I have a talent for it!"

The young people in the group broke out in a quiet laughter. And true to her word at the end of the day she did indeed remember every name.

After a short lunch break the afternoon would focus on a course in small weapons. Most of these young men and women had never seen any kind of weapon so this was completely foreign to them. At the end of the next six weeks they would become experts, all of them, including the two priests from St Casmir and the young girl from the University of Vilnius.

"Is there any one here, Mrs. Massud asked her students that cannot swim?"

Surprisingly only three hands went up.

"Because of the cool October weather it's obvious we can't go in the lake. We will, however, within the next few weeks spent a day or two at the lake concentrating on rowing and canoeing. My past experience tells me at this time of year there could be a few days of warmer weather. We'll wait, hope for the best. It will also give you the opportunity to see the cabins that will be home to you after your courses are completed."

It was rare that Lithuanians did not attach themselves to the water at a very early age. Most were excellent swimmers; majority lived near the Baltic Sea or very close to many of the lakes sprinkled throughout their small country.

As Mrs. Massud predicted the warm days did appear briefly, and all boating courses were completed along with the other survival courses.

"Congratulations to all of you! I am so proud of everyone and convinced when the time arrives you will be in an excellent place to defend yourself."

"Tonight we will have a small celebration. I'm hoping to see all of you—around seven!"

Needless to say the dachas were a welcoming sight at the end of the long day. As October slipped into December the fireplaces would be lit before the group arrived from the exhausting days. The day after tomorrow bags would get packed and moved to the cabins, and the vacant rooms would be made ready for the next group. Tonight would be a celebration, probably the last one for a long time.

Mikael, Justas, and Sophie were among the first group to be shuttled across the lake and assigned to one of the cabins. Every effort was made to keep the groups together, the ones who lived together in the dachas. There were a total of forty-eight cabins. The majority were scattered throughout the forest, a few, one dozen or so, lined up close to the lake's waterfront. These cabins would be home to one hundred ninety young Lithuanians. The majority were students and a delegation of priests and nuns.

The cabins were built almost in duplicate; the only difference would be the manner in which they were heated. The cabins in the forest had fieldstone fireplace, the ones closer to the lake had wood stoves.

Each cabin had two sets of bunk beds pushed against the wall. A small pine table sat in the middle of the floor with four chairs pushed under it. The chairs were carved in a folk style, a labor of love by some old Lithuanian perhaps. There was a pump at the sink. The water would be heated in the fireplaces or wood stoves. Each had a pantry filled with can goods.

Quilts were placed at the foot of the beds. There was a pillow in each bunk. There were willow baskets for clothing that could be pushed under the bed. Two pictures hung on the wall facing each other, two different views of the lake, done nicely in watercolors. A trio of hooks hung behind the door. Every sixth cabin had a small out building.

The cabins were owned by the State and were part of a recreation area rented out to families in late spring and summer. There was a boat house where passengers could wait for the boats to ferry them in and out of the lake area. Row boats and canoes for hire gathered in the boat yard. It was extremely rare that any of the cabins remained vacant, most rented in season, usually by the week. Many of the young people assembled here had spent some summers on this lake with their families.

One of the first assignments for the new tenants would be to cut and chop firewood to prepare for the pending cold months. The plan was to stack the wood on the side and behind each cabin. A plan would later be drafted and put into effect if the Germans were discovered to be within a ten mile radius there would be no fires and existing ones would immediately be extinguished. And the Germans did find their way to Trakai. They came in late winter, a lucky break for the Lithuanians. In the end the good news was the Germans suffered more casualties than these young patriots who banded together and eventually did outwit their enemy.

Mikael and Justas were assigned to one of the lakeside cabins with two young priests from Karinas, the same room mates that shared their quarters for the previous six weeks. Next door Sophie, too, shared her cabin with the three young women from Vilnius University that were together for the training period during the prior six weeks. She felt, however, closer to Mikael and Justas since meeting them on the train. The three had become inseparable. She couldn't remember exactly when her feelings for Mikael changed. It was a slow process, she wasn't even aware of the change.

CHAPTER 8

Christmas was just around the corner and for most of the young people it would be the first Christmas they would be away from home, from their families, from their friends. Preparation would soon begin for the transfer across the lake to the cabins as classes would end in just four days.

Mrs. Massud had compiled a list that she planned to read explaining the events that would take place in the next few days.

"As you all know this is your last week here. I'm dreading the time when it comes to saying good-bye. I will, of course, still have contact with you; but it will not be on a daily basis. A new group is scheduled to be here the first of January. Needless to say; I am so very proud of each and every one of you, and all of you have exceeded my expectations. A small ceremony has been planned, no diplomas, but recognition will be given to the students who have excelled here. Selection will be made to the men and women that have proven to process leadership qualities and have exhibited and have shown a capacity to organize what will eventually become necessary missions, ones that you have been trained to carry out. The leader of each group, there'll be approximately thirty assigned to a group, will select an assistant to help in making some tough decisions, especially when the time arrives for the actual resistance movement. Many of you have the qualifications so my decision is not going to be an easy one. You can be assured the Germans will find their way here. They will make an entrance. It's just a question of when.

During the past weeks you have received training that will become an important and integral ingredient in a resistance force that will eventually join other resistance contingents throughout the country. I believe, without a shadow of a doubt, you are prepared and will succeed in this endeavor. You are an incredible group. You have displayed an enthusiasm under these harsh conditions that contributed and propelled you to conquer a task that was completely foreign to you. Your determination to master these challenges is proof that you will survive these trying times. One very real advantage that you will have over the invaders is the fact that you have knowledge now and will become even more familiar with the area in the months ahead especially the forest which you will soon realize is your true protector. And you may not totally be convinced, but the crossbow, silent and powerful, will become instrumental in saving your life. And, of course, a few prayers couldn't help!"

"I would also like to remind you that there is information posted in each dacha pertaining to your forthcoming move. Please take a few minutes and read it carefully paying special attention to the subject of your weapons. The same rifle and crossbow that you had during training will be assigned to you. For the short trip across the lake the rifles are to remain unloaded. You will meet at the dock, promptly at the time posted, where several boats will be waiting to ferry you across. Before you disembark you will be assigned your cabin number and its location. As you know we have had an exceptional mild winter to date; but if the weather changes and it gets extremely cold and the lake becomes frozen, we will provide sleds for the crossing. I also have made the decision, based on the mild weather, to postpone your move until after Christmas.

Last but not least, the pastor of St. Mary's has invited all of you, regardless of religious affiliation, to attend midnight Mass on Christmas Eve. The church, for those of you who are not familiar with its location, is in the center of the village, just a fifteen minute walk from here. There will also be a Mass on Christmas Day at 9:30 A.M.; and for anyone wishing to go to confession, it's always from four to six every Saturday afternoon. See you tomorrow!"

CHAPTER 9

The news from Warsaw was not good. Casualties were reported in the thousands. All communication systems were severed and the unknown was as difficult to bear as the news that slowly filtered out of the country and would become unbearable to the old priest. Father Ricikas was weary, so tired these difficult days, and the burden he carried became a strain on him. Time seemed to have stood still. The reality of the horrors on Lithuanian doorsteps was taking its toll, draining the little energy he had these days. Being tired became a daily obstacle as sleep would avoid him. Being tired prevented him from performing the most simple of tasks. The gardens he always loved became victim of neglect weeds running rampant spilling over to the grass that needed urgent attention that he was incapable of providing. His appetite had diminished and food did not appeal to him these days. Even having to say Mass became an encumbrance. He would dwell on the fact that the suffering had just begun. It amazed him that the results of the Great War had not resulted in any important lessons, lessons that should have been learned and not to be repeated. But the priest knew in the very end that Hitler could not possibly win this war, but the price of his evil and arrogance would eventually surpass anything history had recorded even deleting the record of the once invincible Genghis Khan, Mongol, 1162-1227, who rode out of Manchuria, crossed the steppes, and invaded most of Asia and much or Europe.

His thoughts would often turn to the young priests now in Trakai. He missed them a little more with each passing day. He tried to make sense of the world that the psychopath, Adolph Hitler, had now created but he knew there would be no answer for him.

Each day more information on the atrocities and horrors of the events raging in Poland especially in the capital of Warsaw would surface to reach the outside world. Would England and France go to their aid? Was it not too little too late? Here the answer was pretty obvious.

The days passed into weeks and Father Ricikas realized he had to find the energy to finish tasks that he had started and needed his attention so on a beautiful fall day he planned to spend the day outside in his garden. He wondered why God could make such a perfect day and then again he would not put a halt to the suffering affecting most of Europe. Again no answer would be available.

CHAPTER 10

Claudia would often hike into the mountains where she and Erik had played as children. She wore her hair in braids in those days; and when Erik would chase her through the birch and pine trees that littered the mountainside, he would affectionately pull on her hair causing squeals and laughter. She realized even at such a young age she would someday marry him, that she loved him.

"Max!" she called to the dog. "It is time to go home now."

They were almost to the end of the path when she turned around and saw that Max was not anywhere to be seen. He was not there. He just vanished out of sight.

"Come, Max! It's time to head back!"

She felt no panic at first but this was so unlike Max who never ventured from her side. She paid special attention to the dog since Erik had been gone as she knew Max missed his master." You are really in trouble if you don't come here right now!"

She turned around and begun to retrace her steps. And in the middle of the pathway there sat Max very still.

"You are a bad dog!" She scolded the big shepherd. She reached down to attach his collar when the dog bolted away running in the opposite direction his leash dragging on the ground behind him.

"That's it! she shouted, but he kept going paying absolutely no attention to her. And it was then that she saw him. He was there in full uniform smiling at her.

"Erik! Erik! Her husband was standing there on the rim of the path, Max turning in circles, tail going a hundred miles an hour, jumping up and down, completely overjoyed to see his master. And without warning they both disappeared back up the path in the opposite direction. She called out but to no avail.

She woke with a start. "My God" Claudia cried out, "It was a dream, only a dream".

CHAPTER 11

My darling, how I miss you! I try to find comfort in reading your letters over and over. You have a special place in my every thought and in my prayers and I pray that God keeps you safe for me. I love you so very much.

I have spent the last few weeks trying to find the courage to make a good decision, one that I am hoping will not worry you, but I cannot keep this news to myself any longer. I am thrilled, I am astatic, I am pregnant. There, I have said it! Please dear Erik do not be disappointed. I could not bear it! I was upset at first not knowing if you would be happy with this news, knowing the war will keep you away possibly for a long time, and I wondering if I shall be strong and brave enough to do this alone without you by my side, but now I am overjoyed knowing that our baby is growing within me. Please do not worry for I am fine, truly. I wanted you to be the first to know, I haven't told either set of Grandparents-to-be but I plan to tell them soon. I think they will be thrilled at the thought of their first grandchild even under these existing hardships. I am feeling just fine, honestly, a little morning sickness which appears to have subsided. Hoping to visit with the midwife real soon, and I shall write with all the details after my appointment. I am hoping you will be as happy as I am when you receive this letter. Take care of yourself, my darling. I will write again soon! With all my love, Claudia

Erik never received the letter from Claudia with the news that she was pregnant. A strict security code was put into effect for all correspondence. She wasn't aware of this newest edit until after the letter had been mailed. Maybe, just maybe, by some miracle it would slip through and eventually would be delivered to him but the letter was returned a few weeks later.

Each night Claudia would pray that Erik would someday return safely to her. She was willing to wait forever as long as he came home to her safe and sound, that this horrible war would end; and at this point she didn't care which side won, she just wanted her life to return to a safe, happy place, and she wanted her husband to come back to her so they could grow old together, make more babies. Sadly these wishes would never come true. There would be no reunion.

CHAPTER 12

As soon as his assignment had been processed and confirmed he was given a portfolio with information that he would need, the demographics of the island, location of the airfield, and other pertinent information. He also was informed that he would have a driver, and the driver would meet him at the airfield. The plane touched down just before noon, a two hour flight from Berlin. The sun was trying desperately to break through the clouds, a good omen Erik thought as the plane started its descent. The entire island was visible from the sky, surprisingly larger than what he had anticipated.

"Captain Mueller?" a young woman approached him as he disembarked speaking to him in German. "I have been assigned to meet you here, I am your driver."

She was in full uniform, her hair tucked under her cap. Erik nodded and followed her to the parked car. He was thinking at the moment how young she appeared; and when she opened the car door for him, he noticed she wore a gold wedding band. There would be no knowing on this third day of October, 1940, that in the years to come, after the war, that their paths would cross in a way that could be defined only as fate, but for now she was a young English woman assigned to be the driver of this German officer, an attractive English woman who spoke fluent German.

"We have a twenty minute drive to your headquarters. There should be a lunch waiting for you."

Erik was looking forward to lunch as he had breakfast early that morning before boarding the plane in Berlin. Yes, the lunch news sounded good to him.

He was aware that the English drove on the left-hand side of the road yet when she pulled away from the airfield it seemed a little strange to him for a few moments, and he felt the driver had picked up on it but said nothing

"You have me at a disadvantage. May I ask you your name?"

"Of course. My name is Mrs. Spencer."

"Your German is very good, Mrs. Spencer."

There was no response from his driver. He was a little curious how she came upon mastering fluent German with no accent. He wondered if she had spent any time in Germany but now was not the time to ask her any questions. He could feel a slight chill, normal under the circumstance. She had a regal-like manner, could be an English trait, though this was his first encounter with an English woman and a very pretty one at that. In fact, this was his first meeting with anyone English. He always recognized the English as an intelligent race far superior to the cultures of Eastern Europe and later by some miracle he had avoided being shipped to the Russian front which probably would have resulted in a one-way trip out of Germany with only a slight possibility of returning alive. Yes, the planets were aligned in his favor on the day his orders were drafted.

The remaining trip was spent in little conversation. But minutes before they reached their destination as if his driver had read his mind she volunteered that her grandmother came to England from Germany shortly before World War I from Berlin to be exact, and her grandmother spoke only German to all her grandchildren; and this of course, the German part, was the reason she had been selected to be his driver she explained.

The sun finally won its battle against the clouds. Erik would soon discover that it was a rare occurrence to see the sun appear on the Island for more than a few hours at a time. During the winter months which were just ahead the sun would almost disappear until spring, and rain would fall almost on a daily basis.

Erik settled back thinking of the trials and ordeals awaiting him in his new role here on the Island, a little curious perhaps as he had never been in a war before, never played a part of an army officer, not really having any idea what to expect. The Island had been captured by the Germans in recent months and being here would certainly give him a better chance of surviving the war and returning home to Claudia. He was missing Claudia but in his heart he never doubted there would be a reunion; but there was no way he could have predicted that their reunion would never take place. And because of the durability of the war, it would be quite a long time before he was delivered the painful news.

"Captain Mueller, we are only a few minutes to headquarters. Major Breuer is planning to be there to welcome you."

Erik nodded thinking she could see him in the rear-view mirror. He had been introduced to Major Breuer in Berlin just a few months ago. At that time neither had been aware that they would be assigned to the same post until final orders were received. It had been a brief meeting, only a few hours, and Erik had concluded that they had some things in common, and Erik could sense that the Major took exceptional pride in his role as an officer of the Third Reich apparent that his loyalty to Hitler was indelible. Erik also learned that the Major was heir to a giant pharmaceutical company. In the post war years Erik would accept an offer from the Major to come work for his company, and his decision to accept would result in paving the way of Erik's destiny and would become a pivotal part, a portion of the puzzle, that would eventually lead him to Vilnius, a place he didn't even knew existed. His life would lead him down roads he could not have predicted in a hundred years. It would be the place where he would meet his brother for the first time, a brother he never knew he had, a twin brother that would take three decades for the two to finally find each other.

"Captain Mueller, we are just about there. The building is there on the right-hand side of the road."

Erik looked at his watch. It would just be about the twenty minutes. He knew one of his duties on the island would include being in command of the airfield and knowing the approximate length of time from headquarters would become useful to him. The island was halfway between England and the coast of Northern France, somewhat closer to the English mainland where the English Channel met the Cliffs of Dover. The location proved valuable for the Germans who now occupied the island; in fact, the name of the island was Half Way Island, so named for the obvious reason. The population he would later learn had a small French settlement originally from Brittany and Normandy, but the Island truly belonged to the English.

Mrs. Spencer motioned ahead indicating that the building was German Head Quarters. There were two flags, one on each side of the entrance, one proudly displaying the swastika and the other black, red and yellow, German's national flag. Erik always felt a special pride on seeing his country's flag, waving or not waving, and reminded him of the reason and scarifies that he along with his fellow countrymen were making to insure that the Third Reich would prove indestructible. The next generations would truly benefit, there was no doubt in his mind. In time, of course, he would come to realize the tragedy of it all, and the role that Germany had played in its efforts to conquer and destroy much of humanity. And in the end Germany would be reduced to a fallen and disgraced nation for the second time in three decades.

As Mrs. Spencer had predicted Major Breuer was there to greet him.

"Heil Hitler! Welcome! So glad you are going to be part of our team. The Corporal will take your bags to your room. It's the building directly behind us. And it's so good to see you again, Erik, it was such a brief time in Berlin. I was only informed a few days ago that you were being assigned here. We'll have briefings but I have scheduled them for tomorrow, not today. I'll give you a short-version tour later after we get some nourishment and make a few introductions."

Erik turned to say good-by to his driver but noticed she had already gone. He was feeling confident he would be spending a great deal of time with his beautiful, young driver; and maybe at some point she would tell him about the island and something about the English, he was curious about both. He knew very little about the English except as he already experienced they drove on the "wrong" side of the road, drank a whole lot more tea then the Germans, and that Queen Victoria married Prince Albert and produced a dozen or so children which made them as much German as English. He also remembered a few years ago in 1936 hearing a broadcast on the radio the speech given by King Edward VIII when he declared his love for a twice-divorced American named Wallis Simpson and abdicated his throne because he was forbidden to marry her and remain king. Erik could not comprehend how a love so strong could possibly exist that a man would give up so much for the woman he loved. David, as she always called him, did eventually marry the woman he claimed he could not bear to live without and they moved to the South of France exiled from the members of the royal family.

And most of all Erik was hoping his driver would agree to a few lessons in English. He had a few short courses in college. He had forgotten more than he remembered, but maybe some of it would come back to him. There was no reason to approach the subject just yet. Even from their short encounter he was well aware that he would have to tread cautiously. There was something about Mrs. Spencer that intrigued him. And he found himself wishing to see her again soon. With some luck tomorrow would come quickly for him.

Spring came early to the Island and everything sprouted a vivid green. The sun made brief appearances almost daily, a welcomed sight following the dismal winter. The war continued, and Erik did not forget his good fortune to be here on this island. At this point Germany's army seemed indestructible conquering one country in Europe after another, but Erik wondered now that the United States had entered the war and joined forces with the Allies after the bombing of Pearl Harbor by the Japanese in December would his country eventually be destined to pay the price. He sometimes wondered what his future would be if Germany did not win this war, but he had no control over this and life he realized would deal him only what he would be entitled, nothing less nor more.

One day in the beginning of May, seven months after he arrived on the island, he found the courage to approach the subject of English lessons. After her arrival at headquarters to take him out to the airfield he waited a few minutes before he approached the subject.

"Mrs. Spencer, I have been thinking, actually for some time now, and I want to know your honest opinion to my question. Of course you are not obliged in any way to accept. I have given some thought to learning English, some lessons if you will, and I wanted to know if you would be willing to teach me, even spend most of our conversations in English. If you do not feel comfortable with this I understand. I did have a few short courses while in college, and I have picked up some here on the island. You can take your time if you need it. As you know I don't think I'm leaving any time soon."

"I had given it some thought recently myself, but I dismissed the idea thinking you were not interested. I really don't know why I assumed that but there were no signs from you that you showed any interest."

"Then you'll give it a try."

"I think I could be up to the challenge. We can start now if you want to, why not."

On their return trip from the airfield back to Headquarters Sara noticed something unusual and quite strange as they approached the building where she was to leave Captain Mueller. There appeared to be huge clouds of dust swirling in all directions and soldiers every where shouting orders. Alarmed at what she was witnessing she pulled the car over to the side of the road.

"Mrs. Spencer, stop here! I'm going to get out and see what all the commotion is about."

It was late afternoon, almost dusk, but Erik could see that the building ahead was heavily damaged. He would discover that a bomb had exploded. There were casualties, among them an officer and three soldiers. He would soon learn that Major Breuer had been spared, but they could not save his leg. The leg had to be amputated. Several of the wounded had been transferred to the local hospital and information on their condition had not been released as yet.

Erik returned to the parked car where he had left Sara, and she could see how visibly shaken he was. He suggested to her to go directly home, and he would give her an update tomorrow.

"There may be roadblocks but your papers should all be in order. Be careful."

There were actually two roadblocks that she had to pass on her way. Soldiers holding huge flashlights; and after checking her papers, flagged her on her way. The whole episode was disconcerting, and she wouldn't be surprised if there was retaliation and someone could be facing a firing squad. What she couldn't possibly know at this time was that those responsible for the bombing were two young boys who would elude punishment with Sara playing a major role in their escape off the island.

She drove down the long driveway thankful to be home. She would fix a small supper for herself, tend to the animals, and settle before a fire, pick up the book she had started recently, and try to get some sleep.

Mornings came too soon. She couldn't remember the last time when she slept completely through the night. It had to be before the war. She missed Paul, especially at night. Not only the love making but the loneliness that the darkness bring, and she wondered if she would ever completely get used to being by herself.

Sara thought back to that night so many times over the years, the night the search was on for the bombing suspects. Just a short while after she had something to eat, she went into the barn to feed the sheep, and this was where the nightmare would begin. Two young men called her name, softly at first but when they knew she didn't hear them, they stepped out of one of the stalls and confronted her.

"Tony, Nigel, what in God's name are you doing here!" never for the moment connecting them to the incidence that just happened at German Headquarters.

"Mrs. Spencer, we need your help! We have to get off the island!" a desperate plea in their voices. And then Sara realized they had to be involved in what had happened several hours ago.

"I can not believe what you have done! What were you two thinking! Did it ever occur to you that you would be facing a firing squad, or the consequences that your families would be facing because of your actions, and the retaliation that will be on top on their venue?"

Sara even in the dark could see these young boys, not even old enough to enlist in the army, were petrified. And how could she become involved. She certainly had no experience trying to assist two criminals to escape the authorities. She was well aware that the Germans would leave no house, barn, or stone unturned to find them, and knew if she were to help them she had little time to prepare an escape route for them. She was already involved the minute they decided to come on to her property. There would be risks, danger for her too, but she decided then and there she really had no choice in the matter.

"And how do you suppose to get off the island?"

"Our brother had anchored his boat down in the cove, and we were headed there but there were soldiers patrolling the coast, as if they already knew we would be heading there. We made the decision we would try again a little later, but when we went back not only was the patrol still there but the boat had lost its mooring."

The next morning Erik realized that he was now in command. Major Breuer was still in serious condition recovering from an amputation of his leg that had been shattered in the bombing. Erik was in full charge, and his first priority was to find who was actually responsible for the recent destruction and deaths. He was convinced there had to be more than one person responsible, and they would still be on the island. He directed every German soldier to search all parts of the island for the suspects and to bring them in for questioning; but the two boys hiding in his driver's barn would not be discovered after days and nights of concentrated efforts to find them. The island would stay on alert until the perpetrators were found. The sun slipped through the clouds after a brief shower, appeared again for a short period and disappeared all together. Captain Mueller was facing his first challenge since replacing the duties of Major Breuer, and he hoped he was up to the test.

Sara had no idea what she had to do but she knew she had to help them, and she had to move quickly as they would definitely have an appointment with the firing squad if they were to be found. There was no sleep for her, even though the house was set back off the road and the barn even farther back where the boys were hiding, she was tuned into any sound or noise that would sound like military vehicles. It made sense to her that their escape would take place at night; but she was well aware that there would be risks involved any time of the day or night, but she did have a plan. She would explain it to her unexpected guests in the morning.

The Germans knew that the only way off the island was by boat, so they would focus on the shorelines. The Southwest section of the island could be eliminated from the search because of the strong tides and rough seas and a boat could not possibly come close enough to the shore to dock or make contact with anyone. So the question remained how she could draft a plan, an escape route for the two men sharing their sleeping quarters with her sheep. She was quite sure Captain Mueller would be too busy tomorrow to need his driver and that he almost certainly would have to remain near Headquarters to formulate a plan for finding those responsible for the sabotage initiated last evening and to get acquainted with the duties related to his new position replacing Major Breuer.

Sara decided to have breakfast along with a small glass of milk and to bring food to her new tenants. They were still soundly asleep when she found them so she left the tray and returned to the house. There was no indication of any impending military traffic out on the road or off in the distance that she could detect; and for just a minute, she was tempted to call Erik regarding the search now taking place but decided not to get him involved in any way a little paranoid perhaps that he would become suspicious.

A short time later she returned to the barn and found the boys were awake, and they had finished breakfast.

"You know that you have to get off the island, and as soon as possible. You must know that you are not safe, that your lives are in danger. Do you have any idea how to accomplish this feat?"

Both nodded but did not appear as frightened as they were last evening when Sara first approached the two young brothers.

"You have little choice. The only way off this island is by boat, but I am sure you are already aware of this so let us draft a plan. One advantage is my house is close to the shore, and I am familiar with this section of the island. The Germans know that anyone planning to leave would have to go by sea, so they will be patrolling the shorelines, but that still leaves us with securing a boat somehow. We always see the fishermen up and down the Coast, some even are able to escape the Harbor Patrol, and come down from Sweden this time of year looking for herring. The Germans also are probably assuming that because England is closer to land as opposed to France they will concentrate on this side for the obvious reasons, and I am guessing that you have already ruled out the French side."

There was no immediate response. The boys took a few ·minutes and then Tony, the older brother, stood and faced Sara.

"You are right. We need a boat, and it will have to be on this side of the island. It certainly would be more dangerous for us to try to reach the Southeast side, the side that faces France. It's too far to trek over there. And I'm sure there are soldiers swarming everywhere looking for us. Trying to reach England is the only way."

"So far I have to agree with you. There are risks regardless of what direction you take but you should try to reduce them as much as possible. I am not totally sure but I think you will find a raft in our tool shed. My husband used to fish from it down in the cove. It's not exceptionally large which might be a good thing in your case, and I am not sure if it's strong enough to reach the fishing boats but we are out of options."

"You may know that I am a driver for a Captain Mueller, a German officer, and because of your deeds last evening he has been promoted to the Commander of this island. Because of your activities I have been granted a holiday today, and I have the car here. It may just be the bonus that we need. With your approval we can take the raft, place it in the trunk, and then both of you can climb in it as there will be room. I'll drive you as close to the water as possible hoping not to arouse suspicion. You can carry the raft to the water and try to make it out to the fishing boats in the harbor. The boats should be deserted at night, and it should be easy for you to stow away. I doubt even at roadblocks that they would not let me through. I speak German, and I am driving a German car plus I have papers. I do not anticipate any problems from this point of view; but of course, there are no guarantees."

So a plan was activated, and the decision was reached to leave in late afternoon. Sara felt a car on the road during daylight was less conspicuous if patrols were out in the area. Returning home minus her passengers should not be a problem. That is if the plan did not fail.

The two boys continued to spend the next few hours in the barn. Sara collected some food for them to take and filled a thermos with water. Just a little after four in the afternoon she summoned the boys, opened the trunk so they could load the raft, climbed into the raft as she had suggested earlier that day, closed the trunk and went on the way, turned left out of the driveway in the direction of the sea. She had decided to leave a little earlier so if she was stopped it shouldn't appear anything but normal. She took her time in the decision as the days were getting longer this time of year; and she wanted to prevent Tony and Nigel from hiding in the woods for too long a time before setting the raft in the water, and she came to the conclusion it was less risky than traveling after dark.

Just a short time after being on the road Sara saw what appeared to be a roadblock up ahead. There were two soldiers armed with machine guns, one on each side of the lane, where two or three oil drums which had been pushed together leaving space for only one travel lane. There were only a very few cars on the road which was not unusual since the Germans had captured the island most traveling in the opposite direction probably making their way home from work. Petro was scarce and rationed making travel by car restricted, and the Germans required a special permit for drivers which also limited the number of automobiles on the roads. The sun had started its decent following a path West toward the sea, and it bounced off the windshield making it difficult for Sara to see what was going on in front of her. She tried to remain as calm as possible but she could feel her heart racing and her foot shaking on the gas pedal. She could see that the car in front of her had been signaled to stop and ordered to pull over to the side. What she witnessed next struck fear into her very soul. One of the soldiers was opening the trunk of the car ahead of her, and the second soldier had crossed over toward her and was motioning to pull up behind the car in front of her.

"Good afternoon. May I see your papers? We have orders to stop all vehicles, including our own."

She produced the necessary papers which he quickly glanced at and returned them back to her.

"My name is Mrs. Spencer, and I'm your Commander's driver. I have been given the day off and am on my way to have supper with a friend over in Cromwell, and I will be returning in a few hours." She spoke to him in German.

"Again I have my orders, Mrs. Spencer. I need the key to your trunk."

"You will have to call Captain Mueller as he has it, I do not."

"There is no phone service over at Headquarters. The power lines are down."

"Let me ask you corporal, do you think I would have anything in the trunk that would endanger your Captain or for that matter, me!" She purposely made no reference to what they were searching for.

The soldier whom Sara would guess was not much older than the two boys in the trunk turned a shade of brilliant pink. He said nothing, hesitated, but flagged her through telling her he was sorry for the inconvenience and actually seemed a little embarrassed by the ordeal. She wondered if she would be stopped on her return but it wouldn't matter to her then.

The two brothers, Tony and Nigel, finally made it off the island, but the search continued for several days. She felt there was no purpose in offering any information or details to anyone; and even years after the war, she decided never to tell the story. There was no reason for any explanation after so much time had elapsed. She did wonder if the boys had eventually returned to the island. She never saw them again. And from that time on in her life she never felt fear as she had on that drive to the sea.

CHAPTER 13

Claudia was exhausted. The labor was a difficult one. The mid-wife was summoned; but knowing the first birth was a long process, she took her time getting to Claudia. When she finally arrived she pulled the blankets back; made an initial observation, and concluded it would probably still be a few more hours before the baby would be born. She left Claudia, contractions still a distance apart, and she joined Frau Richter in the next room and gave her a quick report.

"She is doing fine. I think we still have a few hours before the baby comes. If you want to sit with her, I don't see any reason why you shouldn't."

The mid-wife wanted a cigarette badly, and it explained her lack of patience today. She had always been a chain smoker but not so these days. Cigarettes were scarce since the war and now were rationed. And as predicted the baby arrived just about the time the mid-wife had predicted.

"You have a beautiful baby girl, Mrs. Mueller."

"Please let me see her, hold her!"

And after the smiles and the tears, the joy of seeing her daughter for a few minutes, the new mother fell into a deep sleep. It would be late morning before she awoke and held her daughter again, and it was feeding time.

"Hello my darling. I am your very proud mother. You are so pretty. I think you look like your handsome papa. Yes, I'm sure."

Tears welded up in Claudia's eyes. She missed Erik. She missed him so much, more then any other time since he had been gone so many months ago. Again she cursed the man who was responsible for this fruitless war, Adolph Hitler. There was a hurt, beyond words, that stuck within her like an illness that nothing could cure, clawing at her constantly. She would wake up during the night, unable to fall asleep again, and she would talk to Erik pretending he was there with her. But unbeknown to Claudia she would never see her husband again. Less than three weeks after the birth of Hanna, the name she gave to her daughter, she would succumb from complications of pneumonia and childbirth.

CHAPTER 14

Summer once again came to Trakai. It was late June and Mikael, like he often would, decided to take a break and walk down around the lake. It was a warm summer evening. A slight breeze came from the water, a perfect relief to the day's hot and humid weather. There somehow felt a feeling of peacefulness, of quietness, the only disturbance was the constant lapping of the waves as they moved toward the sand.

He started to walk to the dock where he planned to stay for awhile before returning to the cabin. There was no hurry as he knew on this warm night he would be more comfortable here near the water then in the stuffy cabin. And it was then that he first saw her. He watched as she moved from the water and stepped to the shore, reaching for the clothes she had left there. Mikael knew she hadn't seen him. He stood there for a long time incapable of taking his eyes away from her. No, she definitely was unaware of his presence.

Droplets of water fell from her breasts, her nipples hardened by the slight breeze blowing in from the lake.

"God she was so beautiful!" Mikael thought almost aloud. It was like seeing her for the first time and some inherent force seemed to propel him toward her. He moved slowly as the last thing he wanted to do was startle her, frighten her.

"I'm definitely being tested," he thought, and he wondered if he would fail. He, as a priest, was supposed to suppress these feelings, to be free of any passion.

"Mikael, you frightened me! How long have you been here? I did not see you standing there!" her voice projecting complete surprise and a slight tone of berating.

He did not answer, he could not answer, but remained motionless and speechless looking at her for what seemed a painfully long time, staring at her nakedness, her full round breasts, and he was overcome with a need to pull her close to him! Would God strike him down he wondered!

It soon became apparent to him that not even God and all His saints in the heavens could prevent him from taking this woman. He wanted to take her in his arms, to hold her close to him, to kiss her, for her to kiss him back.

At this moment in time beside the lake here in Trakai, a place far away from St. Casmir, he would make love to this beautiful woman with the long golden hair and eyes the color of the sky on a bright, sunny day. The moment had not been planned, it just happened; and if this would be a sin against his Almighty God, then he would have to pay the price, suffer the consequences for he was incapable of walking away and leaving her.

"Sophie, you are so beautiful!" His words were barely audible. And he reached to her and pulled her in his arms and kissed her, gently at first and then with an urgency and passion that he was unaware existed in him, and she kissed him back with the same passion.

She shivered at the touch of his hands moving gently, softly over her body, and what seemed like an eternity, he lifted her in his arms and carried her from the shore to a small clearing, her arms folded around his neck, and he placed her down on the grass and moved next to her; and as they laid there by the lake, the sound of the waves lapping against the shore, Mikael knew neither Heaven nor Hell could prevent him from making love to her.

Sophie reached over to Mikael and unbuttoned his shirt. She moved her hands over his bare chest and then gradually reached below his waist and touched him, and he moved even closer to her naked body, a whimper escaping from him, setting the way for the lovemaking that was to follow. And when he was completely naked, she moved her legs so he could find her, and she cried out at that moment his hardness awaking every fiber of her being, a passion so completely foreign to her.

His lovemaking became tender; desperate all at the same time, and he stopped for a moment trying to hold on to this feeling as long as possible wanting her pleasure to equate his; but it was not to be, not here, the first time they would make love, and he fell on her exhausted. And when the time had ended they fell into each others arms and lay there together. It would not be the only time they would make love here in Trakai, but for Mikael it would be the one that he would remember forever.

In his arms she felt completely comfortable, and her thoughts turned back to the train on the way to this place. She felt a closeness that felt so perfect, so right. And it was time, there served no purpose being a virgin in these unpredictable times.

"Sophie, I'm so sorry!" he whispered to her. Not for making love to you but I'm afraid I've had little experience in this department!"

"Mikael, it was beautiful!"

He did not answer as he knew nothing could change what was.

They held each other close for a long time, but it would be soon before they would have to head to the cabins. Sophie was shivering from the coolness that had settled in and off in the distance something sounded like gunfire, but it was the rumble of thunder. It appeared perhaps a storm was brewing.

"We must be getting back!" and he turned and kissed her for the final time that night.

"Where or whatever we do for the rest of our lives I shall never forget being here with you." As she knew he belonged to God; and this was just a small detour, and when this time and this place was a distant memory she knew in her heart he would return to his God and be a priest again. Maybe God peering down in the middle of this Hell possibly would forgive us.

Mikael walked her to her cabin, few words spoken between them. They disappeared into the dark. Their secret would remain just that, not to be shared. The rain had started, perfect timing. He could feel the humidity start to disperse at last.

Sophie watched as Mikael walked toward his cabin. She could still feel the warmth of him next to her, feel his breath, the touch of him. She had doubts that she would be able to fall asleep as she was not feeling tired, on the contrary. She wanted desperately to call after him wishing he might turn around and return to her, but she knew it didn't deem possible so she stood outside for a few moments before she went inside. Would Anele guess her secret? She wasn't prepared to share it with anyone. Maybe in time she could change her mind but not now, not just yet. She would bask in her pleasure alone. Would they judge her, preach to her if they knew. Sophie was quite sure she truly did not care but for now she would keep it to herself. Would Mikael confide in Justas? Maybe not she thought. Tomorrow was another day, and she was aware that she and Mikael would be together for the full day. And she knew that there would be a long list of days ahead that she would get to share with him. As she finally drifted off to sleep she wondered how Mikael felt about her. She would soon find the answer. There would be more nights of romance with her priest who would defer his role until the end of the war. He would fall in love with this beautiful girl who gave herself to him and would prevent him in this life, and for all eternity, from having any guilt for abandoning his vow of celibacy, not even remotely. And from their union a child would be conceived on this island, a child that would be born to Sophie eight months after leaving this island, home to them for the last six years, and this secret she would keep from her priest for over a decade. After the birth of their daughter she agonized over the decision to reveal to Mikael that he had a daughter, a girl who was the very image of her father. In the end she decided it would serve no purpose to tell him. She had made a new life for herself after immigrating to England along with a contingent of former resistant fighters. Mikael returned to Vilnius and St. Casmir after the war. God won him back. She knew in her heart she could not win this battle, not now nor never.

Sophie finally fell asleep. She had a dream, but when she awoke the next morning she could barely remember it. She was on a ship, a huge ship crossing the ocean, and Mikael was standing on the dock very still not moving, remaining there in the same place until he was out of sight. She tried in vain to remember the rest of it but unsuccessfully. The next night she had the same dream and again she could only remember bits and pieces of it. It was only years later that the dream made any sense to her.

CHAPTER 15

It was too hot to sleep. Rarely in this part of the country with the proximately to the lake did the temperature elevate to this degree, and there was high humidity also a rare ingredient, a combination that made sleeping difficult. Usually, regardless of the weather, there would always be a breeze off the lake, but not on this hot, humid August night.

Mikael turned toward the window which was wide open, but the heat hung in the room with no sign of relief. There was a full moon shining in the darkness reflecting in the lake; and off in the distance somewhere in the forest, the wolves were in concert howling at it.

He glanced at the clock. It was just past mid-night. By some unknown force, maybe spiritual intervention, Justas was sound asleep in the top bunk. The other two bunks were empty, and Mikael figured maybe they too couldn't sleep and had decided to find comfort by the lake, maybe even take a swim to cool off.

Mikael rarely questioned God's plan, but here in Trakai, a full year since being uprooted from his other life and living here on this humid evening unable to sleep he wondered what God had in store for him and all the other Lithuanians who came to this place. Had He already mapped out their future or was He about to let man destroy himself. He, Mikael, priest first, resistance fighter was well aware that this puzzle couldn't be solved, not on this sleepless night, not tomorrow, or at anytime soon. Revelations says God, not man, in the last days He would destroy this place called Earth.

And finally he went back to the cabin, found Justas still sound asleep, and the two empty bunks now held two men, the missing room mates. They, too, appeared to be sleeping for the night.

Mikael climbed into bed and he, too, soon feel asleep. He had a dream. It was not the first time he had this recurring dream. There was a boy running toward him calling his name. He had a strong resemblance to him. But the boy never caught him and never gave him his name.

Mikael would finally meet the boy in his dream; but the boy would be a man, and the man would be his brother one he never knew exited. And Sophie, young beautiful Sophie, would be instrumental in the reunion.

CHAPTER 16

T he months slipped by and Christmas arrived with a rare sprinkle of snow. For the first time in a long time Sara truly was feeling sorry for herself. She had a small tree complete with decorations, some given to her by Grandma Wagner her beloved German grandmother many years ago along with so many happy memories of her childhood. She had scattered icicles one by one on the branches and finished with tiny white candles, but there was no substitute for the loneliness she was experiencing. Would it ever end, she wondered, the war that separated her from Paul. And though she desperately tried to stop thinking of the handsome German officer; he crept into her thoughts, and it frightened her because she seemed to have no control over it. She often wondered what it would be like for him to make love to her.

On Christmas Eve she reluctantly accepted an invitation for supper and to attend church services with her friends in Cromwell. There were only three churches on the island, a Roman Catholic Church, St. Mary's By the Sea, and the Anglican denomination of St. George which was the largest parish on the island and on the French side was St. Gregory. She and Paul had been married at St. George. They were so happy in those days never anticipating what the future was planning. She would adhere to the fact they would one day again have some joy which had been denied these past years.

It was pitch black outside the cabin except for the full moon that appeared to be held in the sky by the canopy of trees that were stationed in the forest. Sophie could hear the wolves in the distance, their sound sending shivers down her spine. Snow had been accumulating on the ground but it appeared to have melted almost as quickly as it had touched down. The tree branches dipped in all directions from the weight of the snow that was slowly turning into sleet casting an abstract look against the blackness.

The snow brought back pleasant, happy memories of her childhood when she and her sister would spend hours playing in the snow, pulling their sleds up the hill, sliding down, and never seemed to tire. And at the end of the day after arriving back home there would be a cup of hot coco, a batch of cookies that has just been taken out of the oven, and a blazing fire waiting for them. The wet mittens would be dried near the fire along with cold, wet toes. She remembers her mother, auburn hair streaked with gray, blue eyes wide and smiling, a favorite apron tied around her waist as she rolled out the cookie dough, a pie or two already baking in the oven. And many times, senele, (grandmother) who lived with them would make home-made soup filling the house with all kinds of warm, wonderful aromas. Sophie missed her family and knew there would be little chance of seeing them in the immediate future.

Tomorrow was the beginning of Advent and Christmas would soon follow. It would be the second Christmas since coming here to Trakai, and the entire camp was making preparations for the holiday collecting baskets of pinecones and acorns that the wind had shaken from their branches and gathering greens and holly for wreath making. Each cabin would have one to hang on their doors, and each cabin would receive a small Christmas tree, compliments of Cabin No.5 who had volunteered to tackle the task. Sophie tried to blot out the fact that, even if only for a short time, that there was a war raging through out Europe. The Germans had not invaded Lithuania, unlike Poland in 1939, the beginning of a war that would continue for six long agonizing years. But sooner or later the Germans would definitely come; it was inevitable, but let it be later Sophie was thinking. The magnitude of the destruction reported from Poland was difficult to comprehend. Who really were these monsters who had been granted permission to inflict so much suffering on the human race, like a domino effect, invading and capturing one country and marching on to capture and take control of yet one more. There would eventually be few countries in Europe that would be spared from the horror and the destruction planted by the Nazis.

During the next fifteen months the young people who had banded together for their common cause practiced all they had learned across the lake in their training classes. They held mock exercises. They memorized where every river, bridge, stream, railroad track, power plant, road, village and town was located until each and everyone became an expert in it. This knowledge and the combination of their skill with the crossbow plus the protection that the forest would provide resulted in escaping harm and even death. Years later when these resistant fighters would reflect on the war years here in Trakai they were in total agreement these factors contributed in saving their lives and became instrumental in keeping the Germans from digging deeper into their country.

Snow came in full force for the next two days forcing the camp to cancel all practice sessions. Snow piled everywhere, on the roofs, against the cabin doors making access impossible, and blanketing the ice on the lake.

On the third day the snow ceased, the weather seemed to stabilize, the sun appeared making for perfect conditions to strap on snowshoes and survey some of the areas that had been inaccessible by foot. One of the cardinal rules of the camp was that not all groups could disperse at the same time. The reason was fairly simple to explain. If the Germans were able to ascend on Trakai with out any warning, there would always be a contingent behind to defend themselves and deter the enemy from advancing farther into the South where many of the coal mines existed. There was speculation if the Germans discovered the location that the coal would be shipped to Germany and undoubtedly contribute to their war efforts exhausting what the Lithuanians needed as the coal was the prime source of heating their homes.

The days slipped into weeks and months, and there was no sign of the Germans coming to Trakai. In the meantime these young patriots living here beside the lake and on the rim of the forest would practice the skills that they were taught and perfected from their survival courses. And one day everything was about to change. It was the middle of December and the winter so far had remained a mild one but snow had fallen sometime during the night and had melted almost as fast as it had accumulated causing the surrounding area to become one big quagmire. By late morning the snow had turned to heavy rain beating relentlessly down on the earth.

No one could have predicted the chain of events that were about to happen here in Trakai. The Germans finally came to this place and soon discovered they really never had a chance. It would be a huge victory for these young Lithuanians, but it would become their first experience with killing and with death.

The signal came at 11:45 A.M.

"Sophie, Anele, Vytautas, come with us! This is not a practice session!"

And all those long hours mastering the crossbow would now pay dividends on this unusually mild December day.

As the Germans, perhaps a hundred, followed the tanks as they rolled in the direction of the lake soon learned that mud and soldiers were not always compatible. All went better than anyone could have predicted, and some credit had to be given to the snow, the rain, and the mud that resulted. No, a lot of credit!

In the beginning the tanks appeared to move in single file progressing slowly and soon even slower and almost coming to a complete halt barely moving. This in turn forced the soldiers, who eventually became almost ankle-high in the mud, to struggle with each step. Perfect! They would now all become sitting ducks.

As the first flank came into sight the young resistance fighters with crossbows so silent took them down one at a time, one soldier after another. There were no gunshots to warn the next group as they approached. They seemed confused unable to comprehend the full event of what was happening. The tanks which were barely moving rolled ahead completely unaware of the massacre behind them. And waiting farther down the road at the edge of the forest the Lithuanians armed with grenades finished off the tanks. There was no need for silence at this point. It was over!

For most of these defenders it was the very first encounter with death. Though eager to celebrate their victory, it was bittersweet. They felt there were no winners in wartime. History just kept repeating its blunders, nothing gained from all past mistakes. They knew in the end there were really no winners.

For the next few months the young men and young women traded their crossbows for rifles and machine guns, slept during the daytime preparing for the tasks at hand. They blew up bridges, trains, and train tracks, communication systems, and everything and anything that could immobilize the enemy. They banded together and were successful. The

Germans never made it back to Trakai thanks to the efforts and bravery of these patriots that were recognized after the war for the contribution they unselfishly made for their country. In Trakai Castle that was built many centuries ago was a room dedicated to the resistance fighters of Lithuania during WWII. And if you looked closely at the pictures lining the walls you would see that there were more women in this campaign then were men!!

Surprisingly there were few casualties in the years at Trakai. Their biggest loss came only a short time before the war was winding down to the final days. One of the very last patrols that were assigned to the demolition of a small bridge approximately twenty miles West of Trakai, a contingent trained and experienced in this type of sabotage and explosives, lost two men and two women. The plan to blow up the bridge where a section of the train tracks that crossed the bridge was vital in carrying supplies to German troops was to take two days including the time necessary to travel there and then return. Missions were carefully drafted so the actual destruction of the target would often take place shortly before dawn so they had the gift of darkness but just enough light to filter through to ensure the plan would proceed with as little error as possible, or even better, no miscalculations. But on this last day of April, a month ending with an excessive amount of rainfall; the river had risen to its bank, and it forced the young saboteurs to take extra time in selecting the section of the bridge where they would detonate the explosives. They realized that it would become more dangerous as the sun would make its appearance. The two women who where posted on either side of the bridge were the first to realize the situation was becoming dangerous and raced to warn the others to abort the mission, but it was too late. A plane flew out of the clouds and quickly discovered them and commenced firing killing them instantly. The others dove into the river and swam to the other bank where the trees shielded them from the gunfire. The plane circled around several times before disappearing over the horizon. Of the seven who embarked on this mission only three made it back.

They would soon discover that two who dove into the water had been shot, and the current washed them down stream. One of the men who lost his life was Father Judzapas, a priest who came from the city of Vilnius, and who had shared a cabin with Mikael and Justas during their years in Trakai. This day was to become the greatest loss for the young resistance fighters since the beginning in 1939. The next day a patrol was sent out to bring the bodies back to Trakai, but only two, the women, would return and would be laid to rest next to Anele and Peetar for all eternity. Mikael thought of the two men who did not return which made him sad, but he felt it was more important where their souls had journeyed. At the memorial service Mikael once again read the eulogy and said the prayers, tears freely streaming down his face. This would be the last Lithuanian that would be buried here in the make-shift cemetery under the umbrella of birch trees. The war was about to come to an end. Mikael had mixed emotions about leaving this place where he had spent the happiest years of his young life. And of course there was Sophie! He wondered how life could continue without her. God would have to take over.

CHAPTER 17

The snow melted, in the woods, around the lake, everywhere in Trakai, and spring arrived just a bit early. Tulips, the flower of Lithuania, bloomed in all shades of colors, buds made their arrival and leaves would soon follow as always, grass turned a vivid green once more, and the Germans did not return to Trakai, but they did not depart from Lithuania. It became time now for these young partisans finally to put into practice what they were preparing to do for so long.

The next few years proved to be very successful for these Lithuanian resistance fighters. Sophie, Mikael, and Justas, with rare exception, went on every mission together and with the other members of their contingent banded together to destroy communication systems, blow up bridges, railroad tracks and supply trains, proving over and over how a small group could accomplish and make such important contributions to the war effort. And just short of a miracle was how so many of them came away with not even a scratch! Credit would have to be shared by their teacher, Mrs. Massud and their Heavenly Father.

It was during this time that Sophie had fallen in love with Mikael, solider, best friend, priest. She knew in her heart that she could never completely belong to him as he already belonged to another, his God. During the post war years, her relocation to England, the birth of her daughter, Mikael's child, eventually her marriage and moving to the States, she would never completely loose her love for him. It would be over a decade before he would get to meet Amber, his daughter.

There would be no planes airborne today. It started to rain in torrents, and the wind steadily whipped the rain around in circles with little indication it was going to cease any time soon.

"Captain Mueller, I suggest we pull over to the side of the road. I can barely see a foot in front of me. It's been a long time since I've seen it come down this hard, and I wouldn't even take a guess how long it will last. These wind storms come up very fast without much warning."

Erik was surprised how composed she was under the circumstance, but he would later discover it was a characteristic of the British probably developed at an early age not to display too much emotion. The rain continued to pelt the car, was relentless, and showed no sign of changing course.

"Captain Mueller, with your permission, I suggest we wait out the storm at my house which is only a few minutes away. We could wait this out there."

"Your house is this close to the airfield?" he seemed surprised.

"Yes, not exactly next door, but close to it."

"Will there be anyone at home?"

"No, I'm there alone, only my animals I'm afraid."

Erik wondered if her husband was in the war but he would wait again to bring up the subject. But before he could erase his thought she told him her husband was a pilot in the R.A.F., and she had not seen him for almost a year. Of course she was not privileged to know where he was just that he was off fighting this bloody war. Almost immediately she wished she had not given him this information. She must remember in the future not to mention anything at all in reference to the war; but this was her first war, of course, and she would have to learn a few things about it if there were an etiquette required!

Erik did not respond. There really was nothing he could say, but it brought his attention to the fact that the Germans were not the only ones afflicted during these times; and for the first time he started to question the insanity of it all.

"Use your own judgment. Sitting here for the rest of the day doesn't sound like too much enjoyment, and it could become a little dangerous as the mud has already started to slip down away from the hills."

"I'm afraid we are in for a lengthy, early spring storm. The island frequently experiences the scourge of them during this time of year. The roads become impassable often downing trees and the power lines. They probably didn't include this in your briefing here!"

It took approximately ten minutes, maybe a tad longer, to make the trip with the accompanying rain and wind a distance that would take approximately only a few minutes if the storm had not hit the island.

"That is my driveway just up ahead, barely visible. It is a gravel driveway and subject to becoming a quagmire in these rain storms, but I think we are a little ahead of the impending damage."

It turned out to be a long and winding driveway, and Erik could see stonewalls on both sides as his driver had to shift into second and make her way slowly and cautiously in the direction of the house. He would later learn the old farm house had a barn on the back of the property, completely hidden from the road, housing a few sheep. He wondered how this woman could balance all her obligations.

She pulled the car as close to the house as possible and instructed Erik to wait a few minutes.

"Give me a second to turn the light on so you can find your way."

He waited there as she had suggested to him; and when the light had been turned on, he dashed to the house where she was holding the door for him.

"I'll put tea on and fix something to eat."

Did she say tea? Yes, I'm sure she did. He wondered if she had any Scotch.

And once again he would wait for the right time to inquire. He would soon learn that there was no Scotch; or at least that is what she told him, but he would settle for a pint of ale which he drank warm in the German way.

"This weather warrants a fire in the fireplace. Would you mind, there are logs in the basket on the hearth along with the kindling, matches should be on the right-hand side of the mantle."

Erik had lots of experience in getting fireplaces to the place of a blazing, comfortable fire. He also was well aware that luck often was a key factor, but the fire caught almost immediately. He would sit by the fire for awhile hoping his uniform would quickly and completely dry. Just the quick dash into the house left him soaking wet. It reminded him of home and of Claudia in the cabin in Bannenberg, the pine covered mountains where they had spent their honeymoon. It also brought back memories of his father and him, a long time ago when the two of them would trek into the woods, Erik pulling the cart behind him. They would return home; the cart filled to the brim, and father and son would split the wood and stack it row upon row in deep piles. By the time spring would arrive most of the wood in the woodpile would be depleted. Again in the early fall father and son would repeat the trek back into the forest for the fuel they would use to heat their house in the coming winter.

He would later learn from his driver that the two beer steins placed on the mantle were part of a collection her grandmother had taken with her when she moved from Germany and were handed down to her granddaughter after she passed away. Sara had decided to relegate the rest of the collection to the attic until the Germans left the island permanently. Grouped together beside the beer steins were a collage of photographs and a single picture of a young man in uniform that Eric would guess was her husband.

"His name is Paul. We have been married for three years. This house has been in his family for several generations. We moved here shortly before the war. At one time it was a working farm, mostly sheep, a few horses, and in the summer they would plant vegetables and bring them to the farmer's market. I pray everyday that Paul returns safely; and it may surprise you, Captain, I wish the same for you, a safe return home."

Erik wondered if there were any other ties, anything else inherited from her German grandmother beside the beer steins. He eventually would ask her.

"I guess there were a few things she did teach me. Yes, it definitely was her baking skills. I really make the best pastries, cakes sometimes, and pies, but my specialty is strudel. At Christmastime there was always a gingerbread house, lots of gumdrops and frosting, and fond, happy memories of being with her especially as a child. But I always felt her gift to me was her language. As you know languages are so much easier to learn when you are young."

For the moment it was hard to comprehend that there was a war raging somewhere in a far-off distant place. Sara took to the task of preparing and later serving lunch, making a tray for each of them complete with a tiny white doily, little doubt it had been hand crocheted by the young mistress of the house Erik thought. Sara later made herself a cup of tea, added milk along with a teaspoon of sugar plus a biscuit she took from a tin container. It had become an afternoon ritual for as long as she remembered. Erik passed on her offer of tea but did accept the biscuit. His guess would be that they were home-baked and recently so.

"I am hoping we get some reprise soon but concerned about road conditions on this section of the Island, as you already know our roads are narrow and high-crowned and many unpaved. You may have noticed over the last few months since your arrival here that there are no road or street lights making driving after daylight diminishes especially dangerous on some parts of the Island. Fortunately, it is not as bad here when compared to the far end of the island, especially in the southwest corner where the cliffs are. There are some lights at the airstrip but very few as you know."

The rain continued outside in full force pounding the roof top, and a number of times a branch would fly through the air just missing the windows. The wind would manage to rattle the shutters, the few that had not been closed and secured.

At first with all the confusion Sara had little time to reflect on her decision to bring this German officer into her home. After all the Germans continued to bomb London, killing hundreds of its citizens, destroying her beautiful city. She was from London living there until her marriage, but it was not difficult for her to believe that under the uniform he wore there was a decent human being; and like her, had no role in the development of the conflict now existing between their two countries. She felt, like her, he would much rather be at home with his wife and family then be practically stranded on this island with no end to this bloody war in sight. She felt safe and comfortable with this man sitting next to her by the fire wearing the uniform of an officer of the hated enemy. In fact, she couldn't help but wonder what her true feelings had become toward him, and she became very confused over it. She looked forward to the days she knew they would spend together and dreaded the ones she would not be with him. Unknown to Sara at this time Erik, too, was trying to explain how he felt toward his German speaking driver. There would be an answer off in their future, and the explanation would change direction for both the English woman and the German officer in a way neither could have ever predicted.

And time would prove that her instincts about this handsome officer were correct. He was a decent chap and in some ways reminded her of Paul, her husband, and she thought this very strange. It didn't really make much sense to her that they could be so different yet have things in common. But for the present on this damp, cold night she was too tired to try to analyze it.

"Captain Mueller, I am going to straighten up. There is a telephone on the table in the hallway, and you are welcome to use it; that is, if the lines are not down."

Erik noticed a piano askew in the far corner of the room facing two windows framed with long lace curtains. The piano was completely covered with a sheet, an indication to him that perhaps it had not been played in some time. When Sara returned to the parlor to carry off the trays she turned to face him. He had removed his hat awhile back, and she was trying to remember if this was the first time she had seen him without it.

"Do you play the piano, Mrs. Spencer?"

"Yes, I do, or I should say I played a long time ago, before the war." She wanted to add before the bastards started this bloody thing but said nothing. There was no hatred for Captain Mueller, in fact she feared that some chemistry existed between them which frightened her to death, but she despised what he represented, the suffering and misery inflicted on her country. And she found herself feeling guilty at times, even a traitor, for chaffering this German officer on his missions and now he was here in her home. She made a promise to herself that no one on the island would ever learn the circumstances of this day.

The next few hours passed without much conversation between them, and Sara was hoping the rain and wind would soon subside. It was impossible to avoid this man whom she now knew for six months, and she continued not to feel good about the possible discovery of a German officer here in the home of her and Paul. To say it was confusing for her would make it an understatement. She could not dislike this man, but her feelings would have to be put aside. It was an impossible situation, but she could not shake her feelings not quite knowing just how to define it. She loved Paul, missed him terribly, worried about his safety but was lonesome so often. At the end of the day she had nothing to look forward to but going back home to an empty house by herself making a batch of cookies perhaps, tending to the animals. She, too, felt strongly she was contributing to the war effort in her own way. Now she was suffering on two spectrums. God help her! There was no way she would ever succumb to her feelings, and Erik must never know she promised herself.

Erik surprisingly wished he could spend more time in this lovely, comfortable English cottage but the storm was passing by and he had to make an effort to inspect the airfield and prepare for the next days details. Unbeknown to either of them as Sara locked the door behind them, it would not be the last time they would come to this place. Their affair was not planned, it just happened.

He decided he would make an effort to return to the airfield not positive if it would be possible. It had been a long time since he actually got in back of the wheel, and it did seem a little strange for a minute or two; but once he maneuvered the car on to the macadam, surprisingly he was able to get to the airfield without much incidence. The place looked like a battlefield. Barrels were strewed over the entire area. The petro and oil they once contained spilled over the strip. Some of the planes had been removed and placed into the Hangers; but the remaining ones received the wrath of the wind, a few tipped on their side, the others totally turned around facing in the opposite direction on the tarmac. Tree branches had flown over the fence littering the ground. A light post had come crashing down blocking the driveway, glass shattered and blown against the building. On first observation Erik wasn't sure where to begin the project of clean-up and putting things back in order. He certainly had a challenge ahead of him. The rain and wind seemed to be on track to soon subside, but Erik knew he would have to postpone the clean-up until the next day.

CHAPTER 18

Summer came and went and fall made its entrance on the island. The weather was exceptional warm for September bringing with it heavy rainfalls, but on this third week of the month with no sign of any storm approaching Captain Mueller had decided to explore the Southwest section of the island.

"Good morning, Captain."

"Good morning Frau Spencer, you're well I hope." She nodded to him looking in the rear-view mirror as he entered the car and was seated. This was the first time that he used Frau instead of Mrs. But she knew he purposely was not being disrespectful to her.

At this point she knew him too well, and she addressed him in German asking how he was doing.

"I've seen just about the whole island but am curious about the Southwest section. There is nothing on the official agenda today so with your approval think the day looks like a perfect time to drive out there. I understand it is quite different from the rest of the island, a little on the wild side, do you agree?"

"It is probably the most beautiful and scenic area, but be warned it has frequent storms this time of year that come up with very little notice, and chances are more severe then any previous ones including the one we had last spring."

It was Sara's favorite part of the island and only a few kilometers from her house though it really was two different places. It was called Forde Point named after one of the first families to settle here and one of the few places the Germans did not bomb when they invaded the island. It was mid-morning, and there should be enough time to take the scenic route, the longer route, the one on the perimeter which would provide a view of the cliffs and some of the caves that bordered the far end. The story handed down to each generation was the caves have treasures hidden deep within their walls, a place of safe keeping for the pirates who once sailed these waters. Often during the summer months there would be attempts to swim into the caves in search of the pirate's loot;

but the force of the whirlpools inside prevented a total search, and as of this date the treasures said to lie there were never discovered.

"Could you stop along the road? I'd like to take in the view below. Are there any paths close by down to the water?"

"Yes, there are a few actually. There are some paths with steps and hand railings. We should be coming upon one shortly. Look to your left-hand side, you can see the ocean ahead. It's very rough and probably one reason there are so many caves here. The water has pounded the sides of the cliff for thousand of years chipping and carving away the rock letting the water seep in a fraction at a time. This area is riddled with secluded caves; and if you listen closely, you can hear the caves sing!"

Sara parked the car by the side of the road, and she and Erik found a path close by. As many times as Sara had come to this place during her years here on the island, she always felt it to be special; but most of all she loved the smell of the salt water. On some days the sea would send its waves crashing into the cliffs, spray rising almost to the top. Today was one of those days. Sara noticed there were clouds rolling in from the North. They could head out over the sea. It was the area that gets the most rain and violent storms even though it had been some time since a hurricane developed, but it was hurricane season and Sara had experience in this department. She remembered the last storm that completely immobilized the entire island for weeks. The day had started just like this one, sunny and mild.

"You know, Mrs. Spencer, I was a university student before I saw the ocean for the first time. There are lakes and many rivers in the part of Germany where I grew up but of course no ocean. Our school was competing in a rowing race, a regatta, so a group of us decided to take a train to Hamburg to cheer them on. They lost but it was an experience."

"One of the reasons I love it here is because of the water, you can't travel too many kilometers without ending up near it or in it!"

"Be careful on the path. It appears the railing has broken in several places, and it could be slippery."

"It's only a short way down. Look to your right-hand side, you can see the water just ahead, you'll notice how rough it is today."

They reached the bottom without incident. They walked a short distance, found suitable seating on a huge rock that jutted close to the water, and focused on the scenery.

"Not disappointed. It really is a rare place."

"I find it so peaceful here, an escape from the shape the world is in these days. The summer months are best. People will come to soak up the sun as the water rarely gets warm enough for swimming. I like to walk the beach, I find it relaxing."

"We can do that."

Before she had a chance to say anything he reached over and took her hand and pulled her up from the rock they had been sitting on for the last half hour. There was something about this German officer that scared her. There was no denying that she was attracted to him. And what about Paul, did that mean she was falling out of love with her husband. She knew these feelings could only lead to a painful and sad ending for her. And most of all she had to keep this to herself. He could not ever know.

"I'm afraid it will have to be a short walk. Those clouds could be storm clouds, and it could get pretty rough out here. They roll in from the North and within minutes develop into a storm. This time of year it could be a major one, even a threat of a hurricane not foreign to us. If you think of the location of this island it can't surprise you."

"So the walk is off."

"No, I didn't say that, just has to be a short one."

Gulls flew overhead, circling above the cliffs, squawking loudly. Perhaps they were protesting sharing this space with them.

"I had never seen a seagull until I came here. Quite loud aren't they!"

Sara nodded in agreement.

"In late summer pods of whales come from the North to find food. They are such beautiful creatures. They don't stay long, a pity. I sit here sometimes and watch them. It's fascinating. If you turn around and look ahead there is the largest cave, and it has a name, Pirate's Cave, for obvious reasons I would guess. It's behind that row of huge boulders. The shore is very narrow here you'll notice, even at low tide, but it does make walking a bit easier then when the tide comes in. I've been here when there is no shoreline at all probably one of the reasons there are so many caves. The water doesn't have to travel very far!"

They continued to walk the shore listening to the surf as it pounded against the rocks, rushing into the caves, relaxing for a few seconds, and roar back out again into the sea. And for a while the German officer and the beautiful English woman forgot there was a war marching across Europe and that they were on opposite sides of this conflict.

Erik watched as she walked along beside him, shoes removed, the laces wrapped around her hand, occasionally picking a stone from the ground and tossing it out into the water. She was stunningly beautiful he thought, and he wondered what it would be like to hold her close, to kiss her, and even make love to her. Could she possibly feel something for him? He would soon, very soon, have his answer.

He had removed his jacket and hat and left them in the car. Sara, too, decided at the last minute to do the same. She was now feeling cold and wanted to leave, also she didn't like the change in the atmosphere, and she could feel the pressure changing rapidly.

"I think we are in for a storm. I've experienced more in the last few years then I care to admit. We are also in hurricane weather, always a threat to the island. So I suggest we better head back."

Within a few minutes after reaching the car it started to rain. It poured. The windshield wipers tried in vain to keep the water off the windows. The roads would soon be flooded, and the wind would become a full pledged partner with the rain.

"So this is island life, Mrs. Spencer! Didn't we have the experience of one several months ago?"

Sara had to smile to herself. He was right of course. It was in May she remembered, but that was mild compared to what was in store. The wind would become the major culprit. It would cause the most damage.

"Captain Mueller, you know that we will not be able to drive back to Headquarters in these conditions. I suggest we try to make it, once again, to my place which is approximately seven kilometers. There are limited choices, the other one being we stay in the car all night!"

"No other options?"

"None I am afraid!"

The wind started to pick up its pace. Tree branches were swaying and bending rehearsing for the next gusts of wind that should toss the broken limbs to the ground. Fog danced off the ocean and made its way up to the land sharing the conditions that soon would limit visibility.

Sara and Erik rode in silence most of the way.

"I can see the driveway, just barely, there on the right."

The driveway was long and narrow room for only one lane. The dirt had turned to mud as it always did in there storms but whatever saint was in charge during this one did their job. Sara pulled up to the side of the house beside the door and turned off the engine. She placed her hands and head on the wheel and gave a sigh of relief.

"Darn good bit of driving! Are you alright?"

"Half and half I suppose. I am grateful we made it. I had my doubts there for awhile. The door is unlocked. Try to make a dash for it. I'll follow you."

Sara had no problem falling asleep and staying asleep. The day had exhausted her. She knew this storm would linger possibly into the next night.

The chill in the room awoke her at dawn. The logs had finished burning. A few embers still glowed in the fireplace. The wind and the rain had subsided slightly, and she knew it was only the calm in the storm and would not last for very long.

She got out of bed, the clock on the nightstand read 6:10, almost the exact time she usually got up. There appeared to be no evidence of the Captain being awake. She lifted her bathrobe from the bedpost and wrapped it around her and headed to the kitchen. A pot of coffee would be the first task of the day and a little later a hard-boiled egg with sausage and a slice of toast with marmalade.

The coffee pot sat on the coal-fired stove perking away, and the smell of it floated throughout the kitchen. She would let it sit for a few minutes before pouring herself a cup. It was one of several items that were now rationed as well as tea, another reason to hate this bloody war.

Sara didn't see him at first. He was standing in the doorway fully dressed but without a jacket, and he had removed his gun. She hated it that she found him attractive; and over the past year, she enjoyed being with him. The weekends when she did not see him she was miserable and had to admit she missed him. This damn war! It should be Paul here with me she thought not him, not the enemy. She wondered why she had been selected to be his chauffeur. There were other women who spoke German here on this island. She certainly was not the only one. And he did speak English, not fluently, but it would only be a matter of time before he would master it. In fact most conversations the past few weeks were in English as he requested. He was intelligent, it was always clear to her.

They looked at each other without a word. Erik realized he had never seen her in anything but her uniform, hair always pulled back neatly tucked under her hat, and now she stood before him her hair like spun gold falling below her shoulders. "Forgive me. I didn't hear you leave your room."

"Don't apologize. These are not normal times, are they! We can not expect to act in a way society would grant its approval."

"May I ask, Captain, did you sleep well?"

"I did and so did a calico cat that found her way to the foot of the bed."

"So that's where Miss Lily disappeared. I tried to find her before I turned in. She'll be looking for her breakfast soon!"

Sara and Erik sat in the kitchen and had their breakfast, and Miss Lily arrived just like clockwork.

Outside the storm raged, black clouds scouting the sky almost seemed to reach and touch the ground below. The rain flooded the fields, the roads, and everything in between. Trees toppled and brought down the wires with them. There would be no venturing outside today. Tomorrow morning could possibly be the earlier time.

"You're quiet this morning."

"I'm sorry. I was thinking it should be Paul and me. Forgive me."

"I understand. It's alright." And he really did understand.

The storm finally seemed to settle down, and Erik made a decision to try to return to Headquarters hoping the road was passable. He told Sara he would return possibly the next morning.

Erik was pleasantly surprised that all was pretty much the same at Headquarters as when he had left two days ago. They were in the process of restoring the telephone lines and replacing a window that had blown out not much damage considering the force of the storm. Lieutenant Lang provided him with an update from Berlin and gave him a condensed version of the events of the previous days. He also requested a calendar containing information pertinent until the end of the week.

"Lieutenant Lang, do you have any plans for this evening? Would you join me for dinner, let's say 6:30, at the Smuggler's Tavern. I want to visit with Major Breuer maybe around 5. He is leaving for Berlin the end of the week. His rehabilitation here is complete. It's been a long haul, but he's glad to be alive."

"Yes, sir, I will meet you there at six-thirty."

After visiting with Major Breuer and joining the young Lieutenant for dinner Erik returned to his quarters, showered, and went to bed. He planned on returning to Sara in the morning. His last thoughts as he feel asleep were of her. He missed her and wondered how long he could keep his feelings to himself. It had been awhile since he thought of Claudia. He felt he had already been unfaithful to her.

The storm door at the side of the house continued to slam against the house, and Sara supposed that the force of the wind pulled the latch up so she decided to try to secure it. But her plan didn't go as expected. Just as she reached to lock the door a gust of wind ripped between the two doors and caught her hand forcing her to let it go. It wasn't until she returned inside that she felt the pain and saw blood trickling down from her hand and the gash that cut into her flesh.

She headed toward the bathroom where she stored the first-aid kit droplets of blood making a path on the floor.

Eric was in the parlor sitting and enjoying the fire when he heard Sara call to him.

"I may need your help! Please could you come to the bathroom?"

"What has happened?"

"My hand, I caught it in the door. There is a first-aid kit in the medicine chest over the sink. There should be bandages there."

"You will need an antiseptic!"

"There's some in the kit."

Erik reached up and took the kit from the chest, took out the antiseptic, placed Sara's hand over the sink and poured the antiseptic over the wound.

"It's going to sting a bit!"

"Yes, yes it hurts!"

"Sit down on the stool, and I'll bandage and tape your hand. You probably would benefit from a few stiches; but it is not going to happen, so I will tape it as tightly as I can."

At first the bleeding would not stop so Erik instructed Sara to hold the bandage as firmly as possible so he could cut the tape and apply it over the bandage to secure it. Finally the bleeding did stop.

"It's not perfect but will have to do; and you, are you doing alright?"

Sara nodded but the hand started to throb and tears welled up in her eyes. Erik reached down to help her from the stool and took her in his arms, held her and tried comforting her. A shiver ran through her, and she turned and clung to him.

"I think I know what will help, do you have any whiskey hidden some where?" remembering her denial on his last visit.

"I'm really not sure. If there is any in the house it would be in the dining room cupboard."

Erik did find a bottle about half full exactly where she said it would be. He found a glass and poured a drink for her. Then he poured one for himself.

"One thing you English know how to do!"

Sara gave him a slight smile, finished her whiskey, thanked him for taking care of her, excused herself, and went off to bed. She wanted him to follow her but she knew he would not, not this night anyway. She had never been unfaithful to Paul, and her husband was the only man she had ever been with. She was only nineteen years old when they were married. She actually met him for the first time when she was just thirteen years old. They both had attended a rugby game in Oxford where he was a student. She was visiting her brother David and his roommate had a brother. His name was Paul Spencer. Of course he paid no attention at this their first meeting but all changed three years later when both arrived for graduation ceremonies. For her it definitely was love at first sight; and though he would never admit to it, she always thought for him it was love at second sight. Three years later they were married, church wedding and a lawn reception, complete with champagne, canopies, and a roast beef dinner served with blood pudding followed by cake with strawberries and cream for desert. The honeymoon was a trip to the South of France with a brief stopover in Paris. They were in love and happily planning for the future when Paul was called into the Royal Air Force several months after Hitler invaded Poland. The English were an alley of Poland and had made a commitment to Poland in the event Germany invaded their country. The rest is history.

Sara waited for Erik to return, so difficult to admit to herself that she missed him, German officer, enemy of her beloved country, but she realized that she had absolutely no control over the way she felt for him. This feeling now existed for some time. There were times when she wondered if he knew.

Time seemed to be at a standstill, and her frequent check of the clock proved the day was moving slowly for her. The telephone lines were still out of service, and she knew that there was no way of him contacting her.

Finally Sara could hear a car coming down the driveway and went to the window watching as he drove up to the door and turned off the engine. She stood in the entry and waited for him to enter the house. He held the door for a moment staring across at her. She smiled at him, and she could feel her heart racing. He closed the door behind him and walked over to her. Neither one spoke. He reached out to her and took her in his arms.

"Sara, I've missed you!" It was the first time he called her Sara. "I couldn't wait to see you again."

Sara did not speak. She pulled herself even closer to him and rested her face on his shoulder. He reached down and kissed her, gently at first, then with an urgency he was unable to control.

"If you want me to stop tell me right now, or I'm afraid it will be too late. I want you, Sara. I want to make love to you. I have for a long time."

"I'm afraid it is already too late."

He picked her up and carried her to the bedroom, placed her gently on the bed. He reached over to her and removed the hairpins from her hair and watched as it spilled over the pillow. He ran his fingers through her hair, kissing her face, her neck, her lips, her breasts, his mouth finding her nipples, hard and erect, and when he reached down to touch the rest of her body she let out a little cry. He had broad shoulders, a firm body, and when he pulled her even closer to him she felt herself drifting into some forbidden place, and she wanted it to go on forever. Soon darkness appeared and replaced the daylight, and Erik knew his time here would soon have to end.

"You're smiling!"

"This is the first time I have made love in German!"

"Sara, I have to leave shortly. You do know that I do not want to leave you, don't you! It's getting late."

"Will you stay here beside me for just a few minutes longer?"

"I want to stay here forever, but the whole German army will be out looking for me. The telephone service should be restored any time now, and it will be difficult to avoid Headquarters if I disappear for any length of time."

"Erik!"

"Yes."

"There are no regrets for this day. You need to know. Since this stupid war I wanted nothing more then for it to end quickly. Now I am not sure if I want it to end soon. Did you ever hear of anything so selfish and probably border-line treason! And for some reason I have not one ounce of guilt. I have never been unfaithful to Paul."

This, of course, would not be the last time for their lovemaking. At some time in the future the war would end; and Sara knew Paul would return to her, and Erik would go home to Claudia, or so it would seem to be that way.

She watched as he left the room, wondering if her life would ever return to some sense of normalcy. She turned her face into the pillow and cried herself to sleep not awakening until the sun found its way through the curtains in her room.

There were no other choices available but the role that had been handed to her and life would go on, not the way she visualized, but it definitely would move ahead. In a way she was glad she couldn't see into the future. It would possibly frighten her.

After she bathed and got dressed she walked outside to survey any damage caused by the recent storm, a storm that she would have to categorize as a hurricane. To her surprise she found only branches splayed across the field, and there were no trees that had been uprooted. The storm door on the side of the house, the one on which she cut her hand, had its latch hanging from one screw that remained, and below the steps and around the foundation of the house were hoards of twigs and leaves and piles of pine needles that were scattered everywhere.

She returned inside the house. It felt so empty. She would wait for Erik to call.

She knew when the war ended, it couldn't possibly continue forever, that he would return to Germany regardless of whom won in the end and chances were she would never see him again. She tried to think back to what life had been with Paul, what she loved most about him, time they spent together, the nights of lovemaking, and she found it difficult. It was similar to doing a puzzle. The missing pieces just wouldn't fall into place, and there was little doubt that the German officer who shared her bed last night had something to do with it. It didn't seem fair! If there had been no maniac leading Germany in his senseless act of aggression, Erik would not have entered her life. The question haunting her was would she be capable of letting him go emotionally when the time came. The thought of never seeing him again made her sad, engulfing her in emotions that brought her to a place she never knew had existed, but for now he would be here with her far away from Claudia, his wife.

CHAPTER 19

I t was early the next morning when Sophie discovered the note. She had just returned from a two-day mission. She was exhausted, and she was looking forward to catching up on sleep.

"By the time you read this I will be gone, I shall be in a better place. I could not go on without the one I loved, my best friend. Try to forgive me and understand that I could not continue this journey alone. When all these terrible times have ended; and you have a few minutes to reflect, look to the sky. There you will see two bright stars, together for all eternity."

"Thank you for being my friend; and if over the years you think of me, do not be sad. And my wish for you is after the war ends you will find love, be happy, and live a long life."

When they finally found her it was too late. The bed was covered with blood. She had slashed her wrists. Her voice was barely audible, just above a whisper.

"Forgive me!"

Mikael in the meantime had been summoned.

"I will stay with you. I will hold your hand until the angels come and carry you to paradise. And Peeter will be there waiting for you and in the Kingdom of Heaven there will be no more pain, no tears, and you and Peeter will be together forever."

And Mikael recited the 23rd Psalm, "The Lord is my shepherd, I shall not want." barely finished when her hand slipped and fell to the side of the bed.

The next day Anela was buried beside her beloved Peeter, deep in the forest under a canopy of birch trees, a small simple cross marked the grave.

"Will God forgive her for taking her life, Mikael?"

Mikael took a few seconds and turned to Sophie.

"How could He deny her a place in His Kingdom. She has already lived in Hell! It's times like these when our faith is tested, and I believe He has a plan for each and every one of us and sometimes it is difficult to accept and understand; but life continues, a combination of sorrow and happiness. We go on, life goes on, we cope as well as we can, find an inner strength. It's not always easy but given no other choice we somehow are given the strength to bear it and see it through."

"I need to stay here for awhile longer, just a little longer. I'm not sure if I will ever feel normal again."

She watched as Mikael walked away. She desperately wanted him to hold her, she felt so alone.

Sophie did not know how this journey would end, but she knew that nothing would ever be the same again. Everyone would be touched by these times. Mothers will lose their sons and daughters, husbands would not return from the war. Does God ask of us more than we are capable of bearing? Only time will provide the answers. The past year and the next few years will change the course taken by every person in Lithuania. She knew that these years would haunt her as long as she lived. She could never completely fathom the destruction that took place in her world and a veil of sadness would consume her and wouldn't let go of her.

In the years after the war had ended she would never forgot she was one of the lucky ones that survived those evil years that claimed fifty million people eradicated from the face of the earth. And in so many cases the ones left behind had also been handed a death sentence along with the ones who perished as they would never be capable of resuming a life that had once been theirs. In many cases it would take something small to trigger the memories of those days and on rare occasions it would remind her of the happy times, of Mikael and Justas, the three of them assigned to the same mission and the feeling of accomplishment after sabotaging a German station or blowing up a bridge preventing the enemy from transporting troops and supplies. But it was the sad times that she would remember most often, like ghosts from out of the past, and it would pull her into a dark place stirred by memories. They say time heals; and maybe it does a little, but not completely, it leaves a footprint on your soul to carry with you for as long as you live.

Of the one hundred and ninety that started on the journey, one hundred sixty-one, on this day would leave the forest here in Trakai, most would never return. There were tears, hugs, and smiles, men and women together, hands joined. They formed a circle, and one of the final acts would be a moment of silence to remember and pay tribute to those that would remain here in the forest, their final resting place.

Sophie smiled as she remembered Anele laughing and running through the woods, swimming in the lake on warm summer days, sharing the secrets of their first love. She glanced toward the grove of birch trees and spoke out loud.

"Good-by my dear friend, until we meet again in a better place. May you rest in peace. I love you and miss you."

Then one by one this young group of Lithuanians read the names of those that would remain behind. When it became Sophie's turn to read Anele's name tears streamed down her face, and this time she had to turn away from the birch trees where her friend had been laid to rest.

Years from now Sophie would return. She would come in the fall, and she would plant tulip bulbs under the birch trees and say a prayer.

Sophie turned and followed Mikael and Justas, and the three went on their way. It was so quiet, a quiet she could never forget. For now Trakai began gradually slipping away. They would return to their cabins one last time, pack up their belongings, and try to find the way back from where they had come. It was so difficult to comprehend that this had been home for six years!

But it was the sad times that she would remember most often, and it would pull her into a place surrounded by reminders of the past. They say time heals; and maybe it does a little, but not completely and leaves behind a footprint on your soul to carry with you for the rest of your life.

For many of these young partisans they would go on to confront another enemy, the Red Army and life would become unbearable at times even harder then the years in Trakai. Sophie as planned would go to England. Life would improve for her in her new country, and eventually she would go to the United States but the war years would change her forever. What no one knew during those years when Lithuania had suffered beyond hell, between the time the German tanks rolled over Lithuania's soil in 1941 until the Nazi machine was destroyed in 1945, 700,000 would be killed in a country that once had four million people.

CHAPTER 20

It was the beginning of May in Trakai and the night was exceptionally warm. Mikael could not sleep but the weather was just a small component of the sleep problem. He had caught a recent broadcast on the BBC predicting that the war in Europe would be over any day now. The surrender of Germany was immediate. There were rumors that Adolph Hitler had committed suicide and all remaining of this evil psychopath who was responsible for the death of millions of people were a heap of ashes that once belonged to this monster discovered by the Russians as they captured Berlin. Controversy existed for many years after the war as to the authenticity of this actually being his remains but was later proven that it was, and the woman he married just days before was in the same bunker and died just hours before her husband shot himself. The Russians later confirmed to the rest of the world they had removed Hitler's remains several times to different locations to prevent his final resting place becoming a shrine of some sorts.

After tossing and turning, somewhere after mid-night, he left his bunk and stepped outside. Justas on the top bunk stirred but did not awake. The air felt refreshing as he stepped into the night. He walked the few yards to the lake front, found a bench and sat down. The waves had a hypnotic effect as they lapped and found their way to the shore. A full moon slipped in and out of the few clouds that would later open up and spill on to the lake and the forest. Mikael could hear a rumble of thunder in the distance, but it circled around and seemed to head toward the North.

For sometime now Mikael found it difficult to pray. He made attempts but the words had little meaning, just words, and he knew he was in need of divine assistance but it seemed that those with the powers eluded him. He was determined to hang in there being well aware that it could take more time. On this night, sitting on the edge of the lake, the end of the war in sight, he felt a need to pray and ask God to give him the strength to become a priest again. And as he sat there in the darkness he could not wonder what God had in His plan for him. His thoughts turned to Father Ricikas, and he had to smile. He was looking forward to their reunion after so many years had passed, but Mikael had no way of knowing that the dear old priest had been executed by the Germans in the early years of the war. There would be no reunion.

CHAPTER 21

Erik looked over at Sara, and he thought he saw her crying. "I'm sorry, Erik, do you think this war will ever end! I've changed my mind about it. I don't want you to leave."

"I'm afraid it will be soon, maybe just a matter of months. The Allies, especially Russia advancing from the East toward Berlin, are defeating the German forces." It was the first time their conversation touched on the subject of the war itself. Erik realized the collapse of the Third Reich was inevitable and had to admit that he was aware of it for some time now.

"Our generation has paid such a huge price, and there will be no victory for any of us regardless of the winner. Tell me what has our sacrifices really accomplished, what all this nonsense achieved except we are separated from our families, from those whom we love. And think of all the young men and woman who will never come home lying in some foreign place with a white wooden cross to mark their grave. I just don't get this war thing!"

Erik wanted to reach out to this young beautiful woman who had been his driver, his lover, for the past years, to hold her and comfort her, but he held back.

The thought of Germany losing the war frighten him, but he would soon discover life would continue just not in the manner he would have predicted.

The next few months went by and the war continued. Eric tried to convince Sara that the news was pending. The Russians had now captured and occupied Berlin.

"Will I ever see you again?" Sara could not bear to look at him.

He could see the pain in her eyes, in her voice.

"I'm not sure; but I do know that I will never forget you, not ever. I think I have fallen in love with you. I have a wife; you have Paul, and I am not totally convinced our lives will ever be the same as before the war. Claudia and I knew each other for most of our lives, but we were married for only two weeks when I had to leave. It really was such a short time together. It was very difficult for me, but I know it had to be harder for her. She doesn't know if I am dead or alive. All correspondence was prohibited as soon as I received my orders to report here. She would have no idea where I was, and I was forbidden to contact her. And you, too, I am well aware of your pain, your separation from your husband, the worry of him. No, none of it is fair. It will soon be over. The news of Germany's surrender is only a few days away. You'll see! Time we should be getting back, Mrs. Spencer. Thank you for sharing this day with me. I will miss you, you know."

"Promise me!"

"I have absolutely no doubt."

The sun had started to fade slowly slipping over the horizon. A slight breeze blew in off the ocean. It was the end of a perfect day. The sun, not a frequent visitor on the island, its presence had been a blessing. Clouds had been missing, and the sun was the sole object in the sky.

"Sara, let me give you my jacket," noticing a slight shiver as he draped his jacket over her shoulders

"You're trembling!"

"Just a wee bit cold, I'm afraid."

The next few seconds became a blur. He pulled her closer and held her. Tears spilled down her cheeks, and she stared to sob.

"Erik, don't let me go. Please don't let me go!" she pleaded.

She placed her arms around his neck and buried her face in his chest. He picked her up and carried her the short distance to the car, placed her next to him and took over the role as driver. He was aware that their time together was coming to an end, and he wondered how he could make it without her. It would take a little time but Sara the beautiful girl originally from London and the handsome German officer would find each other again.

CHAPTER 22

May once again came to Half Way Island, and the days ahead would become his final ones on this island where he had spent the last five years. He was having difficulty with the knowledge that Germany was loosing the war just three decades after its defeat in WWI. Nothing could prepare him for what he would witness in the weeks ahead after returning to Germany. He wondered how the German people could recover from the humiliation and destruction that was inflicted during the war years. And what role would the Russians and the Communists play now, the group that Hitler hated almost as much as the Jews. He would find his answer; but as he expected, the news would not be good

The day that the Allies and the world had been praying and waiting finally arrived on May 6, 1945, with the surrender of Germany. The war in Europe had now come to an end. It was time for Erik to return home.

Sara, as she had numerous times before this day, made the trip to the air field, only this time would be the final one. Exactly as the very first trip; it took twenty minutes, and like the first trip it was almost in complete silence. One chapter of their lives was closing and another one would begin. They would find each other once again but for now they felt this was a final good-by, not possibly having any inkling that the two of them, this English woman and this German officer, would find each other once again.

"It has been a pleasure and a privilege to have known you Mrs. Spencer. Thank you." He spoke to her in German. "Auf Wiedersehen!"

He tried to keep the farewell as professional as possible. Would those few who were watching have guessed it was anything more then what it appeared to be? Maybe!

Sara tried desperately to keep her composure fighting back the tears as Erik shook her hand. She had fallen in love with him, and she would miss him with every fiber of her being.

She stood beside the car until the plane disappeared over the sea beyond the horizon. It took a few minutes before she realized tears had just spilled down her face.

"God speed my dear Erik." She whispered as she found her way back to the road. She would head home and wait for Paul to return to her from the war and try to make plans for their future together. But Paul would not return. His plane was shot down somewhere over Germany It was just days before the final days of Hitler's Third Reich.

CHAPTER 23

April 23, 1945

The meeting was scheduled for the next morning to be held at the boat house. Sophie, Mikael, and Justas were a little curious and had absolutely no idea what it could all be about. The three arrived a little early and waited patiently for Mrs. Massud to arrive. They knew she was rarely late and did not hesitate to show her disapproval to those that broke one of her cardinal rules of not being on time.

"I don't have even a small clue, do you?"

"No," Justas answered. Mikael shook his head.

Most of the group arrived early, too, and appeared anxious to hear why they had been summoned and guessed it had to be something of major importance.

And ten minutes before eight o'clock Mrs. Massud came in a few minutes before the time that had been posted exactly as predicted, glanced throughout the room, and concluded all were probably present.

"Good morning, everyone! Thank you for being so prompt and responding on such short notice. You may have already guessed that I would not have requested this meeting if it were not very important so I am going to ask each of you to pay close attention.

I will gladly answer any questions but please hold them to the end of the meeting. This will be the first of two meetings I have scheduled. The subject will require some time before decisions can be made as you will soon learn. So let me begin."

One of the young men offered her a chair but she declined saying she preferred to stand. Sophie noticed how tired and thin she appeared since the last time she saw her several weeks ago and noticed her jet black hair was peppered with gray, the war had definitely taken its toll. Sophie wondered how her own mother would look after so many years and even if she were still alive. It always made her so sad when she would think about it.

"Get comfortable everyone. It will be awhile I think. There is much to discuss." She took a moment and glanced around the room. She felt it was short of a miracle that so many of the young people here tonight had survived these last years. She would take some of the credit and give the rest to God!

"I will try to keep this as brief as possible so let us begin. There have been reports that we are in the final days of war and that these horrible days shall end soon. The war with Germany is now in the last days, possibly hours. I for one could never have predicted it would take six long years. However, it seems it will not be finished for us here in our country. It is so difficult to comprehend but almost certain that another enemy has arrived on the doorsteps of Lithuania, the Soviets. Sadly all evidence reveals that it is just a matter of time before we will become a Communist state. The Red Army is now concentrating on the capture of Berlin, and I would doubt if they are paying much attention to our part of the world as yet. We are a good distance from the Kremlin and Moscow and that is an advantage for us. It will affect us eventually, so it is important to consider options that may be available to you."

Mrs. Madssud paused for a moment. She was hoping that the group sitting before her was grasping the seriousness of it all, but she had no way of knowing it yet so she continued.

"Some of you may be familiar with a section, a small section outside of London that was settled by Lithuanians over the past few decades. You may even have relatives living there. Most still speak the language and celebrate our holidays, and a huge percentage marry within the community. So you ask what has this to do with our being here today. We are drafting a plan within the next few weeks to take a group of you to England. I am aware that many of you cannot, for many different reasons, consider taking this course; but for the rest you will have the next two weeks to make a decision, probably the most difficult one of your young lives! It will not be an easy one. The Soviets are not focusing here now but all that will change, just a matter of time, as soon as the war ends the Baltic States will become a priority. The Communists doctrine will be difficult for us, extremely so. Property, your parents, your grandparents property will be confiscated by the State. Land and houses that have been in families for generations will no longer belong to them. They will try to smother all forms of religion. Churches and synagogues will be closed! There are reports that Stalin has already sent his own people to labor camps so our citizens certainly will not be spared."

The young people listened to her every word but most of them not quite grasping the full meaning of what she was describing to them.

"For those of you, after giving this a good deal of consideration, there will be another meeting two weeks from today. All the details by then will have been drafted, and I will pass them along to you. I can tell you that a boat is scheduled to leave from the Coast to Faro an island in Sweden and then to Goteborg and then to the final destination over the North Sea to England. The plans are complete, the contacts already made for the journey, but no definite date has been set or the port from where the boat will depart. One important part of this plan is to know before hand the number of passengers. We have to be certain that the boat will accommodate everyone who has enlisted, and that food and water along with other provisions will last for the entire trip."

Mrs. Massud paused again, closed her eyes briefly and continued.

"What is important now is to give each of you ample time to think this through carefully, to consider the benefits as well as the disadvantages. Your decision will set the course for the rest of your life! We all agree that we do not deserve what has been handed down to us over the past years. Our lives should be getting easier, our future a hope that we deserve and are entitled to have. Unfortunately, we again have another battle that is just starting. Is it fair? Of course not! I for one am tired! I will finish by saying I wish all of you the very best. I am extremely honored to have been a part of your family, and I will never forget you! I look forward to seeing you here at the next meeting for those of you wishing to receive the final information and instructions concerning this subject. Thank you so much for coming!" and she followed by asking if there were any questions.

The next meeting went as scheduled. Their teacher, mentor, instructor, was surprised at the turnout, pleasantly surprised as she was the organizer of the trip, the date now definitely scheduled.

"Let me remind all of you that this will be the most important decision of your life. You have a chance that many of you, if you embark on this journey, will never see your family again, or at most, years. You have been here in Trakai for the past six years with little or, in most cases, no contact with them. The Communists are now preparing to enter our country we are told so we have set the time for departure to an earlier date than we had previously planned. Some of you may not be totally convinced that life could not possibly be harder than before the war or the six years here; but I can tell you inexplicably that you will endure more hardships, your life and conditions will not improve! You will be a slave in their regime, a puppet in your own country. You will not be allowed to practice your religion and all land will be confiscated as there will be no private ownership of property. All property will belong to the State. It may all sound extremely difficult for you to fathom, and this is why I must urge you to take this matter seriously!"

She stopped for a moment and scouted the room. Everyone seemed to cling to her every word. And she continued, her voice emitting sadness. "If you decide to embark on this journey there is no guarantee your future will not lack difficulties and disappointments; but I know without a doubt, you will have a brighter future, a future that will be denied to you here in your own country. Most of all I'm totally convinced that the next generation, your children as well as your grandchildren, will reap the rewards and results of any sacrifices you are willing to make. I'm too old, my health is failing, so Fate has dictated my future for me; but I can tell you without a second hesitation if I were in your position, I would seek a better life in England. There is no future for us here sadly. Before we leave here tonight I strongly urge everyone present to give this your undivided attention, to fully try to understand the consequence of living in a communist country. I cannot stress to you to please consider every option available to you. You, each and every one of you, deserve the freedom to make your own choices throughout your life. It will definitely be non-existent here."

"In closing let me remind you this will be the most important decision in your young life. You have five days to decide if this course is the right one for you to take, not a long time when you consider how important this decision will be, and it will set the direction of your future."

"Good luck to all of you. I will pray that God guide you! May I wish you a good night everyone!"

The dear old lady who guided these young men and women through the war years appeared tired, shoulders slightly bent forward, her eyes looking dull, dark circles rimming them as if sleep were avoiding her, Sophie was thinking as the meeting was drawing to an end, and her hair once raven was peppered with gray thinning near the temples; and it was evident that she had lost a great deal of weight, the stress of the past turbulent years no doubt a major factor. Without her skills, her dedication, the chances that so many would not be here today and having survived was because of the time and instruction given by her, efforts and knowledge uncompromised. In the end she received her wish. More than one half of her students in this group would sail across the Baltic and the North Sea to a new freedom denied to them in their own country. And for many England was just a short detour as many finally immigrated to Canada and the United States but carried with them their Lithuanian heritage. Many would become active citizens and become successful making many contributions to their new country. Unfortunately, in less than a year after the surrender of Nazi Germany, she passed away and was buried near her home in Trakai. Over the years many of her students would come to pay their respects and perhaps say a small prayer. It would be more than a decade but Sophie and Mikael would be among her visitors.

CHAPTER 24

Sophie could not stop the sobs. She was having mixed emotions now that the days were coming to an end at Trakai, the place she called home since 1939, six years ago. At times she had difficulty remembering life before Trakai, and there were doubts concerning her decision, but the decision had been made to leave for England.

"You must promise you'll write!"

Mikael was choking back tears. "I will remember you in my prayers, Sophie, and ask that God watch over you and to take care of you. We have been to Hell and back. I am now wishing you a better life. You won't find it here. The Soviets will instill their doctrines; and freedom, something that should be our God given right, will elude us. You now have been given a chance to find freedom, something unobtainable here in Lithuania. But most importantly your children will live in a world where they will have opportunities and will be able to make choices that will be denied under Stalin rule. In time the Church will suffer. The Communists are atheists, and they will try to impose this doctrine on every denomination, Catholics, Jews, Lutherans, all God fearing, God loving people.

You must stay close to God. And remember, whereever your journey shall end, you will always be a Lithuanian!"

With tears streaming down her face she said good-by to her two best friends, Mikael and Justas, one whom she loved, the other whom she fell in love. She knew in leaving she may never see them again; or if they would be reunited one day, it would be in a very distant time.

CHAPTER 25

Mikael and Justas joined a small group that was going to Vilnius. The train ran daily during the war years; not exactly on schedule, but with rare exception the trains traveled between Trakai and Vilnius every day. He often could hear the train whistle blowing as it approached the station, a good sign as he felt at least some things were not disturbed or interrupted because of the war. And it had a connection to Vilnius for him at times forgetting the hardships bestowed on the young resistance fighters.

Had it really been six years since he, Justas, and Sophie had stepped from the train bringing them here? The train could be heard in the distance, smoke billowing from the stack filling the air, brakes grinding as it made its approach toward the station, and finally screeching to a halt.

The two priests settled in waiting for everyone to board. The conductor signaled all were aboard. He made the rounds collecting and punching tickets as the train slowly pulled away from the station. It was difficult for Mikael to accept they were going home at last having mixed emotions about leaving the place that were with no reservation the happiest of his entire existence.

Mikael had a window seat, and he took a final look at the place he had lived, loved, fought for the last six years.

He turned to Justas who was sitting directly across from him.

"I feel so sad, Justas. I am not so sure I want to leave! We became a part of a family, a part of something that was important, an experience that we will never duplicate. Have you thought about becoming a priest again? Have you asked yourself if you could be a priest again? This will be my greatest challenge. God will have to intervene as I know I am not capable of doing it alone."

The young priest who had accompanied him throughout most of his adult years looked over and nodded. For the second time in his young life Justas would truly be tested. He, like his fellow priest, would be challenged. He would need time; but most of all, he needed guidance from a higher power. But it would not be God that would dictate his future, but the beast from the newly formed Soviet Union by the name of Josef Stalin. He like his beloved pastor, Father Ricikas, would fall victim each to two different invaders of his small country and unbelievably in a short period of time. It would not be until the year 1990 that Lithuania would gain its independence but not without huge casualties suffered during the Nazi and shortly the Communist regime. In the end Lithuania would survive. The Third Reich collapsed and finally came the dissolution of the Soviet Union.

Mikael had to deal with the separation of Sophie, the loss of Father Rickas, and then a short time later Justas. Through it all he felt great pain, sorrow, and loneliness, but he never questioned God. He was aware that God had nothing to do with it. It was the evil that Man had created. He would during these difficult times give credit to Him for helping to deal with these trials and helping to find his way to being His dedicated servant of the Church after so much anguish and turmoil his years after returning from Trakai. Mikael, the priest still a man, would stray again in the years ahead. Sophie would become his partner in sin, his love for her overpowering any vow he had taken.

CHAPTER 26

S ophie read the instruction sheet for the second time. She was to be at the dock on Friday evening between eight and nine p.m. The summer days were getting longer at this time of year, and the decision had been made to embark after dark. She was unaware of the actual number that had signed for this journey, but her guess was perhaps forty from her group in Trakai. She would later learn that a few had to reverse their original decision to leave because of parents or members of their families that were too frail to care for themselves and decided it would be impossible to make the decision to leave at this time. They felt it was a duty to support them in the hardships that confronted them, some with debilitating illnesses. Almost all of the former resistance fighters that signed on originally for the trip to England did stay with the decision they had made, the majority with the approval and insistence of their families knowing that a future for them in their country would become nonexistent.

The women had been assigned to the middle deck, the men to the lower. It appeared to Sophie that there were more men than women on board, most she recognized from Trakai. One young woman turned to her and said, "Have we made the right decision!"

"God I hope so!" she replied. It seemed to her, of course, a little premature to answer.

Room No. 2 was the third door on the right about half way down the corridor. She would share the room with three other women. There were two bunks in the room, facing each other. Folded at the end of each one was a set of sheets, a pillow with a pillowcase, and a heavy blanket. A round window facing the port side was covered with a film of salt water making it almost impossible for any light to enter. A small sink stood in the corner with clean towels hanging on a towel rack, glasses in holders, and a small ice chest placed under the sink with bottles of ginger ale a remedy to help seasickness on the rough seas.

The group was ready to begin the journey, a harrowing, unpredictable, and possibly a dangerous one. They would leave from the Coast, across the Baltic Sea to the island of Faro in Sweden, a stopover in Goteborg, cross the North Sea and finally to the English coast. There was a small colony of Lithuanian immigrants from the Baltic States that settled in London. Many had come from Latvia, Estonia, but the majority was Lithuanian. A huge Russian population had settled a few miles away from the Lithuanian Village where they still practiced the customs and traditions of their mother country. The Lithuanian community had a fairly large Jewish population that had escaped before the outbreak of the war. Many had once lived in Vilnius, the Jerusalem of Lithuania. Many were doctors, lawyers, shopkeepers, accountants, and contributed to the village as well as to their adopted country, and many lost their lives after joining with the armed forces of England.

The sun was in the process of disappearing completely below the horizon. Departure was scheduled in just about an hour if all went well. The weather being the main factor could cause delays. In this part of the world the sea could become unpredictable, but there are no tides in the Baltic Sea so the Captain did not have to take this into consideration.

The Captain had instructed everyone on board to gather on the upper deck by 10:30. The weather was cool but not cold. Patches of stars shone in the pitch black sky. The night was still, little wind, which was a good omen.

"Good evening, I'm Captain Bankauskas, originally from Druskininkai but I now live in Goteborg, Sweden, having moved there several years before the war. Goteborg will become our final destination on this portion of the trip. There will be a small stopover on Faro which is one of the small islands in the archipelago off the coast of Sweden."

The Captain stood on a crate of some sort and appeared much taller at first than he actually was. His beard was sprinkled with gray, and his face weathered from his many years at sea.

"First of all I would like to welcome all of you. To those of you who are not familiar with the rules of being on a ship for an extended period I suggest you read the instruction sheets that have been placed in your cabins. In my experience at sea I can recall but few life-threatening ordeals, and I believe one reason is we never take the sea for granted. Without question it can become a dangerous place if you take unnecessary risks: for example, you are to stay below in your designated cabins from 10:00 p.m. until 7a.m. because this is the time the sea becomes the roughest. Our mates, who I will introduce shortly, are available in an emergency. As there is little way to predict sea conditions, it is imperative that you, each and every one of you, stay below if the seas become too rough, and that includes day light, and there are no exceptions! There will be a lifejacket and lifeboat drill in just a few moments. It will not take long, maybe fifteen minutes, no more, I hope! Now on to the business at hand! When I call your name, please answer "present" and confirm your cabin number. I plan to start with the women first."

"In Goteborg you will have a day's layover before you board a second boat that will take you to England, to the East Coast. You will be notified with updates and all details." The Captain was holding a clipboard with the names of the passengers and their room numbers.

"You will find a form on your berth with information concerning your voyage. Take a minute and read it. If at any time you should need assistance a crew member will be available to help you. If you are prone to seasickness then I suggest you sip a glass of ginger soda. There is a small ice chest under the sink with one bottle for each of you. I'm predicting a pretty rough sea. At no time are you allowed on deck without permission of the crew. Also pay attention to a sheet of paper tacked to your door. You must sign in/out each time you leave your room. Again, read the information we have provided for you. You are dismissed!" He stepped down from the wooden crate he was standing on and motioned the members of his staff to follow him.

Sophie was pleased. Her name was called fourth, and she moved to the space where the lifejackets were stored and waited there until the roll call was complete. She missed one of the names of the girls that would share her cabin but remembered the other two, one she recognized from a mission not too many months ago, one of the last in Trakai, and the other one she met in the cabin, and they had a short conversation before being summoned to the top deck, but she couldn't remember either name.

Sophie learned many years after the war had ended that the Captain had been responsible for the transport of hundreds of Jews from the Baltic States during the war years risking his own life knowing if captured execution would be inevitable. Lithuanian in 1995 posthumously awarded him Lithuanian's highest Medal of Honor.

CHAPTER 27

It was just before mid-night that Sophie settled in her room. Sleep would avoid her she knew. No time in her life, even the years at Trakai, did she feel such fear, but there was no turning back.

The boat rocked gently as Sophie lay there gazing at the ceiling, a hundred thoughts raced through her mind. She was wide awake. Just a short time later the engines started, and the boat slipped from the dock. It was headed out to sea, destination Faro, a small island in Sweden, and then Southwest to Goteberg.

The girl in the bottom bunk called up to her asking if she were alright.

"My name is Ana and I am from the city of Kaunas. I am so afraid, are you?"

"Yes!" she replied. "I am afraid I am! I knew this would be difficult for me; and once my decision was final, I was certain there would be no turning back. So yes, I admit I am afraid. My name is Sophie, and I was in Trakai during the war. I can't remember one day there that I experienced this type of fear."

"I am so glad to meet you, Sophie. There is a group from the Lithuanian section of London that plan to meet us the day we are scheduled to dock. I was told they have compiled a list with names, some background, and have already assigned us to our families." And as it would turn out Ana, her new friend, and Sophie would be assigned to live with the same family.

The boat rocked from side to side making sleep impossible for the four girls sharing the same quarters so they talked into the night exchanging a few things about themselves and a few opinions on what each thought to expect in London.

Just two hours into the journey the wind came barreling down from the North tossing the boat slightly off its course. Huge waves continued to spill over the sides forcing even the crew to remain below deck. The water continued to pound the boat throughout the early morning to tumble over the ladders and into the hold. It appeared pitch black. The

Captain announced over the loudspeaker that everyone had to remain below until the storm subsided and confirmed that the information he had difficulty gathering was possibly the storm would break within the hour. It was a prediction only he explained.

Sophie at this point started to feel nauseated and felt at any minute she was going to vomit. She barely reached the sink. She had never in her young life felt so sick. The small space started to spin around, and she now felt faint. When she awoke the storm seemed to have subsided. It took her a few minutes before she discovered what had happened. The girls in her room managed to get her up on one of the lower bunks, placed a cold washcloth on her forehead, and suggested she remain there until she started to feel better.

The second night into the trip the sea became a tidal wave of unrelenting turbulence. Sophie could hear the water pour over the side of the ship, and she wondered if the weight of it would pull the ship into the icy sea. She watched from her bunk as the ice chest once secured under the sink slip from its space and move to the other side of the room. She tried in vain to reach the chest which had the ginger ale as she suddenly felt sick, nauseated. She would have to share the basin with Grazina who by now was vomiting over the side of her bunk. If only they could get some fresh air but neither could move and the rules forbade leaving during the night. At one point Sophie felt maybe it would be better if she just died, as this was by far the worst she had ever felt in her whole life! In the weeks ahead she would soon learn that she was pregnant, and the combination of seasickness and being pregnant became a volatile duo.

Just about the time Sophie began to think there was little hope for her and the other poor souls aboard; the wind suddenly seemed to shift, and the sea simultaneously regained some calmness. Maybe, after all, she would live to see another day. If the conditions stabilized and the boat stayed on its course Sophie guessed they would make port almost on schedule.

"All hands on deck! Everyone report to the upper deck!" Sophie had just managed to fall asleep when the command from the Captain came over the loudspeaker.

She followed the others, stumbling up the stairs, not quite light as yet, struggling to keep her balance. She was pleasantly surprised to see the sun fading in and out of the clouds. It was a good omen she thought.

The Captain appeared tired. He was a giant of a man, large chest and arms. His hat was missing since the previous times he had summoned all passengers on deck, and his long hair soaking wet fell almost to his shoulders. He stepped up on to the crate. It appeared to be the same one that assisted him the last time to overlook all in front of him. He took a few minutes looking out over his passengers before he shouted out to them.

"Call your names out so I can hear you, one by one, starting with women first." Sophie again was one of the first to call out her name as the Captain had ordered, and one by one the other women followed as directed. He checked each name and then continued on to the men. It took a few minutes longer for the men's roll call as there were a dozen or more of them than were women, but the whole process only took approximately ten minutes.

Captain stood looking over the list, scanning the small group before him, returning to the list before he finally addressed all those lined up in front of him.

"Please listen carefully. Is there a Vidas Norvaisa present?" There was no response.

"Does any one know this young man? Could it be that he did not hear my announcement."

A tall man standing in the back row raised his hand. "He was in his bunk until late last night. He told us he was going to go on deck as he was not feeling well, he said he was seasick. We tried to deter him from leaving the room, but he paid no attention to us. This morning he was not in his bunk, and it appeared he did not return during the night or this morning, and we never saw him again."

"I need all of you to pay attention, to be on the lookout for him. I'm ordering the crew to make a complete check of the ship. Let's hope we have a happy ending to this. It's rare; but one could be swept overboard, especially with the conditions we just experienced."

After a complete search of the entire ship several hours later the Captain had to conclude that Vidas Norvaisa had disappeared somewhere in the darkness of the Baltic Sea.

Sophie could not place the young man among those who had enlisted for this journey. How very sad for a life to end in this manner after surviving the war years and to meet death in such a brutal manner. She felt such sadness. It lingered for a long time, days after the tragic event had occurred, and she felt badly that she couldn't remember the young man whose life had ended so unexpectedly. A few years later in London she would meet a young woman who she would discover was Vidas Norvaisa's sister. It was closure for her and eventually for her family who had lost contact with him. Though deeply saddened by the discovery she told Sophie that finally they could close this chapter and forge ahead with their own lives something missing during the past three years.

CHAPTER 28

This group of expatriates now settled here in England had banded together; and with a sense of optimism and much determination became very successful in the country that welcomed them and adopted them. They carried from Lithuania their customs and made a commitment to practice them so future generations could inherit an important part of the heritage entitled to them. The war, of course, diverted many things important to the expansion of the community but in the post-war years they regained what had to be postponed during those years when England had declared war on Germany. The community had pledged to assist anyone that wanted to relocate after leaving the Baltic States in most cases to find freedom and a better life then they would have in a country now under Soviet rule. This group now arriving from Trakai would be no exception. All efforts would be made to find housing and employment as quickly as possible and introduce them to courses in English. This contingent, however, was the first that did not arrive as a family. These young people who had survived the war had to make the most difficult decision that certainly would be the hardest one of their lives. They knew the chances of ever returning to their country, or seeing their loved ones, would be extremely rare if not possible. The world had rid itself of one monster, Adolph Hitler, and Stalin now had a role that the world would judge as beyond evil. The world would eventually discover that thousands of Lithuanians, after surviving the horrors inflicted by Hitler, would be sent to labor camps in Siberia where most would never return. It was a death sentence that few would escape. Justas was one of them.

CHAPTER 29

When the young freedom fighters from Trakai were finding their way to the English coast, Erik found his way to Berlin, a stepping stone to home in Heidelberg. At first he could not fathom what he saw. The city had totally been destroyed. Rubble covered the streets, the smell of it prevalent everywhere. The buildings that were left standing were no more than shells, impossible to detect what had been there before the bombing. Nothing was left of Nazi Headquarters where just a few years ago he spent months in preparation for the military duties that would follow shortly. There was absolutely nothing that reminded him of the Third Reich, predicted to be Germany's future, an insurance that was predicated to eliminate all that Germany had suffered because of the partitioning of their lands after the end of the First World War, and the guarantee promised by Hitler that Germany's victory now would assure the cancellation of the humiliation the country had to bear because of Germany's defeat.

Erik found a place to sit suddenly feeling overwhelmed. He stared long and hard at the shell of the city that once had been one of Europe's most beautiful and cosmopolitan cities. And for the first time in a very long time, since war had been declared and he had to leave Claudia, his new bride, he became overcome with a feeling of deep sadness. It really became unbearable, and he broke down, put his hands over his face and felt the tears sting his eyes. It was unbelievable. He always felt he would return to a victorious Germany, one in which he would feel proud and with a large dose of joy, one that he would be sharing with all of Germany in the glory of victory. It was, of course, never to happen. Erik knew it was time to concentrate on trying to get home. He was aware it would not be an easy task. The Red Army would be out on patrol everywhere, and he knew this was a dangerous place for an officer still in uniform. He felt some relief as the day was coming to an end, and the darkness of the night would definitely assist in his plan to escape the city. He also knew luck would have to intervene, lots of it. The sun would soon disappear, and the night would become a long one filled with uncertainness. He felt fear, something he rarely experienced. In the distance he witnessed two Russian soldiers raising the Soviet flag, the hammer and sickle, over what appeared to be nothing more than a frame of what had once been a building. It seemed so surreal to him. He could barely grasp the reality of it all. It was hard to remember back what the city looked like before all this destruction. Nothing will change what has occurred, he knew, and he said a silent prayer asking God to assist him in finding his way safely home and to be with Claudia after so many years had elapsed. And then as the sun finally dipped slowly over the horizon and darkness replaced the light Erik noticed an old priest moving in his direction. Erik watched as he found his way into the side of a building that remarkably stood untouched in the middle of the rubble. It was a church, perhaps a cathedral. Erik decided he would follow him and entered through the same door. Surprisingly, there were quite a few people in the church, lighting candles, praying at the altar and kneeling in the pews, and a few going to what appeared to be a confessional located on the far side of the altar and almost completely hidden from sight. Erik was surprised there were so many here who seemingly had not lost their faith in spite of the hardships conflicted due to the long devastating war years. Many probably had lost their homes, even buried loved ones, and no doubt there had to be a food shortage but it appeared at least these poor souls held on to their faith. Where did this faith come from he couldn't help but think. Maybe it was the only thing they had left now in this world. He himself was too exhausted to think much about the subject but he would still pray, as he did earlier, just in case there was a God watching over the mess that Man had just created here on the planet called Earth.

Erik found a vacant pew near the back of the church and in just minutes had fallen asleep there. He had no idea how long he had slept, maybe an hour or so. The old priest he had seen earlier was now in the front of the church having a conversation with an elderly woman appearing to make an effort to console her. She was crying, taking the corner of her head scarf to wipe the tears. The priest leaned over to her, touched her shoulders, and whispered what perhaps were some words of comfort. He moved on having brief conversations with some, smiling and nodding at others as they passed by.

A short time later Erik watched the priest as he moved toward the confessional, the old woman he tried to console following close behind. Erik couldn't help but wonder what in God's name would she have to confess. A few minutes later she came out and knelt in front of a huge crucifix suspended from the ceiling. She appeared to say a few short prayers, which confirmed Erik's suspicion that her sins had to be minor ones, made the sign of the cross, and left through the side door, the one Erik had entered. There was at this point no evidence of any more tears. Erik couldn't help but wonder if she had a safe place to go to. He realized she could be one of thousands that perhaps would become displaced in weeks and months ahead. The Russians would confiscate all that was left in the city.

When the priest first noticed Erik he had been asleep in the pew; but now seeing that he was awake, he approached him. The church was cold and damp, and the priest was carrying several blankets, one which he offered to Erik.

"There are cots in the basement and you are welcomed to spend the night. The stairway is in back of the church on the left-hand side." And before Erik had a chance to thank him he went on and continued to make the same offer to a young German soldier that had only minutes earlier entered the church.

After finding the stairs to the basement he selected one of the empty cots and joined the other soldiers already sound asleep. It was only a few minutes when he too fell asleep almost immediately, results of an exhausting and emotional day.

In the early morning, as rays of sunlight flooded the basement, he was pleasantly surprised to see a long refractory table on the far side of the room with several large bowls filled with cereal, a basket of fresh rolls, a small dish of strawberry jam, and a pitcher of milk. A small sign in the center of the table read, Help Your Self. There appeared to be more than enough for the dozen or so that had spent the night. Erik thought how lucky he had been to have found this place; but this was another day, and he would now have to make an attempt to get out of the city hopefully without incidence. But first he would have some breakfast. He suddenly realized it had been quite a long time since he had something to eat, nothing since he had left Half Way Island. As he was finishing breakfast, one of the soldiers approached him. "Sir, we suggest you change your uniform before you leave. Father has left some clothes. They are behind that door. Because the Red Army is on patrol, it will be less dangerous not to be in uniform."

He thanked the soldier as he opened the closet door. It certainly was a good idea he thought hoping he would find something hanging there for him. He did, and he changed leaving his uniform behind. He would return upstairs, knell at the altar, and for the second time in less then several hours he would say a prayer. And for the second time in that same period he became overwhelmed with a feeling of fear.

CHAPTER 30

It was obvious to Justas and Mikael the small kitchen hadn't been in use for some time. Dishes sat in the sink. To their surprise the faucet was in working condition: and on turning it water dripped, and after a few minutes it flowed without interruption. Drinking glasses shared the space with cups and saucers, bowls and plates, stacked in the cupboard above the sink. The tiny pantry that adjoined the kitchen held pots and pans, canned goods, and on the top shelve were rows of jars in all sizes and shapes containing an assortment of vegetables that had been preserved, a toaster covered with mold, and a tea kettle with a missing cover. A half-empty salt shaker and a sugar bowl rested on the table on an oiled tablecloth covered with layers of dust. It was evident that no one had lived here in a long period of time. Draperies tattered hung off their rods.

Anxiety started to settle in. Mikael and Justas shared the same opinion. Could something terrible have happened to their beloved priest? They were both aware of the Nazi's treatment and killing of the Jews in Vilnius and Lithuania, but they were unaware of the murders in other ethnic groups and religious orders. In the next few days they would learn of their pastor's fate, his murder by the Nazis.

In the corner of the hall stood the grandfather clock covered with layers of dust and cobwebs. Mikael smiled to himself when the old clock chimed exactly on the hour as if it were welcoming them back. The pendulum was almost invisible as the glass was barely noticeable from many years of neglect, but the almost silent movement could be heard. Remarkable he thought glancing at the clock.

"Mikael, what do you make of all this? It frightens me. Father would never leave here, definitely not of his own free will. This was truly the only home he ever knew, and everyone here loved him."

"I, too, agree he would not just up and go somewhere else. I don't think we are going to have a happy ending here. Tomorrow we will ask around and maybe there shall be an answer. Possibly there could be a logical explanation, but I wouldn't count on it."

The journey to find what had happened to Father Ricikas would not have a happy ending and in their hearts and minds they knew he would not return.

Mikael decided to go next door to the church. The path from the rectory to the church was lined with weeds, twigs, and leaves piled on the stone walkway, another clue that the old priest had not been living here for a long time. The rose garden that was his pride and joy tumbled over the flower beds that gathered on the level below. The vegetable garden had completely disappeared and now nothing but weeds covered the ground where the prized tomatoes would ripen on the vine. Mikael dreaded going into the church. The windows were all in tack but were barely visible. Dirt and dust had accumulated over the years, and the shrubs and vines had grown and attached themselves along with the dirt. Paint was peeling making it difficult to decipher what color it was supposed to be originally.

The front door was locked so he tried and entered the side door. It was dark inside and an odor of dampness permeated throughout, the source a huge hole in the roof which he suspected was caused by rain common this time of year allowing it to drip down through the opening. He took a moment to scan the room as if he half expected to see Father Ricikas. He suddenly did not feel well. He knew it had something to do with the old priest. It all became so overwhelming. He knelt in front of the statue of the Blessed Virgin, her blue dress faded and several stars missing from the space above her feet, made the sign of the cross, and he prayed. He prayed for the missing priest, and he prayed for guidance on being a priest once again. Then he returned to the rectory and Justas.

CHAPTER 31

Mikael removed the cassock from the linen press, inspected it closely, and placed it back in exactly the same space where it had hung for the last six years. His transition back to being a priest was not going to be an easy or expeditious one. He felt he was in a strange, unfamiliar place.

He was not the same man who had worn it before the war, and he suspected it would be awhile before he could find whatever necessary course he needed to pursue in solving the problem before he could be capable of wearing it again.

It had started to rain, gray-black clouds floated across the sky. Mikael crossed the room to the window overlooking the garden. Tree branches littered the ground covered with weeds and leaves. The section of the garden where the rose bushes had once climbed and clung to the old stone wall, some stationed on wooden arbors, were now tilted or had fallen in all directions. Pieces of paper once tossed there by the wind were embedded in their thorns. Daffodils, early messengers of spring, were barely visible. The fence had crumbled, but the posts were still standing vines twisted around them. A birdbath in the very center of the yard had toppled and laid in several pieces on the ground. On the side of the church leading to the entrance of the gardens was a statue of St. Casmir still standing watch over the once well kept manicured grounds. The statue appeared to have suffered no damage; and if there had been any harm resulting from the elements, it was not visible.

The weather was a factor in Mikael's mood, but he knew he couldn't put all the blame on it. He had been a resistance fighter longer then he had been a priest, and now he wondered how he would be able to return to his role of being a priest, he always thought, a vocation chosen for him by God. He dwelled on Sophie, and the memories of her that he brought back from Trakai with him; and he also missed the young men and women with whom he shared the precarious times of the last six years. Was he capable now of returning to the religious life, a life that was not supposed to have been elected to interruption, especially by a war? But most of all he missed Sophie, beautiful, radiant, vivacious Sophie. Not even a week had passed since he had last seen her. He couldn't focus or concentrate on the smallest detail. Sleep eluded him. When he did sleep it was intermittent. And he had a recurring dream. Sophie was swimming toward him, calling his name, but he couldn't reach out to her and pull her to shore as it was evident she was in some sort of distress. He realized it would be a long time before she could write to him, but it didn't help him in any way to stop obsessing over it. He became concerned that he might never see her again. He prayed that she would make the trip to London safely and all was fine. He would eventually receive a letter from her, a letter that would alter his life. It would confirm she was well after the arduous trip at sea. She wrote that she missed him and hoped all had turned out much as he expected it and with Justas, too, hoped he was doing fine. She also wrote she had made a remarkable discovery, one he would find difficult to comprehend. For the first time he would receive information that he had a brother, a twin brother, Sophie would confirm to him. The rest of the story would come a little later, a story that had all the twists and turns of a mystery novel. He, like his new found brother, had made the decision to do everything possible to find him and eventually meet him. Unfortunately, it would not be in the near future. The new Soviet Lithuania would restrict travel in and out of the country.

To add to his despair he was disappointed that Father Ricikas was not here to welcome him and Justas. He needed the old priest for reassurance that all would pass and to assist him and help guide him toward being a servant of the Church once again.

Justas, too, found it difficult to resume his role as a priest; and like Mikael, he suspected that Father would not be returning, not anytime soon, perhaps not at all. The two would soon learn that their fears were confirmed. The details leading to his death, the murder of the dear old priest, became untangled over the next few weeks. It would prove to be another test of faith for the young priests.

The two priests upon their return soon learned that no Mass had been said at St. Casmir for almost three years. There had been no priest assigned to the parish. Father Ricikas, the parishioners had witnessed, was brutality carted off by the Germans, pulling up to the rectory one early morning in a large transport truck. They had given a description to Mikael and Justas of the events that followed that morning. The dear old man was never seen again. Mikael and Justas were determined to trace his journey. They would try to solve the mystery doubting it could have a happy ending.

The two priests wondered how the Church could survive here in Vilnius now that it was under Soviet rule; but tomorrow was another day. They had little choice but to tackle each problem one day at a time. Today they would not dwell on the subject. There was too much work to be done.

"Justas, why does so much of this seem out of place?"

"I really cannot give you an answer, but I am convinced we need time to readjust. It will take time, but we will get there!"

CHAPTER 32

After several days, walking, hitching a ride with a local farmer on his hay wagon, finding shelter in a barn during a torrential rainstorm and spending the night there sharing the space delegated to the farmer's horses, and thinking he was as exhausted as he possibly could be, in the distance he could see the mountains ahead certain they were the mountains that surround Heidelberg. Yes, he was absolutely sure of it!

As he approached the City, and from his first observation, he determined that it had been spared from even minor destruction. There appeared to be no damage contributed to the war. It was evident that the Allies had not bombed the old University City, unlike the industrial sites that were almost completely razed, and of course the capital, Berlin.

A feeling of relief spread over him, tears welling up in his eyes. He stood there, quietly, overcome with emotion. Finally he was home. There was no way of contacting Claudia since his return to Berlin, but hopefully she would be there tonight when he arrived. He vowed never to tell her about Sara. It would serve no purpose and would only hurt her, and there was always the possibility she would never forgive him. But before the day would completely disappear he would discover the devastating news that Claudia, his wife, had passed away. She would not be there to welcome him home from the war.

Erik guessed it would take an hour or so before he could reach his destination. He was surprised and took notice on this final portion of the journey that confirmed there was no war-related damage, but he could clearly see the results of neglect. Obviously there had been little or no money available for repairs to the homes. And when you add to the equation that the men had been off fighting for what most thought would become a victory for the Third Reich the neglect would become almost inevitable. Eventually when the Hell on earth came to an end a total of 50 million people had been wiped from the planet. But for many the enemy was not in uniform. It came in the form of T.B., pneumonia, polio, and a host of other killer diseases. He would soon be told that Claudia had fallen victim to this enemy.

His feet were in pain, and he was tempted to remove his boots as he was sure they would be covered with blisters, probably blisters upon blisters, but he hesitated knowing it would be impossible to put them back on his feet. How strange he thought that during the war years there was no pain to endure; and now that the war was over, he was experiencing his first bout of pain.

He would tolerate it just a little longer, he was almost home. He had left this place almost five years ago and wondered why it felt like he had been gone forever and in another way it seemed only a short time ago that he had left.

Erik hardly recognized the house. Even in the darkness he could see the field of weeds that flooded the yard that once was a manicured lawn with palettes of flowers in every corner. The shutters hung down off their hooks, and the paint almost completely peeled away from the wood. Ivy covering the brick front was overgrown and badly in need of pruning. But it was home after all, it was home.

Erik knocked softly on the front door, but there was no answer. He waited awhile and knocked once again. It became obvious no one was going to come to the door so Erik tried the latch and found it locked. Maybe with a little luck the back door would be unlocked, and he would let himself in the house. Just as he stepped through the doorway he was greeted by a very pretty very young girl, her long blonde hair framing big green eyes.

"My name is Hanna. What is your name?"

"My name is Erik.

"That's my papa's name. His name is Erik Mueller, like me, Hanna Mueller."

He felt as though he had stopped breathing, a vise squeezing in his chest.

In all those years he never once gave any thought to the possibility that Claudia could be pregnant, how very stupid, how selfish of him. He was more concerned with Sara and worrying about her becoming pregnant.

"My papa is in the army, and my Oma told me he would be coming home to see me soon."

"Hanna, I'm sure she is absolutely right. Is your Oma home? Is your mama here?" The young girl did not answer, just stared up at him. After a few minutes had passed she motioned toward the bedroom. "Oma is lying down. She's not feeling well, but I'll go and tell her you are here. I'll be right back. Wait here!"

A few minutes later Oma entered the room. "Oh, my God, my dear Lord, Erik, is it really you! You made it home! I've prayed every day for your safe return. And I see you have already met Hanna, your daughter!"

"You're my papa!"

"Yes, I'm afraid I am!"

"May I give you a hug?"

"I would like that very much. And is your mama here? I would like to give her a hug too!"

The two women, one so little and one much older, did not answer. They did not say a word, like something had spun around and struck them.

"Oma, is she here? Is she well?"

"Erik, come in the parlor with me;" and he followed her lead into the front room. She turned to her son-in-law and hugged him, and when she started to talk, her voice trembled.

"Sit down. I'm afraid there is no easy way to tell you my son. I have very bad news. Claudia is not with us any longer. She passed away three weeks after Hanna was born. Medicines were unavailable during those years and the few doctors had been drafted and gone off to war. Though there were complications from the birth at the end her death was caused by pneumonia. She was so ill at the end. She was so concerned and she worried about the baby. I could never explain the pain of those days. If it wasn't for Hanna I'm not sure if I would have had the will to go on, but I needed to do it for the baby; and of course, for Claudia. Seems I have been exhausted from that time on. If you wish I will take you to her tomorrow. I am so, so sorry!"

"Yes, I would like that." And he fell silent. There were no words. His heart felt as if it had stopped beating and had broken, both at once.

In the days that were to come he went through the motions, got acquainted with his daughter who had become such a joy to him. And a new feeling had engulfed him, one that was new and one he had never experienced, it became his constant companion and he was unable to bury it, to let it go. He felt a feeling of guilt, and it was consuming him.

For the next few weeks and months Erik settled in the role of Hanna's father. He and Oma did their best for her channeling their energy and time into caring for her. Erik and his daughter would take long walks down by the river, occasionally rowing across to the other side, sharing a picnic lunch that Oma would prepare for them. And each morning they would take turns helping her with her lessons. Hanna was bright and displayed enthusiasm for all her subjects. School would start again in the fall, and she had told her proud father that she was looking forward to it.

"I'm thinking you have little choice, Mikael. It's not fair to either you or your parents to keep postponing going home, especially if you think how long it has been since they have seen their son. You know I was planning on going home soon myself, but I need a little more time. This is a difficult adjustment for me. I've been praying for guidance every day since we came back here. I truly want to remain a priest, but I'd not be telling you or myself the truth if I were absolutely sure I want this vocation for the rest of my life. The years in Trakai were the happiest years for me. I was a completely different man; and with all the hardships we endured, I have to admit it probably would have to be the best years. Strange, I suppose, I can't explain it, could be the social aspect of it, the feeling I was really accomplishing something important. The role I had been given made me feel content, again hard to put into words, and I was contributing something, even in such a tiny role, to expedite the war's end. And yet there were times when I had hoped the war would not end soon, selfish and stupid I know. You and I are well aware that once the Soviets issue their edits, they will try to enforce them and eradicate all religions, not just the Catholic Church. So, the decision will not become mine in the long run though I honestly hope it never comes to that."

"Justas, you are like a brother to me, one I never had. It's difficult, as you might imagine, for me to foresee a life without you in it. I had to let Sophie go, and God only knows how I miss her. And I have faith that God will lead you in the right direction. It's too early to put this much stress on yourself, take it a day at a time, put it on hold for awhile. There will come a time for a decision, a little later, not now. When I get back maybe you will decide to go home too for awhile. You might feel differently by then. You don't have to mention this to your family just yet, just go and enjoy your days with them. Now let's draw a plan to start the necessary repairs to the church, agreed?"

The next week was spent scrapping, plastering, painting, sawing and hammering. The improvements did not appear quickly, but it did become obvious and the young priests did feel a sense of accomplishment. Mikael, again, put his visit home on hold and put all his efforts into finishing the task at hand.

The parishioners realizing that St. Casmir once again had a priest, two priests actually, returned to hear Mass on Sundays and the Holy Days of Obligation. Infants would be baptized, children came for catechism to prepare for their First Communion, the young adults for their Conformation. And the two young priests even noticed a few extra moneta (coins) in the collection basket!

As time passed the priests almost had forgotten that Moscow was now issuing orders to close all churches, synagogues, and anything connected with the worship of God. But as time passed St. Casmir remained an active and flourishing parish. The Red Army did not come with lock and key. It was short of a miracle.

The front door, badly in need of repair and of paint, was locked so Mikael tried and entered the side door. Inside it appeared dark with an odor of dampness and mustiness the source probably being a huge space in the roof at the back of the church. He suspected it was caused by the rainfall especially common in early spring and snowfall during the winter months. A statue of the Blessed Virgin Mary stood guard at the far end of the altar, her blue dress faded from the sun peeking through the windows over the years, and there were stars missing from the space above her feet. The plaster had crumbled falling on the floor in a heap revealing a few missing toes. Sadly, she too, had become a victim of the war years taken its toll on her as well.

He genuflected as he passed over the aisle in front of the cross of Christ suspended from the ceiling, made the sign of the cross, and knelt in front of Mary. It was not the first time since he returned from Trakai that he experienced a feeling of complete loneliness, and he was well aware of the reason. He missed Trakai, his family there that had bonded together for so long, and most of all he missed Sophie. And he could not help but wonder if he would ever see her again knowing he played a part in her journey to England by encouraging her to take a risk and seek a new life there. He asked Mary to help him now in his darkest hour and to watch over the woman he knew he would always love. A gloom had descended over him, wrapped him so tightly he could not escape, not without divine help he knew. He was incapable of letting it go at this point by himself. He was aware that there was no magical solution that could dissolve the pain and despair that existed in him. The feelings and the pain would only increase, become more intense, when he and Justas finally discovered the fate of their beloved pastor who had been murdered at the hands of the Germans. God did eventually lift the burdens from him and the demons that had followed him. Now it was time to be a priest again, put his problems aside, and get on with his life, his life here at St. Casmir, and yes, to be thankful for making it back here healthy and alive.

CHAPTER 33

It was late afternoon the day he had received the letter from Sophie. It was warm and sunny a welcome change from the rain that had drenched the city for the last few days. He placed the letter in his pocket and walked outside to the garden. Here on the old wooden bench, perhaps hand-carved by someone who came to St. Casmir many years before him, he sat and read his letter.

My dearest Mikael,

Let me begin by saying I am well and hoping and praying this finds you the same. The journey was long and difficult, and there were times when I wondered if we would make it safely here.

Grazina had a bout of pneumonia, and she spent her first few weeks here in the hospital. It was a difficult struggle, but she pulled through and now is fine and completely recovered. She is staying with a family in my neighborhood, and we do get to visit often.

I was offered a position in a bookshop owned by the family that I am living with. I have been taking English courses at the Lithuanian church along with most of the group that came over on the ship with me. The course is two nights a week and works just perfectly. The priest is from Kaunas originally. He's been in London way before the war years.

I am praying that this letter reaches you as I know you worry about me.

Give my love to Justas; and of course, to you, Mikael. I am missing you both so very much. God willing we will see each other again—in this world I hope!

With all my love, Sophie

There would be no mention of her pregnancy. It would serve no purpose for him to know a baby was due. It would be many years before Mikael would meet his daughter for the first time, a spitting image of her father.

Time seemed to move slowly and Mikael wondered what God had planned for his small country not sure if He would be remotely involved in it. The Soviets replaced the Nazi occupation. Both were forms of the Devil's advocate. With the future so uncertain Mikael knew it would be a test of faith for all Lithuanians.

Slowly the faithful came back to the Church attending Mass on Sundays and Holy days. Their children were being baptized, attending Sunday school to prepare for First Communion, and the number of adults going to confession on Saturday afternoons took Mikael by surprise. It was apparent that the war did not destroy their faith as during the last four years there had been no priest here at St. Casmir. Throughout the Soviet Union the majority of the churches had been closed by this new regime; but Lithuania, a good distance from Moscow and the seat of power, escaped many of the new edits that were being imposed in other satellite countries now under communist control. Mikael wondered if that would change in the future.

St. Casmir was in dire need of repair, the result of being closed for so long. Plaster fell from the walls and paint was peeling throughout the church. The roof needed to be replaced. When it would rain water would spill over on to the altar exactly where the Virgin Mother stood watch. Her toes had already started to crumble; and the stars that once encircled her head were barely visible. Repairs would have to be made before winter arrived accompanied by cold weather. First on the list would have to be the roof. He would worry about the plaster and peeling paint at another time.

There could be light at the end of the tunnel! They were finding their way one step, one day at a time, becoming priests once again, difficult for them; but as they were finding out, not impossible. It appeared they would give God a chance after all, and He would reciprocate. Not a bad partnership it seemed. Time would tell.

CHAPTER 34

As the time slipped from months into a year he wondered what the future would bring for him. The country was recovering from the war, and it was a slow recovery. He took on the task of tackling repairs on the house; but supplies needed to complete the projects were not always available, and it would become frustrating not being able to finish what had been started. And just about the time when Erik felt the future appeared dim with little end in sight for him the letter arrived from Berlin, the letter from Karl that would result in a better life for him and his daughter and be the key to being reunited with the young British woman whom he couldn't get out of his mind.

The following Sunday, three days after arriving from Berlin, Erik, Hanna, and Oma would make the short trip to the cemetery where the young wife, mother, daughter had been laid to rest. Fresh flowers in spring and summer and a basket filled with branches of evergreen and holly in winter were always placed on the grave; and always a prayer or two, mixed with a few tears, would be said before departing. When Erik and Hanna arrived Oma was already there as she always came directly from Mass, a place she tried to visit every Sunday since loosing her daughter. Several times a year she would bring her granddaughter to church with her and then come to the cemetery after Mass.

She smiled as she saw the two as they approached her and then reached down to take Hanna's hand. Erik knew there would always be a special bond between the two, and he was so grateful for the years that his mother-in-law had spent in raising her. He strangely felt at peace here but was peppered with sadness thinking of what life would be if Claudia were still here with him. The two would share their lives with Hanna and probably there would be more children. They say that time should heal, maybe, he wasn't so sure about that. He knew he wasn't alone in his loss. The war intervened

and destroyed thousands of families but right now at this moment
he felt only his own sorrow. And the guilt he felt became even more
intense. He tried in vain to shake Sara from his thoughts but he could
not conquer it.

CHAPTER 35

It was just over one year since the end of the war, and Erik wondered if life would ever remotely be the same as there was so little joy for him with the exception of his young daughter, Hanna. He felt completely alone the majority of the time. He missed Claudia, but he missed even more the beautiful woman with whom he spent the war years on Half Way Island. To him it felt like only yesterday, and it felt like a hundred years ago all at the same time. He often wondered if he would ever experience happiness in his future. The answer was yes but not for some time yet. God had a plan for him. He would be reunited with Sara, but he would have to be patient.

Hanna seemed to sense her father's mood; and she came over to him, put her small arms around him and gave him a hug. He hugged her back. She resembled her father, blonde and blued eyed. Even though she never knew her mother Erik could feel she missed having one; and he tried to play two roles for her, and with some success. She also had Oma, her beloved grandmother, Claudia's mother, and a handful of aunts and uncles who doted on her and her cousins that lived on the same street and in the nearby village. She was a happy child; and she was very bright, reading was her favorite pleasure.

Erik was preparing to visit his aunt when the phone rang. It was his uncle asking if he could visit with his aunt today as she was asking for him. He was well aware of his aunt's failing health, and he felt guilty as it had been several weeks since he had a visit with her or had even made an effort to call her.

"Uncle Christian, believe it or not I'm practically on my way there now!" he spoke into the phone. "I was planning on seeing you today." He continued.

His uncle had always been slightly hard of hearing but Erik noticed the problem was getting worse. Uncle Christian requested Erik to repeat what he had just said to him.

"Uncle Christian, I will come by this afternoon. Tell Aunt Ingrid it should be around 2 o'clock."

"I'll give her your message."

His aunt and uncle had always been devoted to each other. They married quite late in life, had no children, and Erik became more like a son to them than a nephew. His uncle had become his wife's caretaker since she fell and broke her hip a year ago; but as she was making progress, she was diagnosed with lung cancer and facing the future with little hope for recovery.

Originally when Erik planned to visit he thought he would bring Hanna but decided against it wondering if his aunt was up to dealing with a busy and restless inquisitive 5 year old that probably would sit no longer than a minute. He would bring the most recent photograph of her. He tucked it in his wallet so he wouldn't forget it to bring it with him.

"Hanna, he called, "come say good-by."

"Good by, Papa." And he reached down and kissed his daughter.

"Be a good girl for Oma."

It was raining as he stepped outside as it had been since early yesterday morning. The weather didn't help his mood.

When Erik arrived at his aunt's house he was surprised to see how her appearance had drastically changed since he last had seen her. Her hair had turned almost completely white, long and straight, hanging over her shoulders. She had lost so much weight that her skin hung off her body in small wrinkled folds. The green eyes Erik remembered always bright and sparkling were now dull and sunken, and she barely resembled the woman who as a boy took him hiking through the Bavarian Mountains on school vacations, baked his favorite cookies, and gave him hundreds of hugs over the years.

At first she wasn't aware that Erik had entered the room. When she finally saw him she smiled across the room at him.

"Oh, Erik!" she reached out to touch him. "I am so very glad you could come today!"

"You know you are my favorite aunt, don't you! And you know I still love you!"

"You are here. I am so glad you were able to visit today." She repeated, maybe slightly confused for a second.

121

Always a heavy smoker she reached for her cigarette which lay smoldering in the nearby ashtray, took a deep puff, and then snuffed it out. The end table was covered with ashes. She completely ignored the mess and turned again to Erik.

"Tell me how is Hanna, and your mother-in-law?"

"Both are fine, Hanna growing up so fast its hard to keep up. And I just happen to have the latest photo for you, one that you can keep".

"She is just adorable." And she beckoned her husband who had just entered the room to come over to admire their beautiful grandniece.

"She is so like you, Erik." She smiled, and her husband nodded in agreement.

"I am preparing a salad and some sausage for lunch. Will be awhile I'm afraid. Excuse me. I'll call you when it's ready. I hope you can spend some time with your Aunt Ingrid today, Erik. She often mentions how she misses you. I suspect even more so since her sister, your mother, passed away."

"Erik, there is something I have wanted and have needed for you to know for a long, long time; and finally as I am afraid that there is so little time left, today I must tell you what has haunted me for so many years. I don't expect you to grasp and absorb it right away, but what I am about to tell you is the whole truth. You may believe that I'm an old and senile woman, but I swear on your mother's soul it is the truth." His aunt spoke slowly and softly as she wanted her nephew to hear her every word. "There is no easy way to tell you. I believe you; and yes Hanna, have a right to know. I have anguished over this since your parents passed away." She paused and looked at Erik who appeared to have no idea what she wanted to say to him. Tears welded up in her eyes as she remembered the circumstances of those years." I will start the story by telling you that you have a brother, an identical twin brother."

"My God, Aunt Ingrid, what are you saying? How can this be true! Did he die?"

"I don't know. Of course there is that possibility. Naturally if he were alive he would be your age, but let me get on with the story so you understand a lot more. Years before I met your uncle I lived in Latvia. At that time they were many Germans living in Riga. It was not unusual; it was a beautiful city, but after a few years I decided to move to Lithuania where I met and married a young man, his name was Arlandas. We were married for a very short time. Even today it is painful for me to go back to that time. He was killed in a boating accident, he drowned. The months that followed were difficult. I somehow remembered he had an uncle who was a priest. I wanted the pain so much to disappear, and I thought maybe the priest could help me. I had met him briefly at the funeral services, and it turned out I was right. He provided a great deal of comfort for me. Part of it was that we were both connected to Arlandas, and we both had lost someone we loved. On what was to be our last visit, the last time I saw him, was several days after you were born. The old priest told me a young woman found her way to the church; and it was pretty obvious she was about to give birth, her time was near. He summoned the village mid-wife. There were two babies, twin boys." She stopped for a moment and glanced at her nephew. He didn't say a word.

"Your mother died the next day, and she was buried in the cemetery behind the church. Father and I were the only two present for the burial. The priest didn't know who she was or how she had found her way to the church. He wouldn't agree to my taking you to another country or taking just one of the babies. I knew my sister, your mother, could never have a child of her own and would love you from the minute she saw you. Unfortunately because of the distance involved on the trip to Germany, I could only bring one baby."

"You are telling me I was born in Lithuania, I have or had a twin brother, and my mother, your sister, was not my birth mother!" The old woman nodded. There was a long silence in the room. "And why was I not told a long time ago!"

"So many times your mother and I wanted to tell you, but we wanted to spare you the pain. Your mother was adamant and made me vow I would never reveal this to you, but after her passing I made a decision that I would tell you. Please don't have me regret it, Erik! This has been the most difficult thing I have had to do with the exception of taking you out of Lithuania so many years ago and making my way here."

It wasn't enough he had survived the war years, lost Claudia, but now he had to deal with all of this, or could he. He just could not deal with it now, maybe tomorrow or the day after tomorrow but certainly not at this moment.

"I've kept this all to myself for all these years and there were days when I considered taking you aside, telling you, but I truly thought it would make you sad so between the war and all the other hardships, I just could not muster the courage. I was well aware that someday you deserved to know. Forgive your old aunt. I never meant to hurt you. When you were younger I truly felt there was no purpose in telling you or upsetting my sister who begged me never to reveal the truth to you. There never seemed any right time."

"Did Uncle Christian know about this?"

"No, he does not. I never told anyone, just you tonight."

Erik could see how trying this was for his dear old aunt and wanted to tell her he understood, even though he wasn't sure if he did, but nothing was going to change so he walked over to the sofa where she had been sitting, put his arms around her, hugged her, and told her it was alright. Erik knew the story had to be true. It was too incredible not to be true.

"I hope you can forgive me. I have carried this with me for so long knowing I had no choice but to tell you someday. I hope in time you will make an attempt to find your brother. Father Kapocius would have had died years ago but I knew he kept a journal. He wrote in it every day. It may hold some clues to what happened to your brother. Of course the journal could be long gone, destroyed, hidden and never found, or it could still be in the rectory in the desk where he always kept it. I know you need time to absorb all of this, but you are still a young man. That is in your favor. You do not need to make any decisions now."

"I'm not sure I'm up to this, this test. I find it hard not to forgive you, I truly understand why, I do, but it doesn't make it any easier for me."

He stayed a while longer. His uncle was a little disappointed that he wasn't too hungry not knowing of course the reason for his lack of appetite. He wondered if his life would change drastically with this new knowledge. He would eventually reunite with his brother, a priest in Lithuania, a place that he couldn't find on the map on the first try. He would repeat the name, a country where he had been born, a country he would have to research more thoroughly. He didn't even know exactly where it was, but he would make an effort to find out. And most of all he was determined to find his brother. He believed his brother had to be still alive. He would make every possible effort to find him. It did not matter how long the journey would take.

Mikael always knew that he had been adopted, and he remembered the day well as if it were just yesterday instead of 15 long years ago. He became curious why Sister had excused him from his chores on this summer day. Sister had told him to say a special prayer as there were two very important people who would be visiting the orphanage after lunch, and they were very anxious to meet him.

"Now remember, Mikael, be a good boy and on your best behavior, remember to say please and thank you and if they like you, you could become their son. You will have a home with a real mother and a father. Wouldn't that be wonderful?"

"But, Sister, this is my real home, and I would miss all my friends!"

"I understand my child I do understand, and we would all miss you very much; but I know you would learn to love them, and I know you will be so happy. And you could come here often and visit."

The hours seemed to move slowly but finally the time came to go to the parlor and wait for the visitors to arrive. Sister came into the room, and Mikael rose from his chair. His knees and legs wouldn't stop shaking, and he felt his hands trembling. His stomach, too, didn't feel quite right.

Mikael couldn't remember the first few minutes of their meeting. He just remembered the pretty woman with the straw hat angled on top of her head smiling at him. Sister asked the couple to be seated and get comfortable and said a few words to them before leaving the room.

"Mikael is a wonderful boy as you will soon find out for yourself."

So it was at six years old he gathered up his few belongings, bid good-by to his friends, and left the only place he had ever known.

And the dear Sister had been right. He learned to love the two people who had adopted him and were now his parents. They doted on their only child, loved him unconditionally, and instilled in him a love for God; and many years later when he acknowledged that he was serious about becoming a priest and entering the priesthood, they were supportive to him.

CHAPTER 36

T he letter arrived three days after Christmas. It would be responsible for changing his life.

Dear Erik,

I hope you are well. I'm writing to you to offer you a position with our company here in Berlin. As you know my father founded the business several years before the war; and of course, was interrupted during those years. My younger brother, Klaus, and I have taken over the helm since my father's retirement, and the company is expanding rapidly beyond all expectations.

The purpose of this letter to you is to offer you a position with our firm with the stipulation that you could start in the immediate future. Please contact me as soon as possible. I will schedule a meeting with you so we can discuss this matter at length. I am hoping you will give this your full consideration, and I am looking forward to hearing from you.

Sincerely, Karl

Erik re-read the letter. To say he was surprised and elated would be an understatement, and he couldn't think of a single reason why he would not accept the position. It was the first time since returning home and discovering he had lost Claudia that he felt even a ray of optimism about the future. He would have to travel to Berlin so Karl could fill in the details before he would make a final decision. There was little doubt in his mind that this was a key to a brighter, better future, a future he had become pessimistic about for so long now. There were days when he would feel depressed, only Hanna gave him some purpose to face each day, providing the small dosage of hope that maybe life would improve in the near future.

Later that evening after Hanna had gone to bed, in the stillness of the room, he sat at his desk and drafted a letter to Karl and planned to mail it the next morning. He lay awake long into the night; and for the very first time since he had come home, he experienced a feeling that was not one of despair.

A meeting between him and Karl had been scheduled for Monday, the second week of January; and as Karl had suggested, Erik planned to spend three days in Berlin. His potential employer also insisted that he stay with him, he had a small apartment in the same building as corporate headquarters.

"Papa will be home soon, in just three days, Schnukele." He kissed and hugged his daughter good-by. "And be a good girl for Oma!"

"Yes, Papa, I promise!" sending him kisses as he walked away from her.

And so Erik was off on the journey that would drastically change his life.

Erik boarded the train to Frankfort and at the train station there he changed to an express to Berlin. Karl would meet him there upon arrival. It was shortly after 11 a.m. when the train pulled into the station leaving clouds of black smoke behind. Karl was waiting on the platform when Erik stepped out and extended his hand to his friend whom he had not seen since his visit at the hospital in Half Way Island.

"Erik, it is so good to see you! It's been quite a while, hasn't it?"

"And you, it's so good to see you!"

"Let's have a little lunch, shall we, and a beer perhaps before we go to the office."

As they left the station Erik noticed Karl exhibited a small limp as he turned to walk away, and Karl seemed to notice the attention.

"I now have two legs, one old and one new, but it's not so bad. The new one was the last gift to me from the Fuhrer along with a medal for my honorable service to Germany."

"Do you ever wonder how we ever got caught up in all that, that madness? But we are thankfully rising from the ashes, slowly, but we are forging forward. Our company is a perfect example. We are growing so fast it is difficult to comprehend. And now hopefully you will join us and become part of our success story. I'm truly wishing your decision will be to definitely come aboard, and I'll even give you the next few days to agree to the plan. Our lives were put on hold for a long time, something we had been given no control. But now we do have a choice, now we can make decisions concerning our future."

Lunch followed and the meeting that came later went well. Karl explained the job description in full, salary, and talked briefly about the plans to open a branch in London within the next year the position that would put Erik in full control.

Karl later managed to arrange a short tour stopping to introduce Erik to the employees and explain the responsibilities of each department. Erik was impressed how quickly the company had been given the opportunity to elevate to such a large firm.

"We have done extensive research in England. As you might guess there is, of course, still animosity because of the war. It's been only a little over a year and perfectly normal; but because of the nature of our business, it is one that the English have a real and urgent need, and there is no competition there for us. They may be willing to accept us just for that reason aware that we are a German company. The country has no pharmaceutical companies on our level to date and might explain why they are willing to accept us, not completely willing to embrace us, but they are aware they desperately need our products especially the drugs which will be made available to hospitals and medical facilities. You would be the perfect candidate, Erik, and you already have command of the language. No decision has to be made immediately but I think you will make the right one. The journey should be an incredible one."

"No need, Karl, I am truly grateful for your offer, and I would be a fool not to accept it. Yes, it would be a privilege to be part of the team of Breuer Pharmaceuticals, and I want to say thank you."

Erik was feeling as if he had been awarded a second chance on life, but he could not remotely begin to imagine how this decision would alter his future.

The following days moved swiftly, and it would be two weeks before he would return to Berlin and report for work.

"First, I accepted the offer. It is an opportunity I'm afraid will never come my way again. If there is a negative it would be in time I will have to relocate from Berlin to London, and there is Hanna. I'll have to make important decisions concerning her. Her age is an advantage; children learn and adjust quickly, and she will have to learn to speak English. And, Oma, we would not have you in our daily lives. That will be the most difficult thing for us."

The mother-in-law and grandmother smiled up at Erik from the sofa where she was seated. "My darling son," as she often called him. "You are still a young man, a man who has his whole life still ahead of him. The war years are behind you, and now you have been given a second chance to be happy again, to have some purpose for your life, an opportunity to prepare a better life for Hanna, and to get on with your own life. Of course I will miss you, and my Hanna! It would be selfish of me not to let her go. In my heart I know she deserves to be with her father, wherever her father goes. And maybe arrangements can be made once you are settled to have her come visit once in awhile!"

Erik was silent for a few minutes before he answered her. "You are right, I know. I only wish that Claudia was here to share in this with us. I miss her, Oma."

And he almost spoke aloud, "And I miss Sara!"

How strange, he thought, that now at this time he would be thinking of the woman that he had not seen for a year and one half, and he couldn't help but wonder if he would ever see her again. And what became a puzzle to him was how often she would find her way into his thoughts. He would think of Claudia and with no explanation Sara would unexpectedly enter that place. He wondered where she was, did Paul, her husband, return from the war safe and sound, was she and Paul happy together, and did Sara ever think of him. There was no way he would find the answers at this time' but not too far off in the future, he would have all his answers. Fate had a plan for Erik and Sara.

CHAPTER 37

The next hours moved quickly. Hanna and her papa hauled the old red sled out of the shed and filled the remainder of the day pulling the sled up the hill, sliding down it, and repeating the drill several times. They returned home to the smell of fresh baked pies and a roaring fire. It had been a good day Erik was thinking as he tucked his daughter into bed.

He started the process of sorting out his papers, documents. Most he would leave behind. The remaining would be packed and shipped later to Berlin. He planned to spend the rest of the week organizing and also making every effort to being there for Hanna each day and to be available should any problems or questions his mother-in-law might have for him. And the days passed without incidence, and the time to leave for Berlin quickly approached.

Erik had been assigned his own office with an assistant to do the typing, filing, answer the telephone, and additional secretarial responsibilities. He would later discover that her husband had been killed on the Russian Front, and she now lived with her sister just outside of the city. He also learned she spoke English. Her father had remarried after her mother died, and the new wife was an American from Boston, Massachusetts, where she lived until a few years before the war broke out. He felt this would be an opportunity to practice his English, but his time in Berlin would be brief as the plan for the London office was moving ahead of schedule. As predicted the English accepted the company's proposal resulting in a request from them to move the London project to even an earlier date. Unfortunately, the secretary had not been able to accept an offer to transfer with Erik to the new location, but she kept her promise to Erik and did speak to him in English most often during their time in Berlin.

For the next few weeks Erik would make plans for the upcoming transfer and worked frantically to juggle tasks at home. It was the last days of March, the winter making way for spring. Berlin winters consisted of rain, clouds, more rain on a daily basis. The city worked hard to come alive as the weather tried to warm up. There were still reminders of the ravage that it had suffered, scars from the war still visible, but there were signs everywhere of the city making attempts to reconstruct. Berlin appeared to be pulling itself out of the ashes.

Erik forged ahead days filled with arrangements for the move to London, scheduling meetings, reviewing reports, ordering supplies and office equipment deemed necessary for the new branch. His evenings, however, were filled with loneliness. Social life was nonexistent, one exception. Karl and his wife, Heidi, on occasion would insist on his presence for dinner at their home. Every other week-end he would go home to Heidelberg. He explained to Hanna and Oma his first priority once he got to London would be to find a flat. He was surprised how much he missed his daughter on their long separations. Hopefully the search would be a quick one. He wanted to get Hanna settled during the summer months and before school would begin. He had also planned on hiring a tutor for her for English lessons. He had already spent time with her on the subject and found she did extremely well and seemed to really enjoy the challenge.

CHAPTER 38

The walk to the cemetery seemed just a bit longer this Sunday morning knowing that he would soon be leaving for London. He could not predict when he could return for another visit but certain it would not be for awhile. When he first was given the news that his wife had passed away; he would come here daily, but as time marched on by to the next day, to the next week, his visits became less frequent.

The sun out in full force this Sunday morning seemed to have a routine all is own. It would usually make an appearance late morning, and fade away, then repeating its procedure until it disappeared into the night, but today it erased all routine and hung in the sky for the entire day. It was a rare but welcoming sight for this city surrounded by mountains. Erik was thinking the weather in London had to be similar maybe a little cooler in the summer months as it usually had been on Half Way Island. Erik felt the sun was always an unexpected bonus, a nice surprise. Today was one of those days.

Oma smiled at Erik as he and Hanna walked toward her.

"Good morning, Darling!" She reached down and took her grand-daughter's hand. She wondered how long it would be before her son-in-law and her grand-daughter would be leaving for London.

Time moved forward, not too swiftly, not too slowly, Erik focused on finding his way at work and making arrangements for Hanna to join him in London. It was late spring, summer was on her way. As predicted the English accepted the German pharmaceutical company's proposal, and Erik drew up plans for his transfer to London. The most difficult part was in having to leave Hanna even if only temporarily. He explained to his daughter he would make every effort to find a flat so she could join him, hopefully very soon. He wasn't sure just how much she could comprehend; but between the tears and the hugs, she told her father she would see him next week!

The London weather, rainy and damp, peppered occasionally by fog, was not unlike what Erik experienced in Germany. The first week it rained unrelentingly and Erik thinking this island, his new home called England, would sink to the bottom of the Atlantic Ocean if the rain didn't cease real soon.

Erik spent his days at the office and his evenings and week-ends taking on the task of finding a flat so he could get settled and send for Hanna. The city was still recovering from the Blitz so housing was at a premium. It was approximately two weeks into the search when a young man in his office approached him and told him he thought there would be a vacancy coming soon in an apartment building on the street where he lived.

"It's approximately a twenty minute walk to the office and just two subway stops. It's a second floor flat and completely furnished. I'll write the address down with directions and the landlord's name and phone number. Her name is Mrs. White. She lives on the first floor, right-hand side."

"Thank you, I appreciate it. I'll plan on going directly from work. I'll call Mrs. White and check if she'll be available to show it."

In the weeks ahead Erik would discover the young man to whom he would have to give credit for finding him housing had been a prisoner of war in England, and he learned to speak English quite well while there. He had been here in London just a short time before Erik had been assigned to the London Division and discovered the young man had recently became engaged to an English woman. He had confided in Erik he had not mentioned this to his parents now living in East Germany. His father had lost an arm during the war and not quite forgiving that his only son was living with the enemy and completely unforgiving for accepting a position in the enemy's country! He realized that at some time in the future the announcement would probably become inevitable. Maybe time would heal the wounds.

On more than one occasion in the weeks and months ahead Erik would reflect on the total insanity of the war. The English probably would not forget but it seemed to him they were willing to forgive. There were a few exceptions, of course, but for the most part this was how he perceived it. Before Erik left the office for the day he called the number and spoke to Mrs. White who confirmed the flat was still available, and she agreed to show him the place this evening. With the directions given to him he had no trouble finding the building. After introductions she took him on a tour through the four-room apartment: a kitchen, parlor, and two bedrooms, a large bathroom. The landlady explained the terms of the one-year lease. Erik took out his pen and signed the papers. He could hardly wait to give the news to his daughter. As he left he noticed a swing hanging from an old oak tree, the wind whipping it slowly back and forth. It brought back memories of the swing his father had built for him,

CHAPTER 39

Erik and Hanna embarked on the Underground with a changeover in the North section of the city; and within approximately ten minutes, at the fourth stop, stepped up and out into the area known as the Lithuanian Village. This was the section of London settled by the expatriates of Lithuania. Erik was determined to remain optimistic hoping he could find someone to unlock some of the questions he had about finding his brother.

Erik helped his daughter up the steps and out to the street. It looked similar to some of the German villages he remembered from his country.

"How are you doing, Hanna?'

"I'm fine, papa!"

"Not tired?" The young girl nodded. "Then it's time for us to be on our way."

Erik had no idea what direction to take or where he would begin but noticed a sign with an arrow pointing to a church named St. Casmir. He would learn in later years that St. Casmir was the patron saint of the country where he had been born, and it was extremely rare if in a Lithuanian community that the church would not be named in honor of him.

He would begin at the church as was suggested to him. The church was small, built of stone, manicured grounds, hedges neatly clipped planted all in a row, ivy clinging and almost completely covering the church, rose bushes rambling over stone walls that possibly were decades old. He stopped and searched for a rectory and realized it had to be in back of the church. The rectory, a cottage style house, sat in the middle of a beautiful garden, a brick walkway leading to the front door. A brass door knocker in the shape of a fish had been nailed directly to the front of the door; and just as he was about to pull up the handle an elderly woman opened the door. She took a few seconds before she introduced herself.

"I'm the housekeeper here. My name is Mrs. Idzeljavitsus, and you are?"

"I am Erik Mueller, and I was wondering if there was a priest available for me to see this morning. I only require a few minutes of his time."

"Father is probably hoeing in his garden, over there by the fence, she pointed. I am sure he would be willing to see you "

Erik with Hanna in tow turned and walked down the path in the direction given by the housekeeper. Huge, bright red geraniums planted in clay pots and a variety of baskets in every shape and size were placed along the path every few feet. Violets nestled against rocks along with chicken and hens. In the far corner a cluster of bird houses stood on brightly painted posts giving the look of being wymsical. Erik's guess would be the priest was responsible for this magical place.

As Erik moved closer to the priest he turned as he heard them approaching, rose from his kneeling position and greeted them.

"Good morning!"

"Good morning, Father. I was hoping you have a few minutes."

"Yes, yes I do. What brings you to our church?"

"My name is Erik Mueller and this young lady is my daughter, Hanna. I work with a woman whose husband was born in Lithuania; and after hearing my story, her husband suggested that I come here to speak to someone, a priest perhaps. He said the church keeps records of baptism, marriages, and other documents and possibly these may lead to finding my brother. I am German; but I was born in Lithuania in 1915, and I was adopted by a German family and only discovered recently that I have a brother, a twin brother, probably living in Lithuania. I do know we were born in a town called Klaipeda, and that's the limit of my knowledge."

The priest listened carefully as Erik told him a condensed version of his story.

"I have been living here in London since before the war and I regret, unfortunately, I am not of much help. If he is still in Lithuania there would not be any records in our church; but I'm going to recommend you go back up the hill to the bookstore, Knygynas, on the same side of the street and find a young woman, Sophie, that works there. She came here just a month or so after the war, and she was in the resistance. I'm pretty certain she was originally from Klaipeda. She may be able to help you."

"I know it will take something short of a miracle. I don't even know his name; only where we were born and the date and year, but I want to pursue this as far as possible, hopefully with a happy ending."

"I wish you luck, my son. God works in many ways, and I for one believe in miracles. May Our Heavenly Father guide you and lead you to your brother."

"Thank you, Father. Now I'm going to try to find Sophie. It should definitely be a starting point."

It was a short walk up the hill and Erik saw the bookstore in the distance, a sign in bold black letters, KNYGYNAS, hung out in front. It appeared to be suspended by chains on both sides attached to the side of the building. As he got closer he could see the small-paned windows, bull's-eye glass over the door, and another smaller sign with pictures of books and something he thought was written in Lithuanian. He would soon learn the store was much larger on the inside than it appeared from the outside of the building.

A small bell hung above the door, and it jangled as they entered. Erik was thinking it resembled a miniature library. There were ladders spaced along the bookshelves, and a young woman greeted them from the top of the one farthest away where she was engaged in placing the books in some kind of order.

"Hello, welcome to Knygynas. I'm Janna!"

"Hello, I'm Erik and this is Hanna!"

"So very nice to meet you both." She replied in English and extended her hand to both. Please look around and feel free to ask any questions. Are you looking for anything special?"

"I am really hoping to find a woman, Sophie. As you probably can detect I'm German and have been living and working in London. I discovered I had been born in Lithuania, in Klaipeda to be exact, in 1915 and was adopted by a German couple. I lived my whole life without knowledge of being adopted until very recently. And I learned that I had a brother, a twin brother, who could still be living there."

"This must be very difficult for you."

"I didn't know how I would start my search. I was hoping by some remote chance that someone might mistake me for my brother; or if I could find someone from Klaipeda, they might be able to give me information about my birthplace. The priest at St. Casmir told me he was quite sure Sophie was born there."

"I came here when I was only five years old, but the priest is right. Sophie came here from a place called Trakai where she spent the war years, but she is originally from Klaipeda. If I remember correctly she didn't live there for too long. Her family moved when she was quite young. And no I am not she! She will report to work today at noon. You are welcome to stay and wait for her or get some lunch and return."

"Yes, sounds like a good idea. We will get some lunch and come back."

"I hope she can help somehow. I won't see you again today. It's my half day, but I certainly wish you luck on this journey. There is a small pub just around the corner and also a lunch counter with both an English and Lithuanian menu. The lunch counter serves lighter courses, lots of soups including cabbage soup, always a favorite, served with home-baked bread. I hope you will find what you came here for but don't give up. I have a strong feeling you stumbled into here for a reason."

It was 11:10. Erik planned on returning at twelve or shortly after. He could not have anticipated in his wildest dreams that his pending visit would lead him to his brother. He would later give credit to the planets being lined up in his favor and a little credit to the stars too. He could think of no other explanation except maybe he was in the right place at the right time. Or maybe after all it was the priest's theory.

An hour later Erik and Hanna returned to the bookstore, the bell again announcing their arrival. Behind a mahogany desk in the middle of the room filing what appeared to resemble index cards sat a beautiful young woman. At first she didn't look up to acknowledge the pair.

"Hello I'm looking for a woman named Sophie and was told I could find her here."

There was complete silence. "I am looking for Sophie, and my guess you may be Sophie!"

She sat there for a moment unable to move or to speak, her heart racing, her body completely numb.

She was convinced she would pass out and reached over and held on to the desk knowing at any time soon she was going to faint.

"Are you alright? Are you feeling ill?"

"You're not Mikael!" Her words were barely audible, her face loosing its color.

"No, my name is Erik, Erik Mueller, and I will give you my explanation of why you might think I'm Mikael. He could be my twin brother. That is why I came here today. Janna told me you may be able to help unravel this mystery."

"But you are not Lithuanian, German?"

"Yes, I am German, but I was born in Klaipeda the same place that I was told where you were born. Until a few months back I did not know that I had been adopted and had a twin brother possibly still living in Lithuania. It took a long time for me to come to terms with this; and honestly, I am still a little in shock as you can well imagine."

"You are identical. He always knew he had been adopted. He was five or six years old. This is truly amazing! He is a Roman Catholic priest, Father Mikael Savickis living in Vilnius. And like you he has absolutely no idea about you, none whatsoever, not even a clue!"

Now it was Erik's turn to feel ill.

"May I sit down? He's a priest!" It took a few minutes for him to grasp what the young girl was telling him. "He is a priest!" he repeated not sure if he fully registered the information given him.

"Yes, yes he is. He's in a parish called St. Casmir in Vilinus."

"My God! This is truly amazing. It will take awhile I'm afraid for all to sink in, to comprehend the reality of it all."

"This certainly has to be a shock for you, and also for me. Mikael and I were very close. During the war we were in the resistance living on an island in a town called Trakai. We were there for the duration of the war, for six years. There was another priest from the same parish, Justas, and the three of us were inseparable during those years."

"My goal, of course, is to meet him, possibly in the near future. Do you think he would agree to it?"

"I certainly can't answer for him, but I find it difficult to comprehend why he would refuse. I'd be surprised, it wouldn't make any sense. The negative is that Lithuania is now a satellite nation of the Soviet Union. It would be almost impossible to obtain a visa. The post also is unreliable but not to be completely disqualified. This could be a start, worth a try I would suggest. If you like I will write to him. I assume you have not learned to speak our language as yet! I will also write down his address and give it to you."

"I cannot thank you enough. Would you mind if I stop by again?"

"I promise you I will do everything possible to assist you, but you must be aware that it will be difficult, not impossible however, to accomplish your plan to meet Mikael. And it will be my pleasure to accompany you on this journey if you wish. And you are always welcomed here! I will give you my home address along with the telephone number. You can reach me most evenings. I usually leave the store about 5:30 or 6 p.m. and you may want to leave a number where I can reach you."

CHAPTER 40

It was sometime after mid-night Mikael guessed but the small clock ticking on the nightstand revealed the time was not yet twelve o'clock, a few minutes shy of another day. Sleep had eluded him so he decided to walk over to the window, pulled the drapes aside. He noticed the moon, like him seemed restless. It appeared to slide in and out of the clouds; but it was the clouds, dark and dismal, that raced past.

He could barely see the rose garden from his window, the pedals fading, like him he thought. His life seemed to have no purpose. Everything had become shades of grey. He experienced bouts of loneliness and often depression. He wondered if God would ever return to this place. It would have to be soon, very soon he was thinking feeling like he was being reeled into some dark corner of despair.

Sophie was on his mind as she often was since leaving Trakai, beautiful, warm, intelligent Sophie; and he was well aware that it was she who invaded his soul, longing for something that could never be. He knew beyond a shadow of a doubt that it was she who was to blame for these feelings and the inability to fall asleep at night, and he also knew that he and only he alone would have to climb his way out of this place.

The room was cold and damp, and he shuttered to think of the impending cold winter just ahead. He would close the rooms upstairs and sleep near the fireplace in the parlor. There would be little or no coal for the old furnace, not the forthcoming winter anyway. He could pray for a miracle, but he knew it would not be in His plans. There would be no miracles in Lithuania in 1945. The new Communist regime had other plans for this small country. He at times wondered what His priorities were as it was obvious it had not been included in this part of the world.

Mikael survived the winter and was surprised his task had not been more difficult; and in April as the trees pushed their buds out on the branches a tiny miracle did occur. It was in a form of a letter, a letter from Sophie postmarked March 10, London, U.K., and arrived the first week of April. There was no return address on the envelope but discovered Sophie had written it on the back of letter possibly because she feared it would be too risky to post it on the front. It obviously did work. He would write back to her being aware that there would be a slim chance any letter would ever leave the country; and if it did, it probably would be opened and inspected. He would write the letter and be brief omitting any mention of the current political situation; and with some luck, maybe, just maybe it would pass through the system. And maybe this was a miracle in a different form that Mikael had prayed for because there would be more letters exchanged over the next years. He was absolutely convinced, sure that a greater power was responsible, no doubt in his mind.

Several months after receiving the first correspondence from Sophie a letter would arrive that totally devastated him and would change his life forever. She would write and explain the visit with Erik.

Mikael reread the letter and before the day had ended he had read it a dozen times trying to fully digest the reality of it all. She described in condensed form the circumstances of how he and his brother had been separated at birth. He was definitely an identical twin. I think you would approve of him, she wrote, and he is anxious to meet you. And, Mikael, you had better sit down for this one. He was raised in Germany and was an officer during the war. He speaks fluent English and is employed here in London by a German company. He has a daughter, Hanna. His wife died, and he is raising his daughter alone. He admits he had no idea exactly where Lithuania was until he located it on the map just a few months ago.

I explained Lithuania was now part of the Soviet Union and getting in or out of the country would be almost impossible; but I encouraged him to apply for a visa, probably a complete waste of time and money but what other choices would you and he have of ever meeting each other! Maybe God will answer another of your prayers. Make this your top priority, Father Mikael!! I am afraid you both have your work cut out for you. And by the way your brother's name is Erik Mueller!

Since the journey from Lithuania to London Sophie decided she would keep a journal. I'm trying so very hard. It was the first entry in it. And as strange as it sounds, I feel this is where I want to be, where I now belong. Everyone has been so dear, honestly concerned and caring. Mr.Norvaisa, who is originally from Kaunas, has offered me a position in his bookshop here in the village. I have made a commitment to improve my English though most of his customers are Lithuanians; but if I am to remain in this country, it is of course important that I have a command of the language. It is easier to learn to speak the language than to read and write it, but I have been blessed with a rare tenacity, probably inherited from my mother, which should help me. I miss her every day as I did in Trakai. It was such a sad reunion for me. The war years had taken its toll on her, and it was so difficult for me to see the once strong independent woman reduced to this frail old woman, aged beyond her years. She didn't recognize me or remember my name. I was so thankful that my sister, Shaiste, and her husband were there to take care of her. Contrary to what I thought, my sister and her husband encouraged me to leave Lithuania while there was a chance to do so. My sister felt that if my mother were not ill she would not have wanted me to stay in a country that had nothing to look forward to but more misery in the years ahead. Shaiste had no reservations whatsoever that my mother would have encouraged me and have given me her permission to take this challenge. After that night my decision to leave became less difficult for me. And Mikael, how would he react if he knew he had a daughter. To be continued. S.

It would be many years before she had an answer.

Time slipped by and life continued. Sophie was still a stunningly beautiful woman and perhaps this was a contribution to what was about to happen.

She tried in vain to forget Mikael. She knew in her heart that he could never completely belong to her, that he belonged to God and the Church. She could never have him, not as a lover, not as a father to Amber.

She continued to write in her journal as she did most every night after work, when Amber was settled in bed after her bath and prayers were finished for another day.

I must get on with my life. Mikael is a ghost sitting on my shoulder. It is extremely difficult for me as I compare all the young men with him. I pray the feelings for him will someday dissolve, but I am not so optimistic. I want to find someone to share my life with, to have more children, and to fall in love with, mad passionately like the way I felt about Mikael. Well, let's just wait a little bit longer before I panic. I'm not exactly an old maid–yet! To be continued. S.

And then soon after the entries in her journal complaining about the injustices in her life, her lack of a love life, something totally unpredictable, something unexpected happened to her. It started like any other day. She opened the bookshop for business, rolled the awning down that framed the window at the front of the store as there appeared no threat of rain on this Monday morning.

The next step was to count the money in the cash register, sort out the mail, turn on the radio, a local classical music station, and finally she would telephone Mr. Norvaisa to confirm she had arrived at the store. The dear old man had become caretaker to his wife who had a stroke several years ago leaving him little time for the business. He constantly would praise Sophie and never forgot to express his gratitude to her. Sophie adored him, he was kind and thoughtful and she would often witness a zest seldom seen in a man his age. She always looked forward to his rare visits at the store, but she would see him every Sunday at Mass. His wife had been confined to a wheelchair when she had taken ill but would make the effort to accompany her husband to St. Casmir on most weeks. Sophie often thought she had to be an extremely attractive woman once perhaps before she had the stroke. She had violet eyes framed by flawless complexion. When the few times she would remove her gloves from her hands her fingernails appeared flawlessly manicured. Sophie had no doubt she took pride in herself even with her disabilities.

It was only a few minutes after arriving at work that Sophie heard the small bell attached to the front door jangle announcing that someone was entering the store.

"Good morning!" Sophie addressed the man as he walked toward her.

"And a good morning to you! And how are you?"

"Thank you, I am fine."

CHAPTER 41

"Papa, will Oma know who I am?"
"Of course she will, my darling!"
"You are sure?"
"Yes, I am very sure."
"Are we almost there?"
"Almost. Very soon."

The train was running on schedule, and they should be arriving in Heidelberg shortly before noon. It had been almost a year since Erik had left Heidelberg for Berlin and that period of time since he and Hanna had seen the dear old lady that his daughter called grandmother. There had been letters and pictures over the months, but today would be a special time.

The train slowed as it approached the station and within minutes the doors opened and Erik and Hanna stepped to the platform greeted by the grandmother who eagerly awaited the arrival of her only granddaughter and her son-in-law.

There were so many memories here Erik thought. The war had changed so much in this country, defeated with the added burden of having to recover from the humility imposed upon them for the second time in just three decades. So many lives had been lost, and the ones that survived were desperately trying to adjust to these difficult times. There was a shortage of everything, even the farmers unable to obtain what they needed to farm. With a limited supply of oats came a shortage of beer a staple on every German's table. It also affected one of this country's major exports, an industry that had strived for many decades.

The visit in Heidelberg was brief, but Hanna enjoyed her time getting re-acquainted with the woman that raised her after her mother had died. There was no doubt the young girl who had just turned seven years old and the older woman who was well into her seventies adored each other. They promised to see each other more often in the future each extending invitations to the other to visit both in Heidelberg as well as in London. Erik told his mother-in-law he would make all the arrangements to England any time she would like to visit him and Hanna.

CHAPTER 42

Erik immersed himself in his work, the raising and attending to the needs of his daughter and trying desperately to escape the loneness that would not elude him. The days he could endure but the nights left him feeling empty and confused. He had absolutely no doubt that he once loved and adored Claudia but his thoughts were consumed with Sara. Was she well, did Paul return to her, did she stay on the island? Would he ever see her again? Did she think about him, miss him? Soon Fate would have his questions answered. Fate would intervene and map out the course of his future. Sara would play a major role in it.

His first trip to Berlin since being assigned to the London office was scheduled for the first week in July. He found Berlin slowly rising from the ashes, and its citizens took to the task of trying to restore a life that was familiar to them before the war.

Erik's days were spent attending meetings. The evenings were often with Karl for dinner, and he then would appropriate time to tour the city amazed at the progress of rebuilding this once vibrant and one of Europe's most cosmopolitan cities.

Life settled into a routine, and the extra hours required of him started paying dividends. The London office paved the way for additional branches throughout Europe and consideration was being given to Canada and eventually the United States. In the next decade the company would become the largest pharmaceutical company in the world. Erik was enjoying his life; but the missing component was he did not have someone to share it with.

Just days before the end of February he received a telegraph from Karl in Berlin: Need you here. Please make arrangements to be in Berlin the second week in March. Reservations have been confirmed at the Esplanade Hotel. Looking forward to seeing you, Karl

The week in Berlin would change his life. He would find Sara there. It would be just two years short since their farewell at the airfield in Half Way Island.

Erik tucked his daughter in bed for the night; and after the dishes had been washed and dried, stacked in the cupboard, he sat down at his desk, found pen and paper, and started a letter. It was to Claudia.

My darling Claudia, he began. I am missing you, and I know Hanna misses the mother who gave birth to her but wasn't given a chance to get to know her. You would be so very proud of our daughter!

He hesitated for a few minutes, tears welling up in his eyes.

I have been given a position with a German pharmaceutical company with a branch here in London. It is a new adventure for me and quite challenging. Who would have ever guessed that I, once an officer in the German army at war with England, an admirer of our Fuhrer once upon a time my hero as well as all of Germany, a dictator who will be go down in history as one of the most evil monsters of all time, a madman who has brought disgrace to our country who will be etched in German consciences for all of eternity, would be offered a position and now living here in London? And surprisingly the English have accepted me quite well, and I am grateful. Most are busy trying to reconstruct their lives. London, too, is shaping up, as in Berlin. I do miss Germany. The company has arranged for me to go to Berlin next week for a meeting at their headquarters. I have made arrangements for Oma to meet Hanna and me in Frankfort, and Hanna will go home with her for the few days I am in Berlin. I know how much your mother misses our daughter, and it will give Hanna the opportunity to be with her if only for a short visit.

Time is moving along at a fast pace which I am grateful. It is close to mid-night so I'll say good-night. I will write again soon. Tears had spilled down on to the paper. He struggled to find the words to close, knowing the foolishness of it all. He took the letter, crumbled it, and tossed it into the basket under the desk. He truly felt that some magic potion would be sprinkled on him; and he would feel better, but it did not happen. Fate was drafting a plan for him. It would be almost two years since he said good-by to Sara. It would be just over one week before he would see her again. And surprisingly the meeting would not be in London. Their meeting would take place in Berlin.

He had no way of knowing that he would be given a second chance at finding happiness; but on this dark dreary night, heavy rain pelting the windows, he was only feeling a deep sadness. As always he couldn't wait for the arrival of morning.

CHAPTER 43

Berlin had been Erik's favorite city, and early spring here was his favorite time of the year. It appeared that the city was making a recovery rising slowly from the ashes. He and Claudia had spent a week here shortly before Erik had received his orders to Half Way Island. It was here in Berlin that Hanna was conceived. As he walked pass the Tiergarten it stirred memories of him and Claudia strolling through the park, hand in hand, eventually finding an outdoor café and ordering a stein of beer, trying to block out the reality that this would be the last time the lovers would have together for a long time. On the day that Claudia was to leave to return home, waiting at the train station for the next train scheduled for Heidelberg, a small crowd had gathered. He remembered seeing Hitler in a large black open Mercedes and feeling excited as he witnessed him and his storm troopers passing by. Claudia on the other hand paid absolutely no attention. He and his entourage slowed almost to a complete stop as they passed the station. The crowd screamed in admiration at their beloved Fuhrer among shouts of Heil Hitler. Erik turned to glance at Claudia. He will never forget the expression of hostility she had worn.

Karl had scheduled the first of several meetings to discuss the plan for expansion and to explain that construction was already in the first stages. The laboratory was being supplied with the most modern equipment available. Breuer was planning to recruit only scientists having experience in developing drugs with a background in research focusing on new vaccines to combat disease and illness. Prior to the war there had been a surplus of scientists in all fields but now had become a premium commodity. Russia played a major role in seizing of German scientists to the Soviet Union.

It had been a long day and Erik was tired. He had dinner with Karl and planned to retire early. A suite of rooms had been reserved at the Esplanade Hotel for those attending the meetings. The hotel was located in the center of the city and in close proximity to Breuer's headquarters.

The evening light was slowly disappearing as Erik stepped into the lobby of the hotel. A huge chandelier was suspended from the vaulted ceiling, prisms dispersing beams of light. The lobby, however, appeared dimly lite. The floor was heavily polished and huge ceramic pots were filled with early spring flowers and placed throughout. French doors opened to a garden where tables and chairs were set up under umbrellas.

He had just stepped into the lobby when he saw her. She was standing in front of the reception desk talking to the clerk who had just summoned the bell hop. There was absolutely no question it was Sara. She looked radiant, so beautiful. She wore a pale green silk dress and held a straw hat in her hand. The dress fell just below her knees exposing long perfect legs. He stood and watched for a few minutes trying to decide how he would approach her; but she turned and saw him there. The next minutes became a blur.

"Sara!"

"Erik! Oh, my God! I can hardly believe it is you!"

"You look so good. You haven't changed one bit."

"Thank you."

"Is Paul here with you?"

"No, he is not." Erik noticed her expression changed drastically. Sara had decided to omit the story of Paul for the present. Paul never returned from the war. She would later explain the circumstances within the next few months to this man, the man who would soon become her husband. Now that they found each other neither would risk loosing another hour, another day, without being together.

Sara was enlisted by an English company, BMI, British Microwave, Inc., as a translator. The company was building microwave stations in several areas of Germany, and Sara had signed a one year contract, the projected time for completion. She couldn't help thinking of the irony now that she and Erik had found each other. Fortunately, she had spent more time at the London office, reviewing contracts, contacting suppliers, and scheduling meetings. Once a month she would come to Berlin for the meetings.

CHAPTER 44

"Sara, will you marry me? I cannot imagine my life without you in it. I want to spend the rest of my life with you, to take care of you. I never want to be separated from you again. We have been given a chance, you and I, a second chance that I am so very grateful, one that I thought would be denied to us. I truly felt that I would never find you, never to see you again, and God knows I tried to find you. Now I don't want to ever let you go. I love you, and I want you to be with me today, tomorrow, the rest of our lives. Please say you will marry me!"

Sara felt a feeling of joy. It had eluded her for so long, and there were times when she truly believed that happiness would be something she would never experience again. She never stopped loving the man sitting across the table from her; and like him, almost from that day that he boarded the plane on Half Way Island just days before Germany's surrender, she came to the realization that she probably had lost him forever.

"Erik, Erik, I can't believe you are actually here with me. I had resolved myself to the fact that I, too, would never see you or be with you again. I missed you so much. There are no words to describe how I was feeling. I wish to grow old with you by my side, to share every minute of my life with you, and you should know that I have elected you to be the father of my children! When I go to bed at night and I wakeup in the morning, I want you there beside me. If that was a proposal of marriage the answer is yes. I love you very much. And I am convinced that Fate most certainly had a major role in our meeting here in Berlin. I never in a hundred years would have selected this city to be the place we would find each other, to meet again; just think about it for a minute, how credulous it is!"

"Is tomorrow too soon to marry me?" knowing full well what her answer would have to be. "I'm afraid so. The bride has to have a new dress, a very special dress for her wedding!"

"And it will give you the opportunity to meet Hanna. I am sure you will like her. She speaks perfect English, no accent at all. I speak to her in German mainly so she won't forget the language. And as you are well aware, it is a wonderful gift to be able to speak more then one language. If you stop and think about it, it was really the reason you and I are here this evening sitting across table from each other planning a life together. I often think of the journey, from Lithuania to Germany then to England, a short detour to Germany, and once again to England."

They had spent the first hour exchanging full events of the twists and turns of each other lives, the times of deep sadness for both during the past two years. The second hour they shared a bed together the time lost between them spilling away as they made love. The passion that they had discovered on Half Way Island came flooding back. They held each other long into the night. It felt so right, so very right, and a peace descended on Erik that he hadn't experienced for a long time.

"I cannot begin to tell you how happy I am, by God's interference, and I am totally convinced He had something to do with it, I found you. I never really gave up trying you know. My intuition was you were in London somewhere, and I truly believed for a long time I would be able to locate you. I wasn't sure how but I wanted to believe with every ounce of my fiber that I would someday find you. I'd be on the underground scouting every woman hoping that one day I would see you again, just to casually walk up to you, to witness your reaction. Slowly as the time dwindled down I started to believe my efforts would be in vain, that I should give up my search and perhaps get on with my life. But the more effort I put into trying to forget you the more I realized there would never be a life without you in it. I found you now; and I intend to keep you with me, forever. I love you, I love you, Sara. Welcome back into my life!"

The wedding took place three months after their meeting in Berlin. The bride selected a pale blue linen suit, a pill box hat with a short veil, white gloves, and held a small bouquet of white and pink roses sprinkled with lily-of-the-valley tied together with streamers of blue and white ribbons. The bridegroom, familiar now with the impeccable style of British men's wear, selected a navy blue narrow pin-stripped suit with a burgundy tie accented with powder blue stripes. The only member of the family to attend the ceremony was Hanna wearing a white eyelet dress, blue satin ribbon laced through the outlets at her waist. Her long blonde hair was pulled away from her face styled in a French braid a rainbow of streamers attached with a rhinestone hairclip.

A honeymoon would be postponed, mainly to acquaint Hanna with her new step-mom. They seemed to get on well though initially Hanna was a little hesitant to share her father with his new bride. She soon realized Sara was not a threat, and over the following months she became quite fond of her. There was no question in her young mind that his new wife made her father happy, something that had been missing for some time now. The new wife and the young step-daughter shared two languages, shopping together, spent time baking some of their favorite German strudel and ginger snap cookies; but most of all they enjoyed exploring the City of London together. Sara had lived here before the war, and she knew all the places of interest. And many times on a weekend the three would attend one of the popular plays in London frequently performing before a sold-out audience. London, like the German city of Berlin, was slowly digging itself out from the destruction and the ravages inflicted during the war years. And many times Sara and Erik would sit back and reflect on those dark times; and they both agreed what a waste of time and of all things, and they realized it would take years before the countries affected by the bombing would reflect back into any resemblance to the prewar period. Time and the ingenious of man did fix things. Slowly the two countries inflicted during those long years did rebuild and moved forward anticipating the future in their scope.

Sunday afternoons, weather permitting, Sara and Hanna would pack a picnic lunch. Erik and the two most important persons in his life would take a bus out to the countryside where they would spend a major part of the day together. One of Hanna's favorite places was a park with an old-fashioned carousel. She never tired of riding on the horses waving to her father and to Sara as she went around and around. And with a lot of begging and coaxing, her father would climb next to her, try for the gold ring, and on occasion would actually grab for it and be successful in his attempt for it meant a free ride. Erik, of course, was delighted that the two girls were adjusting to their new arrangement. He felt the happiest that he had been in his entire life. He prayed every night that it would never end.

Their first Christmas together was a joyous and a happy one. A small tree had been placed in the living room decorated with candles, Christmas ornaments, with a single angel peering down from the very top. A candle flicked in each window of every room. Sara and Hanna baked every free minute available to them the week before the holiday including the traditional gingerbread house that Sara and her grandmother had always presented as the focal point on the Yuletide table. It was on Christmas Eve, after gifts were exchanged and unwrapped, that Sara made the announcement that she thought there was a possibility that the baby could be arriving sooner then had been predicted. Her guess was correct. On Christmas day, shortly before midnight, the Mueller family welcomed Christian Erik Mueller, a healthy eight pound fourteen ounce baby boy. Hanna, hoping for a sister, concealed her disappointment but all changed when her new brother came home. She felt it was a good sign that her baby brother Christian was born on the same date as baby Jesus! She had never been so excited in her entire life she told her father and Sara in the days following the baby's homecoming. Her school grades suffered temporarily during the next few weeks as she spent every spare minute with Christian, but gradually her routine returned to normal. Nineteen months later, Andrew Mikael was born. And finally Hanna got her wish for a baby sister. Victoria Elizabeth Anne had arrived several weeks early and had to remain in hospital after her birth before she was allowed home. Her weight increased, lungs grew stronger, and appetite became on track. Even before the baby came home from hospital Hanna and Sara spent their time knitting sweaters with matching bonnets and booties, blankets with fringe, all of course, in pink. Unlike her brothers when they were infants, Victoria had colic the first few months; but just as the family felt that lack of sleep would probably not abate for a long, long time, she gradually got better and the colic finally disappeared completely. Plans to return their new sister to the stork that brought her here now were cancelled. The three siblings decided to keep her after all. And one of the proudest days of young Hanna's life was the Sunday Victoria was baptized and a decision had been made for Hanna to be a Godmother to her sister.

The next few years were dedicated to the children who seemed to their parents to just grow like weeds. On one of Erik's trips to Berlin Hanna accompanied her father. She was now old enough to take the train from Berlin to Heidelberg to visit and spend time with her grandmother. At seventy-eight years old Oma was in exceptionally good health and could still dote on her only grand-daughter. And Hanna loved the dear old woman and often felt sad that the special time the two of them spent together was limited. Hanna could not hear enough stories from her, the ones she would tell her grand-daughter about her mother. Sometimes she would experience a feeling of sadness but most often she felt a warm special feeling especially when Oma would drag the photo album out from the bookcase, and the two would spend hours looking at pictures of a mother and a daughter from so long ago. Oma would elaborate on every detail including the color of the dress that Claudia had worn when the picture was taken. Hanna's favorite picture was one of her mother and father on their wedding day. And as if Oma had read her mind she removed the picture from the album and handed it to her grand-daughter.

And on the Sunday morning after attending Mass just hours before Hanna had to return to Berlin Oma escorted her grand-daughter to the grave of Claudia Richter Mueller. Hanna had cut some flowers from her grandmother's garden to place on her mother's grave. "I hope you like these, Mother!" tears stinging her eyes, speaking to the mother she never knew. They lingered for awhile longer, said a few prayers, and then their good-by. Over the years Hanna would come and visit here even after her beloved Oma had passed away. Her grandmother would not live long enough to attend her grand-daughter's graduation from the University of Heidelberg, but Hanna would bet she was watching her from a different place, a place way beyond the clouds. And Hanna would guess her mother was right there too beside her beloved Oma.

On the train ride back to Berlin Hanna thought what life may have been like if her mother had not died, if she and her father were living in Germany, if there had been no war, if her father had not met her stepmother. There would be no answer to this she knew but one thing was certain. She and her father were not unhappy. In fact, the years were very good to them, blessing them with so many wonderful things. It was a home of love, respect for each other. And Hanna could never imagine a life without her two brothers and sister; and as the years passed, they became even closer to each other. She was well aware that a special gift was given to her.

CHAPTER 45

Twenty six years go a wedding took place on the Cape. It was not a perfect day for a wedding. It started to rain during the later part of the week and showed no sign of relenting on this Saturday afternoon as the guests made their way into St. Anne's Roman Catholic Church to witness the marriage of Viktor Paleckis to Jurgita Remintis. St. Anne's was the only Lithuanian church on the Cape built at the turn of the century by Lithuanian immigrants. The location provided a panoramic view of the ocean below. There were no boats visible on this day as the weather discouraged even the most seasoned sailor from leaving dock. Rain and fog were as much a part of the Cape as the sand dunes and the sea and the natives seem to accept as a matter of fact. It provided some leverage as many Lithuanians were shopkeepers; and when the weather was not conducive for the beach, the tourists would flock to the shops. Business would be brisk and no one would complain.

The wedding ceremony was in both English and Lithuanian. Mrs. Sumauskar had been given a front-row seat; because as everyone knew, without the matchmaker there would be no wedding on this day.

Viktor Paleckis was among the first Lithuanian families to settle on the Cape. He had started a small business, a hardware store, selling paints, tools, small building supplies, and implements that a store of this kind sold; but Viktor noticed that it was the brooms that were always out of stock. It wasn't that the store was lacking for business but perhaps he could add to his good fortune by paying more attention to the brooms, perhaps even selling them door-to-door. Matas, his older brother, agreed to mind the store thinking his younger brother would soon become discouraged with this new venture and before too long things would return to normal. But Viktor never returned to the hardware store. In less then a year the younger Paleckis brother added more brooms to the line and offered all kinds of brushes, knocking on doors throughout the Cape. He hired and trained a dozen new salesmen; and before his twenty-third birthday, two years from his very first sale, he recruited fifteen additional salesmen to join the team for the remaining New England states. Two new modern plants were constructed to manufacture more brooms and brushes to keep pace with orders. Business was brisk, and there was every indication his good fortune would continue.

Life was good. Viktor was well on his way to acquiring his first million. Yes, business flourished, his time and energy were channeled to his work. He never really thought about love and marriage during the early years as the responsibility of the business left him little time for anything that was not related to the manufacture of brooms.

In those years he had built a house high on a hill with an ocean view in the style of the Cape houses, but this house was a big house unlike most of the houses on the Cape. It was the early part of June when construction was finally complete when he moved into the new house. The next project would be landscaping which had already been started. He planned on planting several birch trees on the property. He remembered as a young boy in Lithuania the birch trees that lined the back of his house and grew randomly throughout the entire country.

Now, he was thinking, maybe it was time to find a wife, find someone to share the things that he had worked so hard to accumulate. His brother had suggested awhile back that he visit Mrs. Sumauskar, the matchmaker, who lived just outside the town. He dismissed the idea immediately, but something very coincidental and completely surprising was about to happen. Every July St. Anne's would hold an annual Lithuanian picnic on the church grounds. He had considered attending in years past but always found an excuse, usually work related, not to attend. One evening he received a phone call just as was coming home from the office. It was the pastor of the church, and he was personally requesting his presence at the picnic. "I will not accept anything but a definite yes from you, Viktor."

"I promise to think about it, Father, and will let you know."

"That answer will not do! I shall see you next Saturday!"

The picnics were always a great success. Anyone who had a drop of Lithuanian blood would certainly be there. The women would cook and bake all the traditional dishes, the most popular being the ulvinis blynas, (potato pancakes). Most of the women would don their grandmothers costumes handed down throughout the generations having brought them from Lithuania so many years ago. The band would play most of the afternoon, take a few hours break, and then return and play well into the late evening encouraging everyone to find a partner and join in the dancing.

Viktor arrived early evening thinking only to please Father Stoskus who had been so adamant about his attendance. He spent the first hour sampling the food and talking to old friends and to his surprise was really enjoying the company some of whom he had not seen for a long time, some even years.

"Viktor, how are you?"

He was not sure but he was thinking the woman who spoke to him was Mrs. Sumauskar the matchmaker from Watch Hill the one whom his brother had proposed he visit. She certainly mirrored his description.

"Mrs. Sumauskar, I'm fine thank you. It is nice to meet you. My brother insists at some point I should call on you. It seems he thinks you can find a wife for me before I am too old and too grey."

"Yes, I've seen your brother recently. I was in the store one day last week and the subject did come up."

"Viktor, may I introduce my niece, Jurgita."

"Hello!" she smiled at him." My English is not too good. I have been here only for two months."

Her accent was definitely Lithuanian, and Viktor thought of speaking to her in Lithuanian but decided at the last minute to continue in English. He was smitten with her from the first minute he saw her when her aunt had introduced her that day at the picnic. Maybe she was a matchmaker after all, but somehow he felt his brother had played a role.

"Are you staying very long with your aunt?"

"I have a one-year visa here."

The one year would turn into many years. They were married the following summer here at the church where he had first met her. She would bear him four sons in six years. These were happy years, and Viktor knew he had a lot to be thankful for. Adam, the oldest son, was geared to take the helm of the business, and the three youngest, along with their older brother, would continue to work and contribute to the company until hopefully the next generation would take it to the next level and eventually trading the brooms for building supplies. If all went as planned each generation would enjoy more wealth and success then the generation that came before them. The company in later years would have the distinction of becoming the largest building supply company in all of New England and the Eastern section of the United States.

Not everything went according to Viktor's prediction. Lukas, his youngest son, separated from his siblings and the business and enrolled in medical school. He had considered being a veterinarian for awhile. His father had horses ever since the boys could remember, and there were always several dogs in the house. And for a short period of time there was Billy, the watch–dog goat. No one but no one was allowed on the property without Billy's permission. He would just lower his head and that would be all that was needed. On special occasions, birthday parties especially, Viktor would hitch a small cart to Billy, and the boys and their friends would take turns up and down the long driveway. Then one day without any warning the goat disappeared. The children were devastated and with the help of the entire community they set upon the mission of finding Billy. They posted pictures of their beloved goat in stores, on streetlamps and everywhere they could possibly find space. They ran lost and found ads in the newspaper and on the local radio station which seemed eager to get involved in the search and to assist in solving the mystery of what happened to Billy. The weeks passed by and there was no sign of their beloved pet. But just as the boys lost hope of ever seeing their goat again a strange thing happened. On the way to his office one Saturday morning Viktor passed the old Blinn Farm, approximately a mile from the house. On a second glance into the field proved that the goat with the biggest horns that ever grew on a goat, the one that was standing there, no doubt had to be Billy. He would have to postpone a visit to the farm until he finished at the office and hopefully he and Mr. Blinn could find a solution to the Billy affair. As the mystery started to unravel, it appeared the goat had found himself a girlfriend.

The Billy goat story did eventually have a happy ending. At the last minute Viktor decided to turn around and go back to the farm.

Even though at this point he had little doubt that the goat wasn't his, he needed to definitely make the identification and talk to Mr. Blinn concerning Billy. It was 8:00 a.m. not too early to call on a farmer he thought as he headed back up the road. He was thinking maybe he should call ahead, but he was almost at the farm. As he approached the long driveway leading to the pasture where he saw the goat was the old farmer who did not seem to be aware that Viktor was just a few feet away from him, so Viktor rolled down the car window and called out.

"Mr. Blinn, may I have a word with you?" Viktor didn't think the farmer recognized him.

"Do you remember me?"

"Yes, it took me a minute but you are the broom maker."

"Yes, I guess I am. Suppose you are a little curious why I'm calling on you and so damn early. Our goat disappeared a few weeks back. We thought at first that someone had taken him; perhaps a prank of some sort, but on my way to the office this morning, and I usually take the highway but I decided to take the back roads for a change of scenery plus the fog seemed to be quite heavy on the ocean road. Anyway I am pretty sure I saw my goat, Billy, in your pasture."

"Could be. Park your car on the side there, and we will go have a look. I haven't been aware of any male goat. We have Annie, no males."

It took the farmer and Viktor a few minutes to reach the pasture and without any warning, the goat on spotting Viktor, ran over to him and starting bleating at him.

"Well, no question he must be your goat, not mine!" and almost on command Annie, the farmer's goat, made her appearance trotting over to the farmer and his visitor.

"Are you thinking what I am thinking?"

"It does make sense to me. So the mystery is solved. It appears Billy has had his sights on Annie. I will make arrangements to pick him up tomorrow if it is alright with you."

"No hurry!"

So Billy came home the next day, but his stay was short lived. He was able to find his way back to the Blinn Farm, and there was little doubt that Annie was the reason. A meeting was scheduled between the two families to decide the goat's fate. After a very difficult decision it was decided that the two goats belonged together, and Viktor and the boys would get visitation rights for their beloved pet. In the years ahead the goat couple, Billy and Annie, would be the proud parents of four kids, and the boys saw their goat often and agreed to take part in caring for the family. Billy stayed with Annie until he passed on to goat heaven. The boys begged their father to bury their beloved pet behind the barn in their yard. And among tears Billy went to rest under the old chestnut tree. They placed a small marker on his grave, "Billy Goat, Husband of Annie Goat".

CHAPTER 46

The wedding between Sophie and Viktor took place in London on October 20, 1948, at St. Casmir Lithuanian Catholic Church only a short distance form the bookstore where they first met. The couple planned on having a small ceremony with just a few friends in attendance. They agreed to say their wedding vows in Lithuanian.

Viktor after much deliberation made the decision he would not extend an invitation to the wedding to his sons. Even though he did not need approval from them to get married he wanted to prevent any controversy or discussion pertaining to marrying Sophie, a woman who was just one year younger then his son, Lukas. He would postpone the introduction of his new wife until after the honeymoon, followed by a short stay in London to prepare for the 5-day ocean voyage to New York and finally to the Cape.

The bride wore a pale pink satin ankle-length dress, off the shoulder, nipped at the waist with a slight flair to the bottom. Instead of a veil she choose a wreath of orange blossoms and carried a bouquet of white roses encircling pairs of pink and orange dwarf tulips, her favorite flower. Amber wore a white organdy dress with a wide pink satin ribbon tied at the waist. Her long blonde hair was pulled away from her face in a French braid. She carried a basket of pink rose pedals for her role of flower girl to her mother. The groom was handsome in his custom-tailored suit with the perfect tie that his bride-to-be had selected for her husband-to-be. A pink carnation was pinned to his lapel. If he was experiencing a case of pre-nuptial nerves, he did not show it. He appeared extremely happy on this his wedding day.

On clue the groom kissed his bride and whispered to her. "I am the luckiest man on the planet!"

A small reception was held at the Baltic Inn just a few minutes away from the church. He and Sophie had discussed planning a party for his family and friends on the Cape, closer to the holidays which should work out perfectly, a festive time of the year.

During the last few months before the wedding, Viktor had made several trips to London. On each trip he would stop by the bookstore. There was no question he was smitten by the beautiful young Lithuanian, a stroke of real luck he thought.

On his second trip, in early May, he found the courage to invite her to dinner; and on his following stay in London it was dinner and later a play. He could not remember the last time he was this happy, and it soon became apparent to him that Sophie was the key. He wanted her to become a part of his every day life, to share many of the things that he had accumulated over the years. Each time he would leave her it became more and more difficult for him.

Since the death of his wife, Jurgita, he did have opportunities to meet women; but until Sophie came into his life, he never gave any thought of marrying again. On his next trip to London he had made an appointment at Winston, Ltd., and purchased a solitaire diamond ring surrounded by two sapphires on each side of the ring. He planned an intimate dinner in his suite at the Ritz-Carlton where he had been staying and planned to ask Sophie to marry him.

He arranged for room service complete with champagne and also requested candles to be set on the table with an arrangement of pink roses. He practiced his proposal in Lithuanian; and if she accepted, he would ask her to consider having the wedding in the very near future.

Sophie had grown very fond of Viktor looking forward to his visits and disappointed when it would be time for him to leave London. She really knew very little about the handsome seemingly wealthy broom maker from the States, but she loved the time that they were able to spend together. It was apparent that he showed more concern over the age difference than she did. She rarely gave it any thought. Since coming to London her days and nights left little room for dating. Between her commitment for the bookstore, finding quality time to spend with Amber, English lessons twice a week, there remained little time to think about romance, and Mikael was still very much embedded in her mind and in her soul. And for some strange reason she had not considered the time she spent with Viktor as dating. She just knew how much she enjoyed being with him. He was kind, thoughtful, attentive, and most of all he made her laugh. It was the first time in such a long time that she truly felt she had been given permission to feel good, to laugh, and to be happy. She was well aware that Viktor was responsible for once again making her feel thankful for being alive. It had been awhile, quite awhile.

Viktor and Sophie had made arrangements for Glazina to stay with Amber while they were on their honeymoon in Paris. They sat down with the young girl and explained to her that they were going away for a few days, Glazina would be staying with her, and they would return soon, not totally convinced that at three years old she could really understand. And they were in agreement that the subject of moving from London could wait. Neither could predict how the little girl would react to the news; or again, if she was able to fully comprehend it.

Viktor had been to Paris once shortly before the war and he was convinced Sophie would fall in love with the City of Lights. The French, like the rest of Europe, were recovering from the war and the Nazi occupation. Paris had an advantage that so many of the other European cities did not. Hitler had always been fascinated with the culture, the architecture of the city; and believing that Germany would eventually be victorious, no orders were ever issued for its bombing or destruction. Unfortunately, the rest of France was not spared.

"Oh, Viktor, it takes my breath away! There are so many lights. It's so beautiful"

He reached over and put his arms around his wife.

"I love you Mrs. Paleckis! I want to spend the rest of my life with you, if a short one or a long one! And, I have a present for you, there on the bed. You can open it now if you wish."

A silver box wrapped with a pink satin ribbon sat on the bed. Sophie looked over at the box lying on the bed and glanced at her husband, his smile telling all. "I hope you like it" "Yes, I do!" It was a black velvet dress. She would later wear it to the party soon after their arrival on the Cape, hopefully landing in New York no later then the early part of November. Arrangements were almost complete for the trip across the Atlantic. Sophie had some trepidation concerning an adventure at sea after the journey from Lithuania to England, but Viktor reassured his new bride it would be a completely different voyage. He was right. It became one of the best weeks of her life.

"I love it, Viktor! Would you like me to model it for you?"

"No, wait for the party. I want to show you off to everyone." He watched as she folded the dress and placed it back in the box.

"Come here, please. You're too far away!" And she fell into his arms, the lovemaking lasting long into the night. It was perfect, Sophie thought, and she was looking forward to all the next times. She felt, at last, she had a place in the world where she felt safe and comfortable, where she could possibly now have a future, to share it with a man she loved; and maybe finally, she could have a life without Mikael invading her every thought. She knew there would always be a special place in her heart for Mikael, but it was time to free her self. She wanted so badly to enjoy this new life that Viktor was providing for her and Amber, to put the past in a place that maybe one day she could review it without feeling pain.

Though she didn't want to leave Paris or the honeymoon to end, she was looking forward to the next chapter, the one on the Cape. It became so much more then her expectations. She absolutely loved everything about Cape Elizabeth, her new home. She was the happiest she had ever been in her entire young life, and she did not forget to thank God every night for leading her new husband to the bookstore!

CHAPTER 47

Inside the house high on the hill overlooking the bay hundreds of tiny white lights had been strung on the small trees staggered on both sides of the foyer, wrapped around the bannister, and on each shrub and tree lining the long driveway. Poinsettias were grouped on the sides of the staircase and placed along the balcony. Gold ribbons tied in bows decorated flower pots. Hand-blown crystal ornaments from Austria hung on three huge Christmas trees with a trio of angels glancing down from the very top. Laurel ropes were carefully wrapped around and decorated the stairway forming a partnership with the bright red poinsettias. A crystal chandelier also imported from Austria many years ago during the construction of the house was suspended from the high ceiling in the center of the foyer sparkling like a hundred tiny stars. Baskets that were sprayed with gold paint were filled with fresh flowers and doted with branches of holly supplied the final touch. It reflected a beautiful holiday theme.

The new bride welcomed her guests looking radiant in a black velvet dress falling just above her knees showing off her long slender legs. The neckline exposing just a glimpse of her breasts was topped by a pearl necklace that Viktor had presented and surprised her for this special occasion. Her long blonde hair fell just below her shoulders, a diamond barrette clipped to the side. Pearl earrings completed the ensemble. Sophie looked beautiful, and she was feeling extremely happy on this very special night.

For some unexplained reason Sophie did not feel nervous, excited but not nervous. Viktor several times reached over to her and kissed her, a stamp of approval she thought as the evening went on. Viktor still not believing how this very beautiful young woman, his wife, truly belonged to him, and he noticed she displayed a confidence he had never witnessed, and he wanted to believe that he had a little to do with it. It seemed he possessed everything that one would want in this world, and he was grateful for his good fortune. However, in the near future there would be a few obstacles to over come. He just did not have to face them just yet. Tonight would be for dancing and presenting his wife to all his family and friends.

Luke and Susan were one of the last to leave the party. It was 2:00 a.m. Luke was scheduled to work the next day which was actually now Monday morning. Susan turned on the radio. Christmas music was playing on a Boston station. She leaned back in her seat and reached over to hold her husband's hand. He gave a little squeeze, one of approval. They had been married for nine years. The sex was still great. This morning, however, two hours past mid-night there probably would be no love-making.

Luke turned to his wife and asked her, "What did you think of the new wife?"

"Your father seemed extremely happy, the happiest I've seen him in a long time. I suppose this is more important than any opinion I may have about her."

"Did you like her?"

"Yes, as a matter of fact, I did. I thought she was very charming, and she seemed to possess a rare elegance. And I felt she truly cares for your father."

"Did you find her attractive?"

"She was definitely one of the most beautiful women I have ever met!"

Luke was stunned by her candid reply as he felt exactly the same about his father's new wife. There was something very beguiling, some unknown equation he could not decipher. He became well aware of her presence in a very short time. Her beauty alone would draw attention; but it was something else, something he could not just yet define.

A few months ago his father had written from London. He informed his sons that he had met a woman that he had become extremely fond; and yes, he thought about a proposal of marriage. Luke and his siblings felt that the romance would fizzle out and the young woman, he couldn't even remember her name at that time, would decide to stay in London and their father would soon be on his way home. But there was a wedding and the newly weds arrived on the Cape in early November.

Sophie spent the next few weeks preparing for the evening that just passed almost from the time they arrived on the Cape. It would be a perfect time for a party with the holidays approaching. Viktor had suggested that she postpone the idea of hosting a party for a few more months, but his advice was quickly overruled. He quickly discovered how difficult it was to refuse his new bride as he adored her and planned to grant her many of her wishes. He enjoyed spoiling her, doting on her, and he did not want to deprive her of anything that brought her joy and made her happy. He planned to substitute for the hardships she had endured in her young life. He would often wonder what his life would have been if his parents hadn't made the decision to leave Lithuania and come to this country. He knew he had no real way of imagining the sacrifice and the hardships that Sophie had experienced during her years in Trakai, and the courage it had to take at the war's end to make a choice to leave family and country not really knowing what risks she would have to endure getting to England which would become her new country. He could not give his young wife those years back, and he knew it was impossible to erase them. But he could try to do everything in his power to see her happy, for it made him happy also. He had become a new man since he had met her, and he prayed it would never change.

The new wife was named Sophie, his step-mother! The sound of the word sounded so very strange to him. He never had given much thought to his father re-marrying. It was just a subject that he never thought much about. His father had never discussed it; and as far as he was aware, the subject was never mentioned to any of his brothers. And Luke knew his father did not need his or any of his other son's approval to marry. His father deserved to find happiness; and if Sophie filled the order, then it was fine with him. It was obvious that his father was completely head-over-heels in love with his young and strikingly beautiful new wife, now a role that included stepmother to four of his sons.

Invitations to the Christmas party were printed, and they were mailed the day after Thanksgiving. The party would be held on Sunday, December 22, at 6:30 p.m. for cocktails followed by a buffet dinner.

Late fall and early winter were fairly mild on the Cape shortly after Indian summer would have ended. On this evening, three days before Christmas, snow drifted down and sprinkled the ground with a dusting of it. Even Mother Nature seemed to recognize the importance of the occasion adding her contribution to the gala event.

The lighthouse which was manned by the Coast Guard sat above the cliffs that peered out over the Atlantic Ocean where it stood watch for over a century. Its beams weaved their way entirely around the lighthouse hesitating every few seconds snowflakes caught in its beam of light. It made a perfect and beautiful picture postcard. If you looked out the window you could see it in the distance. In the evenings when the fog would become dense, no stranger here on the Cape, it cast ghost like images as the light would slice through.

Sophie had been pleasantly surprised at how quickly the responses had been returned to her, a few with notes enclosed welcoming her and how much they were looking forward to meeting her. Viktor's sons and their wives would attend and had called her and asked if they could help in any way. She was aware of Caroline's artistic talents so she just might take her up on her offer to help with the decorating. Caroline was married to Alex. She had meet three out of the four, Ben, Adam and Alex, the three oldest boys, but not Lukas, Luke as he was called, the youngest and the only Paleckis not associated with the business. Viktor tried to disguise his disappointment when Luke confronted him with the news he had made a decision to attend medical school. He explained to his father it was not a hasty decision. He had thought about it for long time. Slowly Viktor came to terms with the idea realizing how fortunate he had been to have three of his sons to work in the business that he started so many years ago and would someday take it over from him. When he would start to brag to all his friends and associates that his youngest son was now a doctor, the disappointment was eventually erased.

After spending a few years in Boston he was offered a position with John Adams Hospital on the Cape. It was just a mere 7 miles from home and played a role in his decision to take the position there. There were many advantages not having to commute everyday the 40 miles each way. One was he could spend more time with Susan and the boys. He would be able to become more involved in his sons sport programs and even could be allotted time to attend a few games in which they participated.

The day at the hospital moved quickly. He spent most of the morning hours visiting his patients, returning phone calls, scheduling follow-up-visits, and accompanying a new group of residents on their first tour of the hospital. He took a short break just before lunch and then headed across the walk-way to his office.

"Dr. Paleckis, your father called and wants you to return his call as soon as possible."

"Thank you, Adella!"

He sat behind his desk, picked up the phone, and was a little curious as to why his father was trying to reach him. It was rare he would call him at the office.

The phone only rang two short rings before his father picked up and answered.

"Luke, I have a favor to ask of you. I'm going to be on my way to the airport in an hour. I have a flight to London this evening, and I was hoping you could find time later in the day to stop by the house and check on Sophie. She's not feeling well. She said she will rest, stay in bed for the rest of the day complaining of being extremely tired, a little nauseated."

"I was planning to leave a little earlier today so it will not be a problem. I'll stop by the house before heading home."

"I should be back on Saturday, no later then Sunday."

"Don't worry, Dad. I will keep a watch on her. Have a safe trip."

That one phone call would contribute to changing his life forever.

CHAPTER 48

The roads were just about clear as Luke drove along the coast. It was such a beautiful drive. The ocean surrounded the Cape and one tried never to take it for granted. Luke could remember as a young boy he would sit on the beach listening to the surf crash on the rocks, roll back out, and repeat the process. The seagulls would circle overhead close to the shore, the lucky ones would find a clam, slam it against the rocks, and pick it out of the shell.

Luke shifted into second as he started up the driveway. He was surprised to see the long limo in the driveway.

"Hi, Fred." Luke waved to the chauffeur. "My dad hasn't left yet?"

"No, sir."

Luke rolled up the window and parked the car in front of the garage. "Luke," he heard his father calling to him.

"I am running a little late. I will call when I get to London. Sophie is a little under the weather. Keep an eye on her for me, will you?"

"Dad, don't worry. See you soon. Have a safe trip."

Fred opened the door for his passenger and within a few seconds backed down the driveway, and they went on their way. The airport was just about an hour away depending on the traffic situation unable to predict regardless of the time of the day; but most frequently, it took somewhere around one hour from door to door.

This was the first time Luke had been to his father's house since the night of the Christmas party. He still kept a house key, but his father seeing him drive up left the door open for him. Luke noticed the days were getting slightly longer, it was the middle of February, and like all on the Cape he wished the winter would disappear and make way for the next three seasons, spring, summer, and autumn. Luke and all his brothers loved to sail. His first sailboat was a Snowbird. They would sail for hours around the bay, anchor on some of the many small islands, explore, enjoy a small lunch, and then set sail once again. He had fond memories of those days. He and Susan made love for the first time on Rose Island, one of the smallest islands. Over the next years they would come to "their" island and practice their lovemaking. Luke thinking back to those days felt it was a small miracle that Susan didn't get pregnant. The irony was she became pregnant on their honeymoon. Their first son, Nick, was born just nine months later. Luke was in his first year of residency at Boston General when Zach arrived two years later.

Upon entering the back hall Luke switched on the light. He went into the parlor and was surprised to see the room empty, the furniture removed. He would later learn the new wife was in the process of remodeling the room. He thought it a little strange that his father had not mentioned it to him as he spoke to him almost daily.

He climbed the flight of stairs two by two; and upon reaching the top, he saw a light filtering under the door of the bedroom. He knocked on the door, he knew Sophie was in the room, but what he saw on entering totally surprised and alarmed him. "Luke, come in. Your father mentioned that you may stop by. He worries so! I guess you are one of the advantages of having a doctor in the family, but a pain in the neck for the doctor!"

Sophie was propped on the bed with several pillows under her head.

"You're perspiring. You could be running a slight temperature."

He walked over to her, reached out and put his hand on her forehead. No doubt she had a temperature. And he was concerned with her color, she looked so pale.

"Is there any possibility that you could be pregnant?" The thought of her being pregnant, his father making a baby at his age, could this really be happening! This beautiful young girl having sex with his father, he couldn't imagine it. He hesitated a few minutes and turned to her. "Is there a chance that you could be pregnant?" She looked surprised at his question. "I'm not sure, maybe."

Luke wanted to throw something through the window, break the door down, or yell some profanities at the top of his lungs. He tried to keep his composure, to remain calm.

"I am a little concerned. My suggestion is to schedule some tests, the sooner the better."

He tried so hard for the past weeks not to think about the way this woman was constantly on his mind. He couldn't explain any of it. He loved Susan, his wife. He had always been faithful to her. He couldn't remember even thinking about making love to another woman. Yet as he looked down at this beautiful woman, his father's wife, her eyes focused just on him, her hair tumbling over the pillows behind her, he desperately wanted to take her in his arms, hold her close to him, to kiss her long and hard, to make passionate love to her.

"Does my father know, the possibility of you being pregnant?"

"No, he has no idea. I wanted to wait until I was definitely sure. I'm not convinced that he will be pleased. We never discussed or planned on a baby, but I always wanted another child. It's normal, isn't it?"

"Of course it is." Now he wanted to throw up!

Earlier in the day when his father had called asking him to check in on Sophie he wanted to scream back at him. "Don't ask me to be alone with her. I'm not sure if I'm capable of being alone with your wife!" She was amazingly beautiful, but it ran deeper. It was some sort of chemistry, a feeling he couldn't really explain. But he knew he had no choice but to stay away from her. The alternative would only lead to disaster.

"Luke, make me a promise that you won't tell Viktor until I am sure."

Luke walked over to the window. He could see the ocean; and unlike the summer months when the trees full of leaves blocked the view, this time of year with leaves long gone, it became a picture perfect view.

"I will agree If that is what you want, Sophie." It was the first time he had called her by name. He remained at the window for a few moments and turned to face her.

"I have no problem with that but he will guess in time you know. Will you make an appointment with Dr. Adamovitch, he's the best on the Cape. His office is in the Village in the Surfside Complex. It' a brick building, easy to find. And for now it is important you take fluids. What's in the glass on your bed stand?"

"It's ginger ale. Perhaps it's a little flat now."

"Good, and drink plenty of water."

"Yes, doctor!" she answered smiling up at him.

"I don't feel comfortable leaving you alone. Do you want me to stay the night?"

"No, of course not, Luke. You're only a few minutes away if I need you. I wouldn't mind one bit though if you and Susan did stop by tomorrow. We could have lunch if I'm feeling a little better."

"Fair enough, I'll definitely come by. Susan and the boys are away for the week-end, skiing in New Hampshire. Her parents have a house there. But I want you to call me if anything changes. Promise me?"

It took all of his strength to leave the room. He wanted to stay, but he knew he was not capable of keeping his hands off of her. He had a feeling it would become a sleepless night.

She possessed a hold on him, and he had only been with her twice in his life, once at the Christmas party in December, and again today. He wondered in the end if he would fail the test, the Sophie test as he would begin to refer to it.

Luke glanced over at the clock sitting on the mantle. It was just a little before mid-night, and he decided he would turn in for the night not totally convinced he would be able to fall asleep quickly or even sleep at all. Sophie still was consuming his every thought. He had been tempted to call her a little earlier. It had been several hours since he had left her. He decided to wait until morning as he did not want to wake her. He was convinced his life would never be the same, never be able to return to a place where he would not think about her every awaking hour, to a place as it was before he was introduced to his father's young and very beautiful wife.

The phone rang shortly after eight a.m. It was Susan with a brief report on the ski week-end that she was sharing with the boys. They were staying at Sugar Hill, and she confirmed all was well with the boys and with her, snow conditions couldn't be better, and predicted they would be home around seven that night. She was planning to leave approximately around three in the afternoon. Susan had gone to college in New Hampshire and spent many an hour on the slopes as well at her parent's ski house in Sugar Hill. Snow would begin to fall late October and would often continue to early spring a making for tons of extremely happy skiers. All the Paleckis' were skiers; the adults as well as the children, and everyone had collected happy memories over the years as guests of the Anderson's at their home in the snow covered mountains.

Luke was anxious to terminate the conversation as all his thoughts and his energy were focused on Sophie. For the second time since he left he decided not to call her but just shower, shave, get dressed and drive the ten minutes to the house. He was worried about her but did not want to disturb her in case she was sleeping. And he truly felt she would call him if she were in any kind of distress.

It was cold and damp outside on this Sunday morning, a hint of snow flurries in the air. The sea appeared rough, staggered clouds drifted in off the Atlantic, maybe practicing for a full blown Northeaster.

There was very little traffic. The ten o'clock Mass at St. Anne's would soon commence. Luke and his three brothers all had been baptized, made their First Communion, Confirmation, and had been married in this church. His mother's funeral service was conducted here, a memory still fresh in his mind even today after so many years. Her final resting place was a short distance from the church. Tall pine trees staggered throughout the cemetery planted by the first Lithuanian settlers towered above the grounds where they were commissioned to stand watch. There had always been flowers on the grave; and during the Christmas holiday season, a fresh wreath with a huge red bow would be tied around the headstone. He often wondered if his father was the benefactor, but knew it couldn't be anyone else. He remembered the years after his mother had died when his father and three brothers would visit the grave, say a prayer, but it always left him with a deep feeling of sadness. The visits over the years became less frequent, and he felt some relief as the sadness slowly dissipated. Luke on arriving at his father's house got out of the car and walked toward the rear entry. He noticed that the wind had subsided, the clouds reversed direction and now headed out toward the Atlantic, and the sun previously undetected, desperately tried to make an appearance but to no avail.

As he stepped over the threshold into the kitchen he somehow expected Sophie to be there, perhaps sitting and enjoying a cup of coffee or having a late breakfast. He would later learn his brother, Adam, had volunteered to bring Amber to his house when he discovered Sophie was not feeling up to par. That would explain her absence yesterday when he was here at the house.

He took a moment, searched the parlor and adjoining sun room, and not finding Sophie in either room proceeded upstairs where he knew she had to be. When she didn't answer his knock on the door he turned the doorknob and entered the bedroom.

"I'm not feeling very well this morning. Will you stay here with me!" a tone of desperation in her voice.

"Why did you not call me? You knew I would come here immediately. The last thing I said before I left, before you actually requested me to leave, was to call me."

He knew just by looking at her exactly what the problem might be. His suspicions were confirmed when he reached for the covers and pulled them back to find the sheet was covered in blood.

"Sophie, listen to me, we have to get you to a hospital. I'm calling an ambulance."

"The baby, Luke, is the baby going to be alright!" Luke reached and bent over to her, his heart racing, put his arms around her and confirmed she was going to be o.k. careful not to mention the baby. He got up, took the telephone off the nightstand, and made the necessary call for an ambulance. He couldn't bear to see her in such pain; and it was even more difficult knowing there was no way he could prevent it. He would have to call his father over Sophie's protests. It was the right thing to do, the one and only time he would become capable of doing the right thing concerning his father.

CHAPTER 49

"Luke, your father just left with Adam. They have a meeting in Boston later this morning."

"Yes, I know. I talked to my father last night, and he told me they might consider spending the night there depending how long it took to make the arrangements with the suppliers, but I really came to see you."

"Is everything o.k., Susan and the boys?"

"Yes, we are all fine."

"Pour yourself a cup of coffee. I just made it. Let me get dressed, and I'll make some breakfast for us. It's Maria's day off. Give me a minute or two. I'll be right back."

According to the latest weather report the forecast was for a warm day so she pulled a pair of light weight slacks and a short sleeve top from her closet, decided to forfeit a shower and would just get dressed.

She was still in her robe when she turned around and saw Luke standing in the doorway. "Luke, what are you doing here?"

He did not answer, just stood staring at his father's young, beautiful bride.

"Luke, please leave!"

"Take your clothes off!"

"Luke, are you out of your mind! Get out!"

"I said take your clothes off!"

Sophie could not believe what he was saying. What in God's name was he thinking! Could this really be happening?

"Please leave right now. If you lay a hand on me I will tell your father."

"You won't tell him. I know you won't because after I make love to you, you'll want me again and maybe for the rest of your life."

"How can you possibly think that I would sleep with you? You mean rape because it would be rape."

He walked slowly toward her, removed the tie from her bathrobe and with little hesitation he placed both hands on her breasts. She was naked under the robe.

"Stop it! Stop It! Are you insane? Please don't do this! I love your father. You are his son. You are crazy!"

But he didn't stop. He picked her up, her arms and legs thrashing, screaming at the top of her lungs for him to let her go. He carried her to the bed and took her bathrobe from her and held her down.

"I am going to make love to you. I am going to kiss you all over, and you will beg me not to stop! And the next time I make love to you, it will be your idea. You will come to me the next time!"

She knew now that he would continue, and there was nothing she could do to stop him.

When it was over she lay in a heap, legs curled up under her chin, tears falling out of control. He pulled the covers over her, got dressed, and without saying a word he left the room.

"You bastard!" she called after him, not in English but in Lithuanian. She could hear the kitchen door slam behind him as he left, the car leaving the driveway, the gravel kicking up behind.

She stayed there in bed for the rest of the day not remembering if she had dozed off for awhile. The next thing she heard was Amber calling her. The school bus had just dropped her off in front of the house.

Amber not getting a response from her mother climbed the stairs still calling her.

"I'm in the bedroom, darling."

"What's wrong? Are you sick?"

"No, I'm fine. Mommy is just a bit under the weather. Just give me a minute or so and I'll meet you downstairs."

She had to pull herself together. She somehow knew this day would change her life forever. She would have to have a plan so that it could never happen again, but she needed time to think it through. But it would not be today. She was too tired.

"Mommy, Daddy is on the phone. He wants to talk to you. Can you come to the phone?"

"I'll take it upstairs. Hang up after I pick up the phone."

"Amber said you're not feeling well?"

"I'm fine, just a mild headache. Please, Viktor, I'm fine. How did it go today? Are you and Adam staying the night?"

"I don't think so. We have finalized everything, and we will stop somewhere for dinner and head home. Did Luke come by the house? He told me he would try to stop and have a cup of coffee with you. He's putting the boat in the water this week, and he and Susan want us to go out with them some Wednesday his day off."

"Yes, he did, he stopped by but he didn't mention the boat."

Sophie felt sick to her stomach. She knew Luke was right. She would never tell his father. And she had no way of knowing at this point her nightmare was just beginning.

"I am so glad you decided not to spend the night. Hurry home, darling." She turned around, hung the phone back on the cradle, and returned to bed.

The next few days Sophie tried in vain to keep herself busy. Viktor had mentioned to her he had noticed her lack of appetite and noticed she was just not herself. She reassured him that nothing was wrong just a little tired. She prayed that Luke would keep away from her, from the house. She was afraid she would actually kill him, and it frightened her that she could be capable of doing it. She visualized running a knife through him, hitting him over his skull with a baseball bat, running him over with her car, or shooting him with a crossbow. But it didn't alleviate her pain or the guilt even though in her heart she knew she had nothing to be guilty about, or did she?

"Please, please dear God. I need you to help me get through this nightmare, to grant me the strength I need to resume my life with my husband, to be his wife again. I can't do it myself." She would pray repeating the words over and over, day after day, but her demons would not leave her. She wondered if she would ever be capable of enjoying life again and to experience the happiness that she and Viktor had shared, to make love again with her husband. The most difficult part of the day was when she and Viktor would go to bed. She could not make love, she could not respond to him. She hated Luke more for this, a numbness that dulled her body. Viktor never questioned. He would kiss her goodnight, hold her for awhile, and reassure her that it was o.k.

"I love you. I am so sorry. It will pass I promise you."

She truly loved this man lying beside her. Long after he would fall asleep she would still be awake.

One evening after dinner they retired to the parlor, and Viktor took his wife by the hand and seated her next to him on the sofa. He had been concerned about his young wife noticing that there was something different, something he couldn't decipher, and he worried about her. He detected a depression, a sadness in her that seemed so foreign. He had derived a plan, hopefully she would agree to it.

"Sophie, I was thinking, I have to go to London on business in a few days as you know to meet with some of our suppliers, and I was hoping you, and Amber too, that both of you might want to come with me. You could do some girl things, shopping, lunch at Harrods, take in a play, maybe a little sightseeing and visit your old friends in the Lithuanian Village. Amber will be out of school next week so the timing is perfect. Think it over, but not too long. There are airline tickets, a change in hotel arrangements and a few other things to be taken care of before we go if you decide."

"Viktor, are you sure? I don't need to think about it. I'll start to pack tomorrow. And I can't see any reason why Amber would turn down your offer. It would be a wonderful experience for her. You know how much I love you. You are too good to us! You have always spoiled us, really spoiled us, but I am certainly not going to complain!"

"I had an idea you may take me up on my invitation. And we are overdue for a vacation."

Sophie was thinking this just might be the remedy she would need, and it might even be a factor in getting her life back in order, back to some resemblance to the life she and Viktor once had. But it wouldn't take her long to discover London would just be a deterrent, her wounds would not heal and a devil with the name of Luke would re-enter and turn her life into Hell. She hated him but she hated herself even more for the feelings he had enlisted in her, feelings never experienced, and could not no matter how hard she tried to rid herself of them. No amount of anything she did or did not do could erase the passion he had aroused in her. There were times she could feel the touch of him on her. Not her prayers, not her love for Viktor could make the ache disappear. Would he win, she thought, could this be possible? Would the devil win after all? Her perfect world would soon be tumbling down on her, and there was no way she was capable of stopping the avalanche that would descend upon her.

The night before they would take British Airways Flight No 2915 from Boston to London, Sophie had finished packing her suitcase, helped her daughter gather her things together, tucked her in for the night, checked with Viktor inquiring if he needed any assistance with his packing, and now she would try to get to bed early. Within a few minutes the phone rang, and she knew her husband would answer it as she was now preparing her bath.

"Sophie, can you hear me? That was Luke on the phone. He wished us a safe trip; said to say good-by, and he would see us when we returned."

That son-of-a-bitch, she thought to herself, that narcissist bastard. She felt a sick feeling overcome her. Just the sound of his name provoked the memories of that day.

After her bath, shampooing and drying her hair, sleep now eluding her, cancelling her plans to get to bed early, she let her husband know she was going downstairs to read for awhile. When she returned upstairs to their bedroom he was fast asleep. And finally Sophie too fell asleep.

It had to be almost morning as the sun had barely slipped behind the curtains into the room. She sat up in bed and realized she had been dreaming. She was drenched in perspiration, her nightgown soaking wet. She climbed out of bed not wanting to wake her husband, placed her bathrobe and slippers on and went downstairs. It was him in her dream or should she say nightmare. She was running along the beach, seagulls swirling all around her, and Luke was chasing her. It was at night; cold and windy and her feet would stick in the sand, and the waves would come crashing over her. And he finally caught up to her dragging her down the beach yelling her name over and over again. And then she awoke.

Viktor realizing her absence came downstairs. He looked over at the clock on his bed stand. It was 5:35.

"Sophie, are you all right?'

"I had a bad dream. I was running on the beach, and someone was chasing me," she lied knowing she could not tell her husband it was his son chasing her.

"Try to get back to bed, darling, tomorrow is going to be a busy and tiring day."

"I'm not sure if I will be able to fall asleep. I'm going to change my gown and will try. Sorry I woke you. I will be up in a minute."

"I worry about you, you know. You just don't seem yourself lately. You would tell me, darling, if there were anything wrong, wouldn't you?"

"Viktor, of course I would. You know that I would. I'm fine, just a little more tired these days then usual. And I'm looking forward to London. I think it will be just the medicine the doctor ordered. It will be so much fun."

The days in London went quickly, the weather co-operated, only a few sprinkles fell on the day they arrived. The tennis matches at Wimbledon added some excitement to the city as they did every July. Sophie and Amber took in a play, went shopping and had lunch at Harrods, London's famous department store, and they spent a day with their old friends in Lithuanian Village. She also planned to call Erik. She was anxious to learn of his progress in the search for Mikael. She suddenly realized since the Lukas incidence it had erased Mikael from her thoughts.

Erik and Sara were delighted to see her. They exchanged current events in their lives, and Erik gave Sophie an update on his correspondence with Mikael. There still was no visa pending, but he pledged he would never give up regardless of how long it would take. And in just five short months Sara would give birth to their first child. Hanna was now a young lady enrolled in public school and couldn't wait for the arrival of her new sibling hoping for a baby sister. If the newborn turned out to be a boy, they would just have to send him back!

CHAPTER 50

It was only hours after returning from London to the Cape that the telephone rang.

"Hello, how are you? I missed you!"

She felt like someone had punched her in the stomach. The sound of his voice sent chills throughout her entire body. She knew at once, of course, it was Luke.

"Your father is resting, and I won't disturb him. As you already know we just returned. I'll have him call you. Please do not call here. Leave me alone. You were right, of course, I couldn't tell your father the bastard you are!"

"I have this Wednesday off. I'll be at the boat. I want you to come there."

She hung up the phone and stood there for what seemed like an eternity. What, she thought, had she done in her short life to deserve this punishment. And punishment it was. She was in a place she had never been before. How could she possibly feel anything for this monster! There was no doubt that she loved her husband so how could she be feeling this, whatever it was, for his evil son. Was it lust alone? What price would she one day have to pay. Could she live with the possibility of hurting and betraying her husband, and would he ever forgive her. No, it would not be possible. She would have to draft a plan that would stop this nonsense.

Sophie and Viktor had returned from England to a hot, humid, muggy week on the Cape. There was a breeze off the ocean but it was a warm breeze and offered no relief from the heat. Amber was at day camp, Eagle Feathers, and Viktor was at the office. It was Wednesday. Maria requested the day off and the rest of the week to spend with her mother who was visiting from the Azores.

Sophie picked up the phone and called Viktor's number.

"Hello, Jean. How are you? Yes, London was fantastic, even the English weather had co-operated the week we were there. If Viktor is available may I speak to him?"

"I'm afraid he's out of the office, and he didn't say where he was going but said he'd be back around 4 o'clock. The boys, as she always called Adam and Alex, went with him. If he calls in, Sophie, I'll tell him to call you."

"No, no I was really looking for him to take me to lunch, not important. But thank you. It was nice talking to you. Have a good day."

Plan B would go to the beach, take a swim, and work on her tan. She would make a sandwich, fill the thermos with ice tea, and have lunch at the ocean. This would certainly keep her mind off Luke. But as she would soon discover within the hour, her Plan B failed. There would be no picnic at the beach for her today. Nothing at this point would prevent her from going to him, the man she wanted desperately to hate, to completely eradicate from her life. She felt like she was falling into quicksand pulling her slowly to some bottomless pit where she knew that no one could save her.

The boat was just four miles away at a marina where a majority of the boat owners who had their boats moored there were part of the Lithuanian community, peppered with a few Yankees, most descended from the first English families who came in the seventeenth century to escape religious persecution. Surrounding towns had been named for them, many whose names were listed as passengers on the Mayflower.

Luke owned a sailboat, The Vilkas, (The Wolf). How appropriate Sophie was thinking! She was a little confused why it had been given a "male" name as it was rare that boats were not given a female name or something "cute" like Week-end Pleasure". The boat had been given to him by his father who loved to sail the Cape waters, but because of the demands of the business allowed little time to enjoy the boat. Alex, too, had a sailboat docked in the adjoining slip. He would try to make the effort to take his boat out every Sunday. On holiday week-ends all the brothers would gather and sail out to one of the many surrounding islands with their family to swim and just relax in the sand and surf. One past-time was to plan a clam boil. The adults as well as the children would dig in the sand for clams, add onions, potatoes, sausage, a Portuguese kind, cod, and corn on the cob to the huge pot cooking over a fire pit dug deep into the sand.

Today was a beautiful, perfect summer day Sophie thought; and as the natives would say, a sailor's delight. She felt she should be experiencing a feeling of being the most fortunate woman on this planet. She had met and married a man whom adored her and was completely devoted to her and her daughter. Her home was complete with every amenity available. Several cars were at her disposal. She had no financial problems to deal with, unencumbered, and no restrictions on anything she wanted or needed. And she loved her husband. So why was she willing to destroy her life, to betray the man that had given her this life, who represented goodness, integrity. She had no answer, and the question would remain with her for the rest of her life.

She parked the car in the designated lot, a short walk to the pier. She saw him almost immediately. He was standing on the dock glancing over in her direction almost as if he anticipated her coming here.

He wore a pair of faded khaki shorts, a polo shirt the same blue as the color of his eyes, boat shoes, no socks. Balanced on his sun streaked hair atop of his head were sun glasses. He was holding a glass in his hand which later Sophie would learn was some special brand of ale that had been imported from Holland. And it appeared he was sporting a newly acquired tan compliments no doubt of the days of sailing around these waters. Her feet felt like blocks of something heavy, and she had to garnish all her strength to propel herself forward. She realized for the very first time how incredibly handsome he was and possessing an air of confidence perhaps acquired from the privilege of attending the best schools in the East. And he had a smile that dug into her very soul. And there was something else, an intangible that gave no explanation for her, a chemistry that perhaps was a gift from the Devil himself.

"I'm glad you are here! Welcome aboard! You look beautiful!"

Her heart was pounding so hard she wondered if he could hear it. She was terrified. The wise thing to do now was turn around and leave before she stepped into a place where there would be no return, no escape, and certainly be a one-way fare into Hell. And she knew that everyone who would be touched, like characters in a play, would have their lives drastically altered, or worse, destroyed.

Luke stepped down into the boat, held out his hand for her as she followed.

"You're trembling. I'll pour you a glass of wine", and he motioned for her to sit on the sofa.

"Please sit down. Are you o.k.?"

She nodded. "I feel a little warm." He reached over to her and felt her forehead.

"I'm going to get you two aspirins, and I'll wet a cold facecloth. Stay there. I'll be right back."

He came back with the aspirins, a glass of water, facecloth, and a glass of white wine.

"Just sip the wine."

She took the water first with the aspirins, her hands still shaking. A breeze coming off the water rested on her face, and she started to feel a little better.

"Feeling slightly better, I hope."

"Yes, I am, thank you."

"I wasn't really sure if you would come here today."

"This is the most insane thing I have ever done in my entire life! You know as well as I do that we will not escape unpunished. The most difficult part for me is the betrayal to Viktor."

"Did you think I planned this, to fall in love with you?"

"I am married to your father. He's a fine, wonderful man, a good husband. And you, Luke, you have a wife, a beautiful wife, and a family. It's not just me and you involved in this. Did you ever stop and think of all the people that will be hurt because of us? And for God's sake you are his son! I do love your father, you may doubt, but I do love him. And I may never forgive you!"

"Then tell me, say it as if you mean it, tell me you don't want me to make love to you!"

He loved everything about her. Yes, she was beautiful but it went way beyond that. There was something sensual in the way she moved, the way she walked, her smile, a special style she owned, elegance and sophistication that could only be inherited. And when he thought of his father making love to her it made him completely mad. He would dwell on it, and he was powerless to let the vision go. He began to hate this man.

"You do not have to forgive me, but I will tell you without any hesitation that you will never regret it. I promise you, dear Sophie. I knew from the very first time I saw you that night at your party that one day we would be together. You remained constantly on my mind. And I won't lie to you, I tried, I really tried to stay away from you, but I will never apologize to you, never."

She listened and tried to form some words to answer, but she couldn't. He had found a place where she had never been before, and now she had come to him willing knowing in her heart he could lead her wherever he desired.

Luke watched her as she settled into the sofa making an attempt to get comfortable the glass sitting on the table beside her almost emptied of the wine. She brushed her hair away from her face; but it proved fruitless as the wind refused to settle down, but the wind did feel refreshing.

He walked over to her, sat beside her. "I am going to kiss you; and I am going to make love to you, but I won't do anything you are not ready to do. I mean it. I know how difficult it had to be for you to come here today, but if you stay I promise you that you will not be sorry."

He held her for a long time, bent down to find her lips, and kissed her. She reached up and put her arms around him, and at this moment she knew why she came to him, why she was risking every thing to be with him. The lovemaking was unlike anything she had ever known, and she didn't want it to end.

"I am in love with you. I think I loved you the very first time I saw you. Your hair, like spun gold, falling over your shoulders, and I wanted to reach out and touch it. Your eyes were the bluest I had ever seen. But the very thing I remember the most was the way you moved, the way you carried yourself. I couldn't take my eyes off of you. I wanted you then, and now, I will never let you go."

"I don't really belong to you. I'm married to your father, and I do love him."

"Tell me he can make you feel the way I do!'

"No, no but I am in love with him. There can be different levels of wants and needs, and I can selfishly want both."

"Some day my Sophie you will change your mind. I will make you change your mind!"

"I have to go, Luke."

"You'll come back again?

"You know the answer."

It was 12:20 when Sophie had arrived at the boat. At 3:45 she got back in her car and headed home. She had experienced Heaven and Hell all within a short period of time. Once home she would shower and prepare dinner for Viktor and Amber. Viktor should be home around 7. She felt some relief that he wouldn't be home when she arrived.

On the drive home she reflected back to Luke.

"I wanted to tell you, to let you know, how sorry I am for the time in your bedroom; but if that day never existed, you would not be here with me today. You possess some innate substance beyond anything I have ever known, like a bolt of lightening igniting my soul, and I can't rid myself of it. And I have tried, I really have tried!"

And somehow she did believe him, but it did nothing to remove the guilt that now consumed her. In those hours with Luke she had been lifted to a distant place far away. And however this chapter of her life would close she knew she would take the risk knowing without a shadow of a doubt that it couldn't possibly have a happy ending. He was a master of what he did, and her addiction for him would last for a very long time guilt being dispersed along the way.

CHAPTER 51

The Cape was beautiful this time of year, a peninsular that jutted out into the Atlantic facing a land thousand miles away. The maples blazed in colors of orange and reds, for many it was a favorite time of year. But the very best of all it was the time of year the Cape returned to those who loved it the most, its year-round residents. Most people living on the Cape were descendants of the early English settlers who had the distinction of being called swamp Yankees, their trust funds not been touched since they were signed and the ink on the paper dried several generations back. They had a reputation of being frugal, but there was little evidence of being deprived of any worldly possessions.

Fans were stored in attics, and it would be too early to turn up the heat in the houses. Boats would be pulled from the ocean as the weather turned cooler usually late October early November. They would be hauled from the surrounding waters and placed in storage until spring rolled around again. The larger crafts would be stored in boat yards and boat houses found lining the oceanfront from the beginning of the Cape to the farthest end, a needle of land protruding into the Atlantic Ocean. Smaller boats, usually wrapped in canvas, were stored in the back or on the side of the owner's property. And the very lucky ones would find the way to Bermuda an island five hundred miles off the coast of North Carolina or to the Bahamas, and a few would venture farther south in the Caribbean and pull into port on one of the many islands there. The Azores, an archipelago of nine islands belonging to Portugal and a half way point to Spain, Portugal, and southern Europe was also a popular winter destination. The Portuguese that settled on the Cape came from the Azores, a few from the country of Portugal, and from the island of Madeira along with a small colony of Brazilians. Many of whom followed in their father's and in their grandfather's trade of fishermen, a main source of industry on the Cape. They had a reputation for having exceptional work ethics, honesty, and living in harmony

CHAPTER 52

The house sat on the side of the mountain nestled in a pine grove over looking the Mohawk River. Susan's father had cut the wood from his land and built stairs, thirty-two to be exact, leading down to the river. He also constructed a small shed to resemble a miniature log cabin that sat close to the edge of the river to accommodate the canoes, kayaks, and rafts stored during the winter season.

The house itself was very large combining a total of three levels. A loft suspended over the huge keeping room had two bedrooms, both with connecting baths, complete with a sauna and Jacuzzi. On the first level, which was at ground level, a two-car garage shared the space with three bedrooms all facing the river. A long hallway was built providing ample storage, a huge built-in linen closet, and rows of hooks for coats and jackets. The main area, on the second level, had a master bedroom with bath, a keeping room with a fieldstone fireplace that separated sliding doors that lead out to a deck that wrapped around the back of the house offering a panoramic view of the river and the rapids below.

The kitchen was state of the art showcasing furniture hand-crafted by local artisans. A long farmer's table that easily seated a dozen people had been placed near the sliding doors to view the scenery. Build-in hutches were on both sides of the room with a collection of pottery, again purchased locally, and a collection from a recent trip to Sweden sharing the space with her Dala horses very old ones that came from Sweden. A light fixture carved from wood in a folk-art style had been hung over the center of the table. Two dishwashers, imported from Germany, were separated by built-in cabinets. Fresh flowers were always placed through out the entire house regardless of the season.

A bunkhouse sat on the edge of the property constructed specifically for the grandchildren who made frequent trips to Sugar Hill both winter and summer. A total of ten bunks lined the walls. A tile fireplace imported from Sweden that supplied the heat during the cold months was placed kitty-cornered in the far end of the single room. In summer window boxes would be filled with geraniums and vinca and windows with screens were rarely shut. The window boxes were hand painted in a style called rosemaling, duplicating a folk-art style very popular in the Scandinavian countries. Mrs. Anderson, Susan's mother, was of Swedish decent and had incorporated the Swedish style of design here as well as her home in Connecticut. She favored blue and yellow for obvious reasons!

Though Susan's father had contracted and had the trio of buildings built with the ski season in mind, he was pleasantly surprised and delighted that the family loved the summer here as well so it actually became a year-round vacation retreat. Plans were already in the making to begin construction of a swimming pool something that the grandchildren had repeatedly requested pretty much convinced that their wishes would not be ignored by their grandfather known to spoil his clan over the years. It was rumored that a small fortune was obtained by the Anderson family through careful and calculated stock holdings over the years and an inheritance from an insurance company that was founded many years ago by his grandfather and later sold by the family.

At the last minute, just days before he was to accompany Sophie and Amber along with other members of the family on the ski vacation to Sugar Hill, Viktor reluctantly informed Sophie he had no choice but he would have to cancel.

The very first plant being built outside of the New England states was now under construction in Baltimore, Maryland. The builder had requested that he needed Viktor's opinion on several problems he was facing that really could not wait any longer to be solved.

"I am so sorry, Sophie. I hope you're not too disappointed but it is only in my best interest to make the trip down there. I was going to ask Ben but he would have to cancel his ski week, and I am not totally convinced he would be able to make all the decisions that need to be made concerning this project. And of course, darling, I too am disappointed!"

"Oh, Viktor, I understand, you know I do, but Amber and I will miss you. I suspect she probably more then I will!"

Susan being familiar with the region made a suggestion that all the families join together for dinner and make a reservation at the Snow

Plow in the village as the food was good, and they catered to children rewarding them with a large selection on the children's menu. But the most popular item was the ice cream clown listed first on the dessert menu. And it could be ordered in your choice of flavor!

So after the last ski run, everyone returned safe and sound, it was decided to pile into the station wagons and set out for the restaurant together forming a small convey down the mountain. It was a beautiful winter evening. A full moon peered down on the snow covered mountains, the tree branches bending in all direction from the weight of the recent snow, smoke curling out from the chimneys in the surrounding chalets and houses, and not a single gust of wind anywhere in the very late afternoon, replicated a picture post card. Sophie driving down the mountain revealed she had never seen anything quite so beautiful.

The ride to the Snow Plow took approximately twenty minutes, and the kids were voicing their request for an early diner as they all were ravenous.

Sophie was surprised at how quaint and pretty the décor, in an Alpine design, her first experience in such a pleasant setting. And music floated through the room compliments of a young talented group in matching lederhosen, bright red suspensors, and green woolen hats with tiny feathers pinned on the side.

Several pair of skis hung on the wall that were characteristic of the early models, no binders but leather straps to hold boots secure. A huge brick fireplace straddled the center of the room, a fire blazing on both sides. Tiny white lights clung to miniature fir trees planted in aged wine barrels. In each of the windows flickered a single candle. Snow had started to fall outside, and the flakes fastened themselves to the small windowpanes.

And if it were not for Luke sitting across the table from her, it would be a perfect ending to a perfect day.

As they were leaving the restaurant among the squeals and sounds of delight from the children, Luke walked over to Sophie and whispered to her, "Leave your door unlocked!"

"Have you gone completely mad!" struggling to keep her tone to a bare whisper. She couldn't say another word to him. She could barely believe what Luke had said to her, thinking he had totally lost his mind. But the problem could easily be resolved. She wouldn't forget to lock her door!

It had to be past mid-night when she heard the knock on the door. Luckily she had fallen asleep almost as soon as she had settled into bed thinking she had the problem with Luke solved. She knew it had to be him and that he would not be easily deterred. Knowing this she got out of bed and opened the door. He stepped inside the room, took her in his arms and kissed her, not giving her a second to protest. He reached over and slipped her nightgown away from her body, picked her up and carried her to the bed. It only took a short time to realize she would be a willing partner completely forgetting there was some risk involved, but it was already too late. And for the first time in a long time, even though it did not make any sense, she wanted to blame Viktor for not being here in bed beside her instead of the wicked step-son.

The next morning at breakfast she could not bear to even look at him. There was no doubt she was paying an enormous price for her transgressions. Luke, she thought, displayed anything but being an attentive husband and a doting father. She could feel her head throbbing, and she wanted to scream. It didn't take long for the throbbing to become a full blown headache.

A few minutes later Amber appeared with the rest of the group that had spent the night in the bunkhouse. Upon seeing her mother she came to her and gave her a full fledged bear hug. "Oh, Mommy, it was so much fun. Do you think Daddy would build us a bunkhouse so I and my friends could come here?" "I'm not sure my mylimasis (sweetheart} but we could ask him!"

They settled in their chairs at the long farm table; and within a few minutes, Mrs. Anderson was flipping blueberry pancakes and stacking them onto plates. It was obvious that dear woman would be on pancake duty for some time to come.

She stepped away from the stove for a few minutes to explain that there were two small pitchers of maple syrup, one on each side of the long table. A pitcher of freshly squeezed orange juice, glasses on the right-hand side of their placemats, sat in the middle of the table. She encouraged all the children to pour themselves a small glass reminding them of the activities awaiting them today, and that the juice was fortified with vitamin C, not sure if they actually grasped the meaning of it. In the meantime Sophie found the pot of coffee aware that it might help with her headache until she could find an aspirin which she thought was somewhere in her purse. She was determined that Luke would not spoil her plan to join the others on the slopes today. She closed her eyes for a moment and visualized an arrow piercing his chest and grasping for air, collapsing, mortally wounded. It did make her feel slightly vindicated as foolish as it sounded. It was a long time since she held a crossbow, but she knew it was a skill she would never forget. If the nightmare kept repeating with no hope of subsiding would she be capable of actually killing him! She definitely would draw a plan just in case, but not today. Today she wanted to ski all day. She would put her plan for murder on hold!

CHAPTER 53

Their lovemaking went beyond anything he had ever known. He would relive the hours that he and Sophie spent together making it almost impossible for him to focus or function on anything else. It was like being possessed by some unknown compelling force. There was an energy filled current that sparked between him and her. A trance-like state seemed to persist. Their senses highlighted by the coaxing warmth of the sun and balmy breezes as the boat would often rock gently anchored in the harbor. Luke often felt transported out of reality into another far-away universe. Sophie's admiring glances would fuel his yearning to touch, and he would slip his arms around her shoulders or waist drawing her responsive body closer.

Alone. Unknowingly, they would gravitate toward the bed. Removing clothes was mechanical. She would curl toward him to become closer. And always his hands would begin to move over her breasts, tapping his fingers from one side to the other sensing her response. Her hunger was apparent becoming intensified. She reached over to him, found his mouth, and kissed him hard and long. It was as if neither of them, the new wife or the son of her husband, had ever made love before this time, but always he seemed to anticipate what she wanted from him.

Sophie gasped as he explored her body, full breasts, nipples hardened. He positioned her on her back; and before moving on top of her he ran his hands over her legs slowing finding a place to touch before he entered. She would explode for need of him bringing his shoulders over hers, and she felt they were joined together becoming as one. The room seemed to shift, the air magnetized with their energy, and as always they reached the end together. The two lovers would collapse in each others arms where they would remain linked to each other, the waves lapping on to the side of the boat causing a hypnotic, somnolent atmosphere.

Sophie was the first to stir aware that she had to leave soon, but it was Luke who spoke first. "Please, stay for a little while longer! I can't stand the thought of you leaving me!"

"Luke, you know I have to go. Amber will be getting home soon from camp, and I have to be there."

He knew he had to let her go. He discovered that each week alone without her became almost unbearable for him. There was a need that pierced his soul, and he had no control over it. He was convinced it was much more than the sex between them. He loved everything about this beautiful creature, everything, and he was afraid that in the near future he would be incapable of functioning with out her by his side. Luke had no way of knowing that the future would only bring heartache and would have a tragic ending for him

CHAPTER 54

She heard him shift gears as he came up the driveway exactly at the time he had predicted. She had to pull herself together, quickly. Could she feign not feeling well, call Prudence and explain she was not up to dinner, but she knew it was already too late to cancel.

He stepped out of the car and opened the door for her. She immediately could detect alcohol on his breath.

"Luke, you have been drinking! I'm not going to get into the car with you! You're not in any condition to be driving!"

"Just get in! Get in!" shouting as he took her by the arm, putting her on the seat next to him.

"Luke, please!" she pleaded with him but her protests were to no avail. Once again he would win she thought, but he would not be the winner this time around. Approximately one mile down the highway Lukas Paleckis, thirty-six years old, doctor, father, husband, son, and the lover of his father's wife, beautiful Sophie, within the next few minutes would take his last breath here on earth.

He flew down the driveway out to the street and headed west, a road with numerous twists and turns that hugged the ocean. It was the Cape's scenic route, and the most popular one; but because the day called for rain and the fog had not quite lifted, the road uncharacteristically bore little traffic.

It was like an augury, she would remember months later, that she felt something ominous that overcame her that frightened her to death. She knew he was highly intoxicated, and she could not reason with him. He ranted and raved about the two of then moving away together possibly England or an island in the Caribbean, a place where they could disappear, spend the rest of their lives together. She knew there was no reasoning with him, just as it always was. One of the last words that he would repeat over and over to her was how much he loved her and how he found it impossible to live without her.

For the rest of her life she could not calculate if the accident had been planned out by Luke or if it truly was an accident. The car careened off the road, catapulted into the air over the cliffs that hugged the side of the road, landing below and bursting into flames. Sophie could hear herself screaming and off in the distance Luke calling her name. By some miracle she had been thrown from the car onto the sand several feet away from the car. She could hear his voice like a crescendo, and then a complete silence. It was the very last thing she would remember before loosing consciousness; and the incredible pain, an excruciating pain that took over her entire body.

Prudence, feeling something was drastically wrong, after making several attempts to reach Sophie and Luke by telephone without success, called the police. It didn't take long to find the car aflame not too far away. Luke was dead, Sophie clinging to life.

Years later when she would reflect back on this day she would wonder if she had loved Luke even if it had been in a twisted way. Was it really possible to have loved three men in one lifetime. The answer became obvious to her.

CHAPTER 55

Indian summer, a transitional season on the Cape, arrived a little later this October, a contender in the formula for making it one of the most perfect places on Earth. Trees were ablaze in their fall colors, a combination of brilliant reds, flaming oranges, and vivid yellows. The breeze would circle off the ocean; rattle the maples, and they in turn would lazily float to the ground. The pines would shed their needles, drift down and mix with the fallen leaves. Days would become shorter and gradually become darker. The sunsets would light the sky on fire before slipping over the horizon.

Sweaters and jackets were removed from closets and chests, and coats and hats would soon take their turn. Children waited anxiously to Trick or Treat on Halloween. Farmers harvested the pumpkins in all sizes placing them in bushel baskets at roadside stands, some having been painted with ghosts and witches, many with miniature felt hats pulled down over their stems. Cornstalks, Indian corn in shades of autumn, bags of apples, acorn and winter squash, jugs of apple cider, and pies with mile high crust would be displayed along the side of the pumpkins, all for sale, with a huge selection of potted asters and mums lined up on old plank tables. Hayrides, available as long as the weather would co-operate, and where age restrictions did not exist.

Houses would be decorated in a fall theme. Cornstalks were tied on fences with ribbon and bows, the Indian corn hung on doors, porches, lampposts. Pumpkins and jack-o-lanterns were staggered on steps, stone walls, and displayed in window boxes. Most would remain until Christmas decorations would take center stage.

Sophie had forgotten how beautiful it was at the Cape this time of the year. The ocean would change color, appeared darker, almost charcoal. The thunder from the crashing of the waves resonated sound that only the sea could produce. The harbor was almost completely vacant, large ships moving a little slower as they entered the Atlantic. A few cars passed by signaling left toward the apple stand. Later toward evening this time of year would constantly become shrouded in fog. The fog would creep in and become so dense that visibility was nearly non-existent. The few cars on the road would slow to a snail's pace anxious to find their way to their destination. In spite of all the memories she frequently wanted to bury, she was glad to be here.

She pulled over to the side of the road, found a space looking out over the cove, and thought back to that time when she was in the hospital and had not been expected to live, and the months following when she had to accept the reality that Viktor was no longer in her life. There was an old Lithuanian superstition that reminded us that death appears in the number three. On October 8, 1954, Lukas Peeter Paleckis was laid to rest beside his mother in St. Anne's Lithuanian cemetery high on a hill next to the church where he had been baptized and later made his First Communion and several years later his Confirmation. Less then one month after Lukas died, Caroline Lister Paleckis, wife of Aleksander, mother of Markus and Stefan, succumbed to leukemia after months of painful chemotherapy and numerous blood transfusions that proved to be unsuccessful in extending and saving her life. Viktor Arlandas Paleckis, husband of Sophie, father to four sons, grandfather to seven, step-father to one, humanitarian, entrepreneur, died from a massive heart attack in the same hospital where Sophie was lying in a coma fighting for her life. Viktor keep vigil over his wife's long battle never leaving her side, but the grief always present after loosing his youngest son in such a tragic manner, and the unrelenting burden he carried in watching over his wife always aware that there may not be a full recovery finally took its toll. Not yet thirty-five years old Sophie had lost the three men who had played major roles in her life. Sophie, who survived the accident that had claimed Lukas's life, remained in a coma for forty-four days. Against the odds and despite the predictions and prognosis of the medical team, Sophie made a full and complete recovery from the accident that nearly took her life. The difficult part of the healing process was to adjust to the loss of Viktor and also to come to terms with the death of Lukas. She tried to focus on Amber and assist her in making the difficult adjustment of her life after loosing the only father she had ever known, a man that loved and adored her and was completely dedicated to her from the first day she came into his life.

Sophie remembered one of her first requests coming out of the coma was to ask for a mirror. She gasped as she hardly recognized the image whose reflection stared back at her. Dark circles rimmed her eyes that appeared sunken and tired. A pale shade of grey replaced the once beautiful color of her complexion, one of her best features she had always thought, a gift bestowed compliments of her Lithuanian heritage. It was obvious she had lost a great deal of weight. And most noticeable was the scar on her temple, red and nasty looking.

When the initial shock wore off she was determined to focus on getting well very aware that she should be thankful and grateful she had been given a second chance and had cheated Death. She didn't need a reminder that she had a very close encounter with death. She knew the road ahead would not be an easy one, especially now her life without Viktor. In spite of her indiscretion; she had truly loved him, and she was grateful for the life he had provided for her and Amber, and she would treasure the special times they had shared as long as she lived, as there many of them.

Amber had been staying with Adam and his wife, Prudence, whose real name was Young Fawn, a member of the Wampanoag Tribe. They were the first settlers and the true founders of the Cape. She was strikingly beautiful with long jet black hair often pulled back in a tight chignon, and eyes almost the same shade. She had taken Amber to meet her siblings, many still active in the Indian Council that ruled over the Wampanoag. She was fascinated by so many things she had learned on her visit, by their accomplishments, their generosity toward the early settlers and credited with saving many lives during the first winter when they arrived here in the New World. Amber was fascinated with the stories that Prudence would tell about the Wampanoag, focusing on her ancestors, and beg her for one more story when she barely finished telling one. And along the way she and Madeline would learn words in the Wampanoag language, a long and dedicated task that Prudence and a few other members of the council were researching to bring the lost language back to their members. It was an arduous, strenuous, time-consuming, difficult feat that Prudence was determined to accomplish. As they plowed forward in this endeavor the children were the first to speak the language of their ancestors, one word at a time. Years later

Prudence would not only receive recognition from the Wampanoag but from the State as well for the years she had invested in this project. Her goal was to return to all the members something that had not existed for close to a century.

Madeline was the only child of Adam and his wife, and the only granddaughter of Viktor. She was eleven years old, three years older than Amber, and Amber loved the fact of having an older cousin as she thought of her that way. And Madeline lived in the most beautiful house and yard that Amber had ever seen! Amber was convinced that there was no other house like it in the whole wide world! The house was situated on fifteen acres of land, ocean front, complete with a dock that had been built to accommodate the guests who came by boat, or on most occasions, their yachts. The yard was a child's fantasy. There was a swimming pool including a slide where the girls would play for hours. A trampoline sat next to the fence a few yards away from the far end of the swimming pool which bordered the tennis courts. But Amber's favorite thing of all was a tree house that had been constructed just for Madeline. On warm summer nights they would raid the pantry stacked with all kinds of treats and fill a basket with candy, popcorn, and other goodies, and sleep for the night in the tree house. Adam would sometimes accept their invitation to join them with the condition he would tell them a story. It had to be a true story. The girls were always fascinated with stories that he or Prudence would tell especially animal or Indian stories.

"One of the stories I remember was when the four of us, Alex, Ben, Luke, and I were young, and Ben had found a stray cat which he had already named Charlie Chaplin not knowing Charlie was a girl and about to have a litter of kittens. Our father was adamant in his decision that we could not keep her. So we derived a plan and enlisted the help of Luke. He was the youngest and had a better chance of success with our father in begging him to let us keep Charlie. Whatever Luke said or did pertaining to the cat adoption, it worked! The mother cat delivered five kittens, and we kept all of them. We named them Annie, Lily, Mitzie, Sophie, and Tabitha! In the weeks ahead my father called and made an appointment with the vet to have Charlie Chaplin spayed, and the very next day the cat completely disappeared, vanished into thin air. All the efforts put forth to find her failed. Three years later, almost to the day Charlie had left, we had just sat down for breakfast when we heard a cat crying outside the back door. There was absolutely no doubt that it was Charlie, and when we went outside to confirm it was really Charlie, it was pretty obvious that she was to become a mother again. We convinced our father, and again credit had to be given to Luke, to let us keep her; and we pledged that we would put the kittens up for adoption. We spent the next week-end building a small carrier with a painted sign in big bold letters, "Kittens for Sale". Dad convinced us it would be a better idea to sell the kittens then just give them away. He felt it would benefit them, and they would most likely be taken better care of. Charlie lived to be an old cat. She had no more babies! Now it is time to say good-night. Sleep tight! I will see you in the morning."

"Thank you, Daddy! Thank you Uncle Adam!" Amber, years later, could almost repeat the story verbatim.

Amber's second favorite part of the small estate was a stable situated on the far side of the property that faced a grove of pine trees that was complete with paddock and several ponies which Madeline had given each one an Indian name. During the summer months on school vacation the two girls would divide their time between swimming in the pool and the ocean and riding the ponies, taking a short break to play tennis and jump on the trampoline. Weather permitting the nights would be reserved for the tree house, favorite thing of all.

Three dogs were part of the family as well Amber would soon discover. A pair of raccoons that had been adopted would come every night to foray for food. Amber discovered her love for horses and horseback riding here, and she continued to enjoy riding for the rest of her life. Even now Sophie would smile when Amber had confided that Madeline and she had secretly named the stables, Hobby Horse Ranch.

Amber who had been staying with Adam and his family welcomed her mother home from the hospital with balloons everywhere, a banner with the words "Welcome Home", and colored on the bottom, "To My Mommy". Beside Maria, Alex had hired a nurse for Sophie to stay as long as she deemed necessary. The brothers realized that the physical wounds would disappear long before the emotional ones so they had agreed to postpone the reading of the will to give Sophie the time that she would need to heal. Sophie, all were aware, would become a very wealthy widow. Between the investments Viktor had made in his wife's name over the last several years; plus the share of profits from the company that she was entitled and guaranteed, it was pretty obvious she would never have to worry about money nor the privilege it brought with it.

In the weeks and months ahead after her discharge from the hospital Sophie was restricted to a sedentary life style, focusing on building her strength, avoiding as much stress as possible. Christmas was just around the corner, and a short meeting was planned to discuss how the holidays should be celebrated. Finally after much deliberation and heavy hearts the decision was made to allow the children to have a time to celebrate; not the huge gala of previous years, but the Paleckis children would get to visit Santa with their lists prepared just for him, stockings would be hung by the chimneys, there would be a tree in every house, and all would attend Mass on Christmas Eve together as a family.

The hardest part of the day for Sophie, as expected, was not the day at all but at night when she truly was alone. To her dismay her thoughts would turn to Luke more often than she liked. Even in death he had control over her. When Amber had finished her home work, bath completed, and later when she would tuck her daughter in bed, the realty of the months past would settle in, and the memories of that day would come back to haunt her. But it turned into weeks before she was able to remember what really did happen that afternoon. She sometimes blamed nature thinking that this was the way of intervening and perhaps to prevent the pain endured associated with the accident, to dissolve the memory completely. But slowly, in bits and pieces, it came back to her.

It had started early on a Wednesday morning. Viktor had gone to New York with two of his sons, Adam and Ben, to attend a three-day convention relating to the building supply business. Sophie had explained to Luke earlier in the week that she wouldn't be meeting him on the boat this coming Wednesday. The guilt that had eluded her for so long began to immerge. The fear of hurting Viktor erupted. The affair she was having with his son started to weigh heavily on her, and the thought of Viktor discovering it filtered into her conscience and all of a sudden became unbearable. Several attempts and her determination to end the affair had failed numerous times. She would try to take another course and forge slowly. She desperately wanted to find the strength she would need to stay away from the wicked step-son. She would hold on to a small dose of optimism as that was all she would have in this battle.

Sophie heard the back door open, and she knew instantly that it had to be Luke. He walked over to her and kissed her.

"Sophie, I know what you are trying to do. It will not work! You don't understand that I can't let you go. I won't let you go, never. And why, after all this time, just tell me why? What have I done to you! Tell me!"

She remained silent for a long time, really at a loss for words that probably would not penetrate any way. She placed her hands covering her face, and with no warning, tears streamed down.

"You know, no reservation, that you have a powerful spell over me. I have never experienced any thing in my entire life like it. You have aroused a passion in me that I never knew existed on this earth. And I have enjoyed the trip through Heaven and Hell with you thinking only of me not those whose lives will be destroyed when this affair is discovered; and you and I have been lucky, but luck does not last forever. The more I think about Viktor the more guilt I consume. He doesn't deserve this! And, of course, neither does Susan, your wife, in case you have forgotten you are married to her! The price we pay will be steep. Did you ever give any thought of how Susan would be hurt, your children as well! Would she still want you in her life, could she forgive you? We can't continue on like this, Luke."

"You are right on all accounts. Don't you think I haven't thought about this, spent sleepless nights pondering over this. My work, too, has definitely been affected; but as I have told you I'm willing to take any risk to be with you. I am incapable of giving you up!"

Sophie knew at this moment, again, he really wasn't taking her seriously. And why should he. He was not going to release her it became clear. Again he had won. She was well aware what defeat felt like. She wondered what the next chapter would bring. What it would bring would be tragedy, an unforeseen disaster that would explode without previous warning. She always had known that the day would come when she and Luke could not continue even though he would not commit to its end. But never, never in a thousand years, could she have foreseen how tragically it would end for the two of them. And once again she would have to dig deep and find strength to go on to accept what fate had doled out to her.

CHAPTER 56

Another foggy day in old London town Erik thought as he made his way to the Underground. The arrival of summer couldn't come quickly enough. Even though there would be little time to enjoy the warm months just to witness the appearance of the sun in small intervals would be a relief from the cold, damp winter and spring weather. Perhaps he could squeeze in a few days for a holiday, and he and Sara could take the children and rent a cottage by the sea. He would approach the subject and discuss it with her. Later he would request Karl's approval to leave for a week.

He planned to meet Sara and her brother for a late lunch today in a nearby pub. Her brother was a handsome young man impeccably dressed in the British manner, very distinguished Erik thought as he first saw him approaching in the restaurant. He was married with one son, and he and his wife were expecting another child any day now. They lived in the most fashionable section of the city and within walking distance to the firm where he worked, Adams, Wilton, and Thayer, founded by his father-in-law twenty or so years before the war. He was a German prisoner of war and was very reluctant to meet his sister's new husband. Over the post-war years he made it perfectly clear that he wanted little or nothing to do with Erik. But as the years slipped by, time in many situations can eradicate even the worse of times, and he eventually agreed to finally meet his brother-in-law. He like his sister spoke fluent German; and he like Sara, he had to give the credit to his grandmother. So this their first meeting proved to be quite a successful one. David, Sara's brother, thought this German that his sister married was quite respectable and came away thinking he was a good chap after all. He told Erik that he was sorry that it took him such a long time to consent to a meeting and agreed it had been long overdue.

On the way home Erik discussed the vacation plans; and as he thought, she was really looking forward to the week that they would be away. And he must remember to remind her to pack that tiny red teddy!

Three hundred people filled St. Anne's Roman Catholic Church to pay their respects and say good-by to Viktor Paleckis barely two months since he had come here to this church to bury his youngest son, Lukas. He would be laid to rest next to his son high on the hill with the same pine trees standing watch, the same ocean off in the distance the white caps roaring to the shore both day and night. If you looked very closely maybe you could see Neptune standing there with his trident orchestrating for all the souls buried on the hill.

The funeral arrangements had been made by his sons in accordance with the instructions that their father had drafted at the same time that he dictated a new will shortly after his marriage to Sophie. The Mass, as he had requested, was to be in Lithuanian. Adam, his oldest son, would give the eulogy.

"Good morning. My brothers, Alex and Ben, and I would like to thank you and welcome you today in joining us in saying farewell to our father, Viktor Paleckis.

As most of you present here today already are aware, his wife, Sophie, is still in the hospital in a coma; but her condition has been upgraded, and we are being optimistic that she will soon make a full recovery. Luke, just months ago, was killed in a tragic accident, and he was buried here at St. Anne's. This time, as you can imagine, has been an extremely difficult one for our families. We are very thankful to all of you. The support that you have provided and all of your prayers have given us strength to get through these trying times. It has been a comfort knowing that we have been in your thoughts. Our father loved the Cape, and one of the main reasons was all the friends he had acquired and treasured over the many years. It makes my brothers and me proud to belong to the community here on the Cape.

To you who are with us this morning that are part of the Lithuanian community; you know how very proud our father was of his heritage, and he would always, if there were any doubt on his part that you were not aware of it, he would take a minute to remind you. I honestly felt he thought about it like it was a gift from God bestowed only to a special few on this earth and that, of course, included him.

His parents, our grandparents, spoke only Lithuanian in the home. My mother, too, who as an adult emigrated from Lithuania, spoke only occasionally in English and only then to please her sons. Today we are thankful for our parents passing this gift on to us. My father spoke the language, and we remember on many occasions my father bragging to his neighbors and friends that all his sons could speak Lithuanian. He always had a wish to return to his native country; but because of the Soviet Union's rule which came after WW 2, his wish was never granted. And our father was a generous man He always remembered how fortunate he was and how good his adopted country was to him, so it became important to him to give something back. His love of animals was always evident through out his entire life. When we were growing up there was always a menagerie of dogs, cats, horses, rabbits and a goat we named Billy. Over the years he made large donations to many animal shelters here on the Cape. Our father sponsored our little league team always taking time from his busy work schedule, coached our soccer team when the sport was just being introduced in this country. Last, but not least, he worked diligently to raise money and bring awareness about the debilitating disease that claimed his younger sister at age twenty from cystic fibrosis a fatal lung disorder. It was one of his passions, and I and my brothers have pledged and plan to continue in memory of my aunt and of him.

So, Viktor Paleckis, husband, father, grandfather, friend, may you rest in peace. May the angels carry you to paradise where we shall one day be all together. We will miss you all the remaining years of our lives; and when we speak to each other in Lithuanian, we know you will be smiling down on us. I would like to read a small passage that he requested to be read at his funeral.

I'd like the memory of me to be a happy one.

I'd like the tears of those who grieve to dry before the sun.

Of happy memories that I leave when life is done. I hope that I have made just a small contribution to the place I leave behind called Earth."

CHAPTER 57

The years slithered past since the day that Erik was told by his aunt that he had been adopted, and that he had not been born in Germany but in a country called Lithuania. He wasn't sure at that time where it was and if the country actually existed! Now it would be possible to embark on the journey that had required almost a decade of preparation.

Visas were finally issued after years of rejection. Erik and Sophie could now finalize the arrangements necessary for their trip to Lithuania. Sophie now an American citizen would travel on an American passport, but she recognized there were no guarantees eliminating the danger of returning to the country of her birth now under Soviet rule. She knew there would be risks involved.

On September 27th Sophie and Erik boarded a Finnair flight from Heathrow in London to Helsinki, Finland; and after a three hour stopover continued to Leningrad and finally boarded Areoflot to Vilnius, the capital of Lithuania, and if all went as planned Mikael would be there waiting for them on arrival.

Sophie some years ago had confirmed that the brothers were identical twins but neither was prepared for the emotions that tore through him when seeing each other for first time.

Mikael had spent his first five years at St.Jude orphanage in Rumsiskes a distance of just ten kilometers from the place he and Erik were born. Mikael always knew he had been adopted, but Erik's adoptive parents had made the decision from the very beginning that they would never reveal the circumstances of his birth. The reasoning was never totally clear, but they had convinced each other it would serve no purpose, and they did not want to endure the pain if Erik decided to pursue a search for his Lithuanian roots. Only after the passing of his parents during the war years did his aunt feel he had a right and he deserved to know the truth, especially considering the fact that he had a brother and that she had always been aware of it. His aunt had approached her sister on the subject on several occasions over the years, but she remained adamant in her decision.

That day so long ago became the beginning of the journey. It was responsible for the long arduous years spent preparing for this day.

Erik was the first to speak using a combination of English and a few words in Lithuanian. Sophie, of course, was there to translate if needed.

"Hello, Mikael, I'm Erik your brother! It is so difficult to believe that this day has finally arrived! I cannot tell you what this means to me."

"I am so glad you are here, I have no words. I too am having difficulty digesting it. We have much catching up to do, don't we. I am hoping you will stay as long as you can. I have been looking forward to this day forever, for so, so long, praying that one day we would have this special time. And I know, of course, your visit will not be a long one and you will have to leave."

And for the first time in their lives the two brothers embraced each other.

Then Mikael turned to Sophie who was standing a short distance away. She wanted the two brothers to have this moment entirely to them selves, to savor the moment and carry it with them for the rest of their lives.

Sophie moved slowly toward Mikael, stood quietly, tears falling freely down her face, her hands trembling as he put his arms around her and held her, a shiver shooting through her body.

"Sophie, Sophie I am so happy and thrilled to see you after all these years. You are still so beautiful. I have often wondered if I would ever see you again! You are well, happy?"

"Yes, I am. I have dreamt of this day for so long not knowing if it would ever happen. I've missed you, you know, I think about you, always wondering if you were in good health, if you too were happy. I can only imagine how difficult these past years have been for you, and Justas, I am so sorry. It was such a tragedy,"

"Yes, you are right. It was a difficult period for me. I miss him every day. I try not to question God's plan for each of us. Justas always told me the best and happiest years of his life were the ones in Trakai.

He had a most difficult time readjusting to life after the war. And I will never know if his life was the one he truly wanted, to be a priest once again."

Mikael turned back to Erik who was watching the second reunion of the hour, smiling. It had become a joyous day for all, and he was happy, experiencing emotions unknown to him. He had no doubt whatsoever that he and his brother could learn to love one another, and the reunion would meet all his expectations. He had immediately liked the man who was a carbon copy of himself.

"It's time to move on. Let me help with your luggage. It's a short walk and about a fifteen minute ride. Sorry I couldn't order a better day. It's been raining since early morning."

On the way to the rectory Mikael described the events leading up to the arrest of Justas when the Red Army marched through Vilinus.

"I had decided to visit my parents as it had been over a year since I had been home, and his plan was when I returned to St. Casmir he would take a few days for a holiday and thought he also would visit his family. We still had projects at the church and in the rectory and Justas was still going through a difficult period. He never completely found the peace he had been looking for since Trakai always desperately trying to chase his demons away. He was still having doubts about the priesthood though I thought maybe he was coming to terms with it. The facts were never completely clear; but after investigating the best I could, I came to the conclusion that somewhere, sometime he was arrested probably on the train to or from his visit with his parents. I wasn't aware that the trains had been monitored by soldiers in the Red Army, and I am sure neither did Justas. I had recently returned by train without incidence, and I had no recollection of anyone in uniform.

A little over two years later I received a letter from him. He had been arrested and taken to a labor camp somewhere in Siberia. He was not well. He asked me to pray for him, he had made peace with God, and he knew he was dying at the time the letter had been written. He described the conditions there comparing them to what Hell must be like. He never mentioned the circumstances of his arrest. I never heard from him again."

CHAPTER 58

"You know Mikael, this is the first time I have ever been in your home!"

"You are absolutely right of course. I hadn't given it any thought, until now that is."

"And my first trip since the end of the war, 1945. It seems so long ago for me. We have so much to catch up on, don't we?"

"Mrs. Baumanis has set some dinner for us. You both must be hungry," Mikael said leading them to the dining room. "She comes on occasion to check up on me, but I really don't know what I'd do without her. Her husband passed away a short time ago, and she reassures me that coming here to help is actually a form of therapy. I think she may be right. I remember the feeling that I had of isolation and the sadness that refused to leave after I experienced the loss of Justas."

And so during the early evening and long into the night they tried to cram all of the years into a few hours before turning in for the night. Sophie witnessed and listened to such joy in them, not a hint of sadness present. The two brothers discovered in a short period of time that they were really very much alike. They covered their childhood years, the war years, and briefly the last few chapters of their lives. Sophie deliberately refrained from interfering in their conversation as she knew there would be time to tell her story. Tonight would be reserved only for the priest and his brother. Maybe their story would have a happy ending after all these years.

Tomorrow would arrive soon enough. Mikael had arranged a short excursion to University of Vilnius before taking the train to Klaipeda and on to St. Jude where Erik and Mikael were born three decades ago. Mikael made the decision not to disclose the final chapter of the journal to Erik until both he and his brother were together in the rectory where the old priest had written and stored his journal.

Sophie, too, had decided to postpone her story for another day. This would not be a good time to tell Mikael he had a daughter, a beautiful young girl who bore a strong resemblance to her father. It would not be an easy task for her. She had no logical explanation for waiting so many years to tell him; and if there was a reason for it, it would be to spare him any pain it may have caused him. Amber had known that Viktor was not her biological father, but Sophie never revealed who her real father was.

"I have some good news, Erik. I have done some research and have found the location of our mother's final resting place, and I am hoping you will agree to go there with me, perhaps tomorrow. It's in a town called Klaipeda just outside of Kaunas. There are trains from Vilnius running almost every hour. There's a rectory and a church called St. Jude, a Roman Catholic Church, and the grave is in the cemetery there. There's a young priest, who happens to also be the pastor, who has been instrumental in this journey. He's agreed to meet with you and me. He found a journal written by Father Kapocius years ago when he was the pastor there, and it discloses information relating to us. I'm anxious to see and read it. This, of course, is obviously where you and I came into the world!"

Mikael purposely omitted the last chapter in the journal that Father Norvaisa suggested he read to Mikael during their phone conversation. Mikael did not tell his brother, an ex-officer in the German army and possibly an anti-Semitic, and he himself now an ordained Roman Catholic priest, had been conceived and born to a young Jewish girl. Tomorrow would be soon enough to approach this subject. It would not be this evening, the first the two siblings would spend in the same place at the same time since their birth.

Sophie was surprised and pleased at how well Mikael spoke English and only rarely needed to interpret for him. He later confided that he had studied English over the last few years upon learning that his bother was now living in England and with the hope of seeing him one day. He, however, had limited opportunities to practice it. He had also mastered Russian a language being enforced in all the schools in Lithuania which currently was a satellite country of the Soviet Union. It would remain under Soviet rule until March 11, 1990, when the Supreme Council of the Republic of Lithuania declared the restoration of Lithuania's independence. It was the first country to free itself of the Soviet Union. The other two Baltic nations would soon follow. She would tell Mikael also that his daughter spoke both Lithuanian and English fluently, but first she had to find the courage to tell him she existed, that he had a daughter.

So one by one the three said their good-nights and retired anxious to get a good night's sleep to prepare themselves for the next day and the impending business at hand. It was Mikael who did not fall asleep right away. He was laying there wide awake thinking back to the beautiful girl he met on the train to Trakai, their swimming in the lake and later making love by the lake. And she was always by his side in the forest and on the many missions they had been assigned. He wondered how much information pertaining to their years in Trakai that Sophie told to her husband.

Tomorrow would change the lives of the twin brothers forever in ways that they could not possibly foresee. In the morning after baths and breakfast they started the day at the University as planned, where Sophie's college years were interrupted because of the outbreak of the war. She was awakened by so many memories; some sad but mainly most were happy ones, but she wondered in what direction her life would have taken if there had been no World War II, if the monster by the name of Adolph Hitler had decided to become an artist instead of Chancellor of Germany. She wondered where the path would have led her if she had graduated and had not spent those years in Trakai. But the road she had traveled, the very one where Fate intervened and had changed her destiny, was one with no regrets for her. She had fallen in love with Mikael; a love that would last as long as she lived with absolutely no regrets.

After the short excursion at the University the three boarded the train. Mikael estimated they would be at St. Jude within the hour. Mikael had made an appointment with Father Norvaisa for around noon time. The young pastor had found the journal in a drawer of a desk several years ago shortly after the old priest, Father Kapocius, got ill and passed away. Father Norvaisa could not comprehend the full reason for all the entries until he read the sections about the twin boys born at the rectory. Several years later Mikael contacted him requesting any and all information that the church may have kept and if there were records pertaining to the birth of the twins. Mikael always knew he had been adopted but showed no interest in researching information pertaining to the circumstances of his birth until he received the letter from Sophie with the news that he had a brother. It was during this time his interest had peaked to the point that now he was determined to gather all that was available to him. It led here to St. Jude. Erik's aunt, also, mentioned to her nephew that the priest had kept a journal and perhaps he had mentioned the babies in it. Now Mikael needed some closure for him as well as Erik.

Father Norvaisa had written to Mikael and had been willing to send the journal by post; but Mikael being afraid it may get lost or censured or possibly confiscated by the communists now in control here, made the decision and requested the priest to keep it there until arrangements could be made to personally come for it and take it back to St. Casmir with him. Mikael and his brother were now able to unlock some of the mystery surrounding that day, November 29, 1915. It really had been a long journey to this day.

When Mikael learned that his mother was Jewish he thought there had to be little or no truth to it, and he was having some difficulty accepting it. Like many of the other European countries, Lithuania resented the Jewish population and the old prejudices still remained. In his line of work he rarely came into contact with anyone of the Jewish faith. He did know there actually were more similarities then differences between the two religions. But there were no other alternatives and eventually he had to come to terms with it. Now it would be Erik's turn. Mikael knew Erik would be more affected than his brother the priest and purposely withheld this part of the puzzle from him. But in the end Erik, surprisingly, would be the one to bask in the knowledge of it. The first half of his life was directed mainly on being a loyal German of the Third Reich, and the last chapter of his life he would devote to being a good Jew. But it wasn't accomplished overnight. The process was a slow one and, strangely, he began to embrace it with enthusiasm.

"Well, here we are, brother, where it all began for the two of us! I have a feeling we have embarked on quite a journey. Let's hope and pray that we will find closure here today."

The three, Mikael, Erik, and Sophie, arrived in Klaipeda shortly before noon and were met by the young pastor at the train depot; and after introductions completed, they set on their way to St. Jude a short distance away.

It was a beautiful autumn day, a perfect homecoming for the two brothers Father Norvaisa was thinking as they headed toward the church.

"If you would like to visit the grave first we can go there now. It is near the pond on the side of the church. Later we can have a little lunch, and I'll turn the journal over to you. I understand, Erik, you were raised in Germany, an officer during the war?"

"Yes, I was adopted by a German couple. I understand my late aunt lived here at St. Jude for awhile, and it was she who brought me to Germany. When my parents passed away, it was during the war, she told me the story. Until this time I had no idea that I had been adopted, never any reason to possibly think my parents were not my biological parents. It did take some time before it completely registered. And yes, I was an officer. I was stationed on an English island for the duration of the war. I escaped being on the Russian front fortunately. That was another chapter of my life that was difficult for me, and it still is."

"Were you raised as a Catholic?"

"Yes, my parents were both Catholics. We attended Mass on Sundays, and I spent my grammar school years in a parochial school. My wife and I are raising our children in the Anglican faith whose structure is very close to Catholicism but no Pope. The Queen of England, Elizabeth II, is actually the head of the church."

"Yes, that would be correct from what I have heard over the years. We are almost there. You will actually be able to see the church spire in just a minute or so. If you decide to go to the cemetery first I'll show you your mother's grave then leave you there alone. I'm praying this will be joyous for you, not entirely sad. You have waited your entire life for this day. Sophie and I will be at the rectory. The path from the cemetery will lead you directly back to the rectory. Please take as long as you need. We can have lunch any time."

Sophie turned to Mikael and Erik and explained she would accompany the pastor to the rectory, and she would wait there for them.

They nodded to acknowledge that they heard what she said. "I will see you in a little while!" and she turned and walked away.

A small wooden cross, badly weather beaten, marked the gravesite with a small inscription, barely legible, Known Only To God. Rest in Peace. Below was the date, 12-1-15. It seemed so peaceful here in this place, almost like being in church Mikael thought.

Flowers had been placed in front of a cross that had been erected to face the pond; and just a few yards to the side was a statue of the Virgin Mary in the center of a circle her hands extended toward heaven, and she was surrounded by small scrub pines and miniature holly trees. Two stone benches were placed beside her, one on each side. Across from the cemetery next to the church was a small pond. A mother duck swimming with her raft of baby ducks were going about their daily business. Bordering the pond were rows of pine trees appearing to make an effort to touch the sky forming a border with the adjacent property.

Mikael made the sign of the cross, bowed his head, and said a small prayer. Erik stood silently beside his brother, not moving, just staring down at the grave. It felt so surreal to him, like his body was floating above the ground that he was standing on. Nothing had prepared him, even remotely, of the feelings he was experiencing. He felt overwhelmed and tears welled up in his eyes. Within the hour after the journal had been read to him he would then have to deal with emotions of a different kind.

Mikael was the first to break the silence. "Whenever you are ready, Erik, we can leave. I think it is time." And he turned and embraced his brother, his twin brother, who had made this journey with him.

Sophie and Father Norvaisa waited in the foyer for the two brothers to return. Sophie had described to the pastor how Mikael and she had met and how Erik found her in London and the role she played in connecting the brothers to each other.

"I am convinced that Fate certainly played a major part in all of this, Father, and there was possibly some interference from God's angels, a little help from them didn't hurt!"

The priest smiled in agreement. She briefly gave a small account of the London years and her marriage and move to the Cape. She explained she had been born here in Klaipedia.

"I knew immediately after Mikael had contacted me that he was one of the babies mentioned in the journal, but not until he had contacted me. I had found the journal in Father Kapocius' desk after he died. I was planning on using the desk when I found it tucked in the back of a drawer. I started to read a portion of it, just a very small part of it, returned it to the desk and really forgot about it until I spoke with Mikael several years later. The journal, of course, is really theirs. It belongs to them."

"I can see Mikael and Erik walking up the pathway, Father."

"We'll have some lunch and then get on with the business on hand. The last train to Vilnius is at 5:30 so there's time. Before you leave you may want to see our church. You can decide later. Mikael and Erik are welcome, too. I'm assuming that you are Catholic. Most of Lithuania is Catholic. Before the war we had a large Jewish population, and I have been told that in the middle of the nineteen century one-half of the population was Jewish. It always amazed me of the three small Baltic States we are the only Catholic country. Our two neighbors to the North are predominately of the Lutheran faith with a few who practice and belong to the Russian Orthodox Church. Estonians, more so than Latvia and Lithuania, still practice pagan rites. Though they are referred to as pagan they really have to do with nature and the forest where they are usually held. It is still a part of our culture. Did you know that Lithuania was one of the last countries in Europe to be Christianized?"

"No, I did not know that. Interesting! It would not have been my guess."

Mikael and Erik were extremely silent as one would expect. Father Norvaisa invited his guests to join him for lunch in the adjoining sunroom where a table had been set. The room looked out over the pond and several varieties of shrubs had been staggered on all sides of the water leaving room for a path to the pond. A bowl of kopustas sriuba (cabbage soup) was served first followed by a plate of roasted chicken with boiled potatoes prepared in their skins with a sprinkling of parsley.

In the center of the table was a basket of juodas duona (black bread). Tea or coffee was offered later with an assortment of fruits. They lingered at the table over coffee before the priest invited them to join him on the second floor where the journal had been kept in the desk all these years. He would later explain to the brothers that the room was most likely where their birth had taken place and later where their mother had died.

The room appeared to have recently been wallpapered and painted. A mahogany bed with four carved posts sat against one wall with a bedside table on each side. Across from the bed was a matching bureau minus its mirror that had seemingly been replaced by a picture of the Virgin Mary holding the Christ Child. A beautiful carved desk sat in an alcove along side of two chairs upholstered in dark blue velvet that matched a bench in the same fabric at the foot of the bed. The windows framed in white laced curtains were cracked open slightly, and the soft breeze felt refreshing. The floor was recently varnished and a slight odor still lingered perhaps explaining why all the windows were opened.

"Father Norvaisa, Erik and I have made a decision; and of course you have to be in agreement with it, we would like you to read from the journal. Sophie will interpret it into English for Erik. The other option would be to take the journal back with us to St. Casmir and read it there, but we find it appropriate to close this part of our journey here where it all began."

And to what they thought would be the last leg of their journey that started over a decade ago finally would end, but unknown to both, the journey was not about to end.

All present got seated, the pastor unlocked the desk drawer, and after finding the first section in the journal started to read from it.

Today is December 1, 1915, St. Jude Parish, Klaipeda, Lithuania

My name is Father Jurigis Kapocius, and I am the pastor at St. Jude. I am writing this in my journal in the event that one day by some miracle the twin boys born here on November 29, 1915, should find their way to this place. Their story begins the evening before they were born. It had continued to rain relentlessly from early morning until later that night. Mrs.Subacius, my housekeeper and also the widow off my late nephew, and I had just finished dinner and about to leave the table when we heard what sounded like a knock on the front door. Our first thought was perhaps it was the wind howling full force outside as the wind had accompanied the rain throughout the day. Branches from the trees had been shaken off, a few came barreling down hitting the side of the rectory before they fell and littered the grounds. Pine cones and pine needles blanketed the area surrounding the pond. Rain spilled over the gutters lashing the window panes on the way down. Mother Nature was unleashing her furry on this late November night. Mrs. Sibacius turned to me and said she would check the front door, and she would be right back. So, it is really here where this story begins. I could hear her calling to me, a panic evident in her voice. "Father, come quickly!"

There could not have possibly been any preparation for the events that followed. The wind was not the only culprit after all. Standing in front of me on the steps holding on to the railing was a young girl wearing only a dress covered by a sweater, soaked to the bare skin, her hair mattered down from the rain. I motioned her to come in out of the rain; but she made no attempt to move, so I stepped outside and guided her into the foyer. I watched as she moved slowly, both hands placed on her stomach, obvious to me she was in some kind of terrific pain. Mrs. Subacius, my late nephew's widow, made the assumption the young girl could be in labor. It took me a few minutes to absorb her words, and soon I had to agree with her. It became evident to me the young girl was about to give birth. "My, God, I was thinking, where did she come from, how in heaven did she find her way here!" I later determined there were no answers to these questions and eventually she would take her secret to the grave with her.

Mrs. Subacius tried to comfort the young woman, and suggested I go immediately to find the mid-wife, an urgency in her voice that climbed to a pitch inaudible as she struggled to confirm the address with me. So in spite of the weather, still raining and nasty, I found the mid-wife at home, and she agreed to come back to the rectory with me. I wasn't aware of the name of the patron saint of mid-wives so I prayed to Mary, Mother of God, and picked a few others at random!

After her initial examination the mid-wife announced there was a possibility of two babies. Her calculation was right. Shortly after midnight the first of the two boys came howling into the world, and six minutes later his brother followed. I was allowed to see them within the hour. They appeared so tiny to me, but I was assured they were in excellent health and actually had a good weight for being twins. I finally turned in for the night, or I should say morning, and I had no difficulty falling asleep.

When I awoke the next morning the mid-wife, who obviously had little sleep herself, summoned me and explained that the young mother was not doing well, and she thought there was little chance that she would survive the day, for she had lost a great deal of blood, was hemorrhaging, and the prognosis did not look well. As predicted the young mother just two days after the delivery died.

The two women took on the responsibility of caring for the newborns, but we were all aware that this would not, could not, become a permanent arrangement. We realized within a short period that it would become almost impossible to locate any family after making several attempts throughout the parish, and there would be no choice but to place the twins in an orphanage. The days following the birth of the babies were hectic ones. Sleep was practically non-existent, bottles had to be prepared, feedings every three hours, and piles of diapers to be washed, folded, and arranged in a place close by to the ones wearing them. But soon a schedule fell into place, baby-related things got a little more organized, and the boys seem to thrive.

The day before their baptism was to take place I awoke at approximately the same time of most mornings, 6:15 a.m., to prepare for Mass scheduled for 8:00 a.m. I had now established a routine of looking in on the twins before I went down to breakfast. One of the babies was not in his bassinet. I assumed Mrs. Subacius had taken him with her downstairs. It was unusual for her not to be in the kitchen preparing breakfast and bottles for the twins as they would be awake shortly. I asked Mrs. Siuvejas, the mid-wife, who had just arrived if she had seen Mrs. Subacius and she said no, she had not. She told me the last time that she had seen her was around 9:00 last night after they had given the boys their baths and bottles and finished getting them ready for bed. She explained that the next feeding would be around 1:00 a.m., and Mrs. Subacius being here at the rectory, agreed to give them their bottles. I explained that one of the twins was not in his bassinet, and she volunteered to return upstairs and check again. But Mrs. Subacius and the baby were not there. I had to get ready to say the 8:00 Mass so I had to put my search on hold. When I returned to the rectory within the hour the mid-wife was feeding one of the babies. She informed me not only was one of the twins missing but his clothes, formula, and a blanket was not to be found. The previous evening would be the last time I would ever see them. I was hoping my sister-in-law would eventually drop me a note with some kind of explanation and to tell me they were both well, but no letter ever came. After the initial shock wore off I tried to access the issue, but of course could only guess why this event took place. I recalled my nephew's wife had a sister living in Germany who after making every effort to bear a child realized that it would not be possible and finally she and her husband came to terms with it realizing that at this point they had no chance of ever having a baby of their own. Adoption proved unsuccessful, and the sister suffered from bouts of depression over the matter. I knew Germany would not be an easy trip with a baby just a few weeks old but certainly not an impossible one. It was the only explanation that made any sense to me, and as the years went by I was convinced this was probably what had happened.

The pastor stopped his reading from the journal and turned and explained that he had to search for the remaining entry because the old priest did not continue in any order. There was nothing written for a few years about the twin boys. The last few pages would be the end of the entries, and it appeared that it was written just a few years before he died. It became obvious that there was nothing else to record.

June 5, 1922

I had to go to Kaunas as the bishop had summoned me to review the recent edits issued by the Vatican. On my return trip (bus) I happened to see a newspaper clipping on the seat beside me. I was taken by a picture of a man that I later learned was a professor of history at the University of Kaunas, and the article read that he had recently been a recipient of an award given by the university. His name was printed under his picture, Darius, the last name was partially torn from the newspaper, and I couldn't decipher it. But the thing that I remembered the most was the first name, not a common one, and I thought back to the young woman who had given birth to the twin boys who had as she lay dying would repeat the name. Was it just a coincidence? And as strange as it will sound I could see a resemblance of the twins to his man! It haunted me and puzzled me for a long time. I took the paper with me and cut out the article and placed it in back of the journal. It was the only time I would ever see the name again. I knew if I pursued this that it could not possibly have a happy ending.

April 23, 1928

I have decided after all these years to close this chapter. It has taken me a long time to come to this conclusion, to put it in writing, to actually enter it here, but it is needed as it is part of the story. Before the young mother passed away I had been there with her in the room watching over her trying to keep her comfortable in her last hours. I bent down close to her hoping she could hear me. I asked her name. She didn't respond at first. I waited a few minutes and asked her again. And for a split second she opened her eyes and finally answered my question. She told me her name was Rebekah Diamond. She closed her eyes and within the hour she was gone. I made a pledge on this day, December 1, 1915 I would not disclose that this woman buried beside the church in a Catholic cemetery was a beautiful young Jewish girl. Her real home was in Heaven with her Creator for all eternity so I convinced myself to let her rest in peace exactly where she was and not to disturb her. If her boys should happen to come here to this place in the years ahead they can make the decision I found impossible.

CHAPTER 59

Sophie accompanied the Paleckis family to Sugar Hill over school vacation but she made the decision not to ski. She was truly amazed at how well Amber had advanced from the Bunny Hill to be on the same level as her cousins, as Amber referred to Madeline and the Paleckis boys. She did have "real" cousins in Lithuania; and there were her Uncle Erik's four children, but she really never had the opportunity to get to know them.

During the second night just after dinner time a storm came barreling down from the Northeast burying them in twenty-two inches of snow. Mrs. Anderson dug into the pantry to find several bags of marshmallows which had been stored there for such an occasion. The group, adults included, impaled the marshmallows on small wooden skewers that had been whittled just for the roasting of the marshmallows in the fireplace. It was extremely rare that the State would issue a warning for all ski areas to completely shut down; but before noon the following day, another foot of snow had accumulated. The Paleckis children initially were very disappointed to loose a day on the slopes; but shifted gears, and for the remaining day snowmen would be built, coal for eyes and mouth, a carrot for their nose, and a broom adding the finishing touch. Until a gust of wind blew off the mountain the snowmen wore black top hats never to be seen again. A huge snow fort was constructed by the older boys a few feet outside the bunk house. In just a short time all thoughts of their disappointment in not skiing soon disappeared. A few Bloody Mary's with an extra shot of vodka seemed to have the same effect on the adults resulting in the opinion that they were having more fun inside then braving the elements on the side of a mountain. Everyone later concluded it was more enjoyment then they had in a long, long time. The next day the sun appeared, and all descended on the ski slopes.

Christmas was a sad time for the family; and during the following weeks the decision was made that life should go on, there was nothing that would bring back their loved ones, and the children deserved to have functioning parents. So it was decided that the trip to Sugar Hill would be in February on school vacation. And it became a well deserved distraction. The children especially could temporarily put aside the events of the last year.

Sophie was thankful that another room had been assigned to her for the week, not the same one where she and Luke had made love, but she was not remotely prepared for her feelings as she stepped into the hallway. She burst into tears unaware that Alex, already settled into his room, came out to see if was she was alright. "I'm fine, honest Alex!"

"Do you need anything, a drink of something, a shot of whiskey?"

"No, thank you. I have my moments when I think of your father," she lied to her step-son. Why was it always Luke, why could it not be her husband that stirred her memorizes and not the one person in her live that she became so dependent, the one person she had so desperately fought trying to remove him from her life.

"Sophie, come sit in here with me for awhile. I'll pour you a small glass of Scotch." And she took it from him and sipped it until the glass became empty.

"We both have to deal with our losses, and I know very well the pain, the agony, coming to terms with the knowledge that they will never be coming back to us. We Lithuanians are tough, Sophie, and we will get through it. We are given no other choice. I have an emptiness that not in a hundred years would I have ever imagined existed; and I often think I must be in a hell here on earth where most people could never understand or remotely fathom what it could be like. I think God asked too much of me when he took Caroline, my father, and Luke all within such a short span of time. I truly believed I was not going to be capable of surviving their loss; but I knew the boys needed a father more than ever, and I had to be strong for them. And you have to do the same for Amber; and of course, for yourself. My father loved you more then life itself. I remember how very happy he was being with you and with Amber. I do not think he was ever any happier in his entire life. We, you and I, are still young and have many years ahead of us. And without a shadow of a doubt I know God has a plan for us to be happy again. I know that we will not feel like this forever."

"I think maybe your predictions will come true some day. I'd like to be able to find happiness once again, not to have my heart broken every awaken hour, not wanting to get out of bed and face the day by myself. Father Stoskus had stopped by on several occasions to visit and talk to me since I came home from the hospital. I have never been a religious person. Of course, I had to go to Mass with the rest of the family as the whole village always attended church on Sundays and Holy Days. The penalty of not attending Mass was a harsh one. I soon discovered the one hour at church became much easier for me then having to remain in the house for the duration of the week which was the option. School, of course, was not only permitted, it was mandatory. Father Stoskus was a real comfort to me. I was still recuperating from the accident; not always remembering his exact words, but I always felt a peace that didn't exist prior to his visits. But I do remember him saying that the pain would pass."

"I couldn't function if I thought it would always be this way. And as strange as it may sound I think someday in the future I want to get married again; not to replace Caroline, but I do not want to grow old alone. The happiest, best years of my life were the ones I spent with Caroline."

"I definitely understand. I have not given much thought to this but I know I don't always want to be by myself. As you know, you need someone special to share things with; each chapter of your life. It's something that no amount of wealth can replace."

"I think its time for me to go to bed, Alex. The wake-up call, if I remember, is pretty early. I am not up to skiing just yet, but I have to go with Amber to watch her. I know she would be disappointed if I stayed here. I'll be in the lodge for most of the day, have lunch with her, and take time to watch her ski. And I want to thank you, say good-night."

"Sophie if you want you can stay here in my room. I'll sleep on the sofa, it's a sleeper bed. Remember I'm here if you need me."

"I should be fine, thank you," and she turned and went to her room. Her hands were shaking, and it took a few turns before the door opened. She looked up and saw Alex was watching her but said nothing. She turned and smiled at him before entering her room. It was a long day, and she was hoping sleep would come quickly once she settled in bed. But for some reason it was not to be! The wind was howling outside, and it reminded her of the wolves in the forest, reminiscent of a long time ago. Now Mikael entered her thoughts adding to her sadness. She felt so completely alone even though she was surrounded by so many people, people who obviously cared about her; but it wasn't the same as having someone you loved beside you, to hold you, to comfort you when the world was spinning out of control, and to know that special person would be there beside you when you woke up in the morning. She knew she had no control in what Fate had doled out to her, but she didn't have to like it.

After tossing and turning she decided to get out of bed, put music on the radio, and later make another attempt to fall asleep. She kept the volume on the radio low so not to wake Alex in the next room, unknown to her that he had difficulty, too, and had not been sleeping. The music was not helping; in fact, it worked in reverse. The station was playing love songs, one after another, with no interruptions. She got up and turned the radio off and crawled back into bed. She was beyond exhausted and wondered why she had difficulty falling asleep. And then the sobs came, racked her body, having no control to what was happening to her. At first she didn't hear him at the door, just a soft tap, and then another. She knew it had to be Alex.

When she opened the door he didn't hesitate for a second, walked over to her, took her in his arms and hugged her asking her to explain to him what was happening, why she was crying, what could be making her this sad. He had a feeling it was beyond missing his father.

"Alex, please, I'm fine. I'm just having trouble sleeping. Please don't worry about me. Tomorrow will be here shortly."

"I believe you, somewhat, but I will stay here with you until you fall asleep."

"You will be tired for your day tomorrow, and the boys will be disappointed if you don't ski with them. I promise you I am fine, really!"

"Then go to bed, I'll stay until you fall asleep, and then I'll go back to my room."

Like a small child knowing the situation would not change, Sophie did as he directed.

"Alex"! She called to him and hesitated for a moment. "Alex, would you stay just a short while longer, come hold me until I fall asleep." And this time it was his turn to feel like the child not willing to disobey. He knew it would be a test. He, like his brother Luke, had always thought she was extraordinarily beautiful. So fully clothed, shoes left behind in his room, he crawled into bed and put his arms around her. She fell asleep almost immediately. He, however, did not sleep at all for the entire night. When she woke the next morning to the alarm Alex had returned to his room. She couldn't help but wonder who the sobs were really for and thought they weren't just for Viktor and Luke; but for her, she was feeling extremely sorry for herself!

CHAPTER 60

It had been several months after returning to the Cape before she had heard or had any contact with Alex. One evening the phone rang. Amber picked it up.

"Mommy, Alex is on the phone asking for you!"

"Tell him I will be right there, Amber."

"Hello, how are you doing?'

"I'm fine, thank you. How are you?"

"We're fine, trying to stay busy."

"Sophie, I have a favor to ask you. Ben and I are flying out to Denver on Tuesday to bid on lumber and Caroline's mom, Mrs. O'Brian, is scheduled to have hip surgery. As you know she has been helping with the boys, a big help to me really. I have a big favor to ask of you. Is there any way you could take Markus and Stefan until we return on Friday?"

"Yes, of course! Just pack a few clothes for them, and I'll come by Monday night and pick them up."

"You know I really appreciate it, thank you."

"Alex, and I have a favor to ask you only If you have a little time to spare before you leave on Tuesday. Could you come by and pitch a tent in the back yard? The boys and Amber can have a sleepover in the tent. Your father bought it for Amber just before my accident, but he never had a chance to put it up. It goes on a platform that he had built, and it's close to the house in the back yard. It should be fun for them. We can make a fire and roast marshmallows, I'll tell a few ghost stories!"

"Sunday, you know, is family boat day so I'm thinking Saturday if o.k. with you. And as always you and Amber are more than welcome to join us on Sunday. It's my turn to take the helm this week so we'll be at the dock at twelve."

"I appreciate the invitation but I have to pass. Maybe before the summer ends I'll take you up on your offer. Are you sure that you will have time on Saturday, Alex? And any day is fine. Amber and I may head down to the beach for an hour or so; but other than that, I should be around all day."

"The tent is in the tool shed still in the box that it came in. It's right near the front, just on the inside as you walk in. You can't miss it. So if nothing changes I'll see you on Saturday. I haven't seen you since Sugar Hill so I will be looking forward to seeing you. You're welcome, you and the boys, to come to lunch. I'll throw some hot dogs on the grill, and you can sample my chowder. I haven't made it since your father was here. He was the one who shared his secret recipe with me and showed me how to make it, and now it has become one of my favorites. So Amber and I went clamming yesterday, and I actually just finished with it. It's cooling on the stove! One of these weeks I promised myself I would try a clam boil. I mentioned it to Prudence the other day, and she said she would pitch in and help me. I'm planning on taking her up on the offer. If I don't see you on Saturday, Alex, I'll come by Monday night for the boys. Amber, I know, is going to be so excited! Let me know if any plans should change. See you soon."

When she hung up the phone she realized it had been almost four months since Sugar Hill and the little melt down she had there. No mention of that night ever came about, and she was puzzled why he was avoiding her since then. She was aware of his business commitment, obligated to work extra hours since his father obviously was not there any more. There was just he and his brothers, Ben and Adam, to take the full responsibility of the business which now had grown way beyond expectations. The plant in Baltimore was a prototype for the one now being constructed in Albany with plans for additions to the New England ones. And she assumed that his list of priorities were his sons now that they were without their mother. So she knew he was extremely busy but found it just a bit unusual that he had not made even a small effort to contact her. His two brothers, Alex and Ben, frequently visited or called her to be sure she and Amber were fine, not in need of anything. Soon she would discover the answer, but it was a far cry from what she would expect.

"Amber, darling, after dinner I need to have a serious talk with you. So postpone going to your room for a little while please."

"Am I in trouble, mommy!"

"No, no of course not. It's nothing like that at all."

"After Maria finishes up in the kitchen you and I will meet in the parlor. Go and say good night to her, and I'll meet you in five minutes."

"You have always known that Daddy loved you very much, and I love you very much, all the way to the moon! And to the sun, ninety million miles away! You knew that daddy always took such good care of us. And I think now in Heaven he looks down and watches over us. You know that you actually have two fathers, don't you, and that you have a father in Lithuania that has never met you. You look exactly like him! Do you remember the pictures I showed you of him and me when we were resistance fighters during the war?"

"Yes, I think so."

"I have been doing a little research lately on visiting Lithuania where he lives, and I thought we could go visit him later this summer while you are still on summer vacation. I am pretty sure that the country, Lithuania, where he lives and where I was born would never issue me a visa, that's a paper that gives me permission to enter the country. And if they did issue one it would take a long time, possibly years to obtain it. However, I found a tour company that has been given permission to travel to the Baltic States which includes Lithuania. They are making their first trip there this August; the second week to be exact, and it would work perfectly for you and me. We will still need a visa, but it would be a group visa and be perfectly safe for me. It would not give us a long time to spend with him, but we would be able to have some time together. I didn't tell him about you, that he had a daughter, until just a short time ago, as I thought it would make him sad. I know he really would like to meet you. What do you think, Amber? Would you like to go see your father, to meet him?"

The young girl sat very still not saying a word. It was obvious she had not completely grasped the entire subject.

"Do you think my father will like me?"

"I have no doubt whatsoever!"

"Can I have a few days before I give you my answer?"

"You take whatever time you need, my sweetheart. Now come and give me a hug. You better start your homework now."

So a plan was set in motion. Amber, needing just a day to make her decision, seemed excited about the trip and proceeded to ask her mother a hundred questions. Sophie tried to be as completely candid as possible; but also remembering her daughter was only ten years old. And there were some things Sophie decided it could be a tad too premature to try to explain. The most difficult part for Sophie was when to reveal to Amber that her father was a Roman Catholic priest. She would not make any reference to this without collaborating with Mikael feeling he was the only one to make the decision. She would abide by his wishes.

After the deposit was mailed and the dates confirmed Sophie went about the task of getting the information to Mikael. The Post was not completely reliable and much of the mail going into the country was inspected, telephone service was practically non-existent, could be tapped; and if information was turned over to authorities it would place Mikael in danger, even a good chance of being sent to some gulag in Siberia, a death sentence carrying with it a guarantee by Stalin where few ever returned from that Hell on earth. She had a little time to conscript a plan trying to determine which one would offer the least danger to him. She figured there would be a few sleepless nights ahead for her until she could solve this problem. And just when she knew that maybe she would not be able to make contact with Mikael, a miracle happened. She had stopped at the rectory at St. Anne's to ask Father Stoskus if she could have a Mass said for Viktor, a one year anniversary Mass which was soon coming up on the calendar. While she sat waiting for Father to discuss this matter, Mrs.Yenush came in through the rectory door. She noticed Sophie sitting on the small bench apparently waiting to see the priest and stopped by to say hello.

"Hello, how are you?" Mrs. Yenush was the first to speak.

"We have missed seeing you here, and all of us have missed you. It's been a very difficult year for you, I know, but hope things getting a little bit better for you."

"Yes it has. It's been a sad year for all of us, the boys as well. Viktor was so special. We all miss him very much. I pray and hope we are able to continue without him; but there is no choice. We take one day at a time. I'm actually here to have a Mass said for Viktor. It's difficult to believe but it's close to his one year anniversary. And you, Mrs. Yenush, tell me how you are."

"I'm doing fine. My husband is recuperating from a stroke. It's a slow process, however. Some days he wants to give up but manages to gather the strength to go on, and the children have been extremely supportive to him. He is making progress so that is a good sign."

"I'm glad to hear he is improving. It must be as difficult for you as well as for him, being the caretaker and all."

"And as you know, Sophie, God tests all of us!"

"Yes, I believe that is true. And tell me, how is your niece. Do you remember I told you I was in the resistance with her in Trakai?"

"Yes, of course I do. She is still in Kaunas. She went home for a short time but moved to the city a few years ago. Her mother, my sister, just recently joined her there. She has health-related issues and had to make the move to be closer to Agnes. I am going to make a visit there in two weeks. You know I could never procure a visa. I made so many attempts over the years without any success. Finally, Agnes was able to help me. Shortly after the war she made the decision to join the Communist party; not because she believed in their doctrine, but she knew it was the only way to survive. And it benefits her mother. She receives the best medical care which is not the case for everyone. She was also responsible for obtaining my visa. I never would have the opportunity to go to Lithuania if she hadn't stepped in. It's been almost thirty years since I have seen my sister, and I couldn't be more excited! I am afraid the next two weeks are going to be the longest days of my life."

"I am so happy for you! Please give my regards to Agnes. She and I were assigned to many of the same missions. We had a reputation of being experts with the crossbow. We always scored way ahead of the men in our group. Now when I look back, there were a lot of jealous women!"

The conversation continued for a few more minutes when suddenly Sophie had an idea concerning her pending trip and getting information to Mikael. Would Mrs. Yenush agree to bring a letter to him? She would write it in Lithuanian so if she, Mrs.Yenush, were stopped at customs and the letter discovered, there would only be a slight chance they would even take the time to focus on it. She would make it very brief, probably only one or at most two sentences. It would seem to be the very best plan drafted so far. Could she have any reason to turn her down? By mailing it in Lithuania there would be little possibility that the letter would be opened. She would only write the date and month of the time they would be in Lithuania using a code that they had to learn purposely for the sabotage missions in Trakai.

"I don't need any time to think about it. I see just a very small risk. Honestly, I do not feel concerned. You can write the note without addressing it to anyone; and I fully agree, make it as brief as you can. I'll keep it in my purse along with my other travel documents, in full view so suspicion should not be cast upon it. When I get to Kaunas I'll buy an envelope and address it to the church, St. Casmir in Vilnius. I don't think his name is important. There is really no purpose for it, and I feel less interest would be shown, if for some unknown reason, the letter could be seen by anyone other than Mikael. Do you agree, Sophie?"

"And you are sure! This means so very much, thank you! If you should change your mind I certainly understand. I'll drop it by your house within the next few days. I'll call first. In case I forget to tell you, please have a wonderful stay with your sister. Amazing, you will get to see her after so many years. And please remember me to Agnes! And I do agree with you. I would omit his name on the envelope, just as you suggested."

CHAPTER 61

Amber and Sophie decided to spend a little time at the beach on Saturday but would leave early. Alex had called to confirm he would be stopping by to pitch the tent so Markus, Stefan, and Amber would be able to enjoy it while he was away, and it could remain in the yard for the entire summer months.

It was late afternoon before he and the boys finally arrived apologizing for the delay. He appeared tired, dark circles rimming his eyes, and she contributed it to the new responsibilities that had been allocated to him since the passing of his father. As planned there was a hot dog roast, and her clam chowder received raves. The children spent the remaining few hours of the day in the tent, reading comic books, chattering away, having what appeared as tons of fun. When it was time for Alex to leave Sophie thanked him for taking the time to put up the tent and confirmed she would stop by Monday to get the boys. As Alex loaded Markus and Stefan into the car Sophie could not help but think that there was something wrong. She would soon discover the explanation, and it was beyond anything she was ready. She had always been a little superstitious and at this point she couldn't help but wonder if this family, the Paleckis family, had a curse on them.

So on Monday evening after she and Amber had an early supper the two of them hopped into the car and headed to Whale Watch Estates where Alex lived. It was the most exclusive area on the Cape. The house had a spectacular view of the ocean with a two-tiered terrace, perfect for impromptu cook-outs, and entertaining on warm summer evenings. The lower tiered terrace led directly to a private beach. The porch had numerous windows with paned transoms wrapped around the back of the house featured French windows and doors that framed a view of the picturesque harbor. Cabanas dotted the shoreline with the open side facing the water that would make for a perfect ad in a travel magazine, something out of the Arabian Nights. The interior of the house had been furnished with American antiques. Persian rugs were scattered over pine-pegged floors that had been imported from Iran.

An exception was a braided rug that Caroline's grandmother had made specifically for her grand-daughter as a house warming gift that found its place in front of one of three fireplaces. Caroline, an art major at the New England School of Design, had a collage of seascapes which she had painted in watercolors that were displayed throughout the house. She had spent months scouring antique shops looking for the perfect frames for them.

Blueprints had been drafted by the builder to construct a club house for all the residents and their guests projected to be completed by the end of the year. A special meeting had been held to vote on the construction of a swimming pool even though all the properties were within walking distance to the ocean. The pool would be constructed with the majority voting for it. There would be a whirlpool at one end, a kiddie's pool at the shallow end, complete with a single diving board. Several bath-houses were planned and chaise lounges would be set back a few feet from the pool. The committee also voted to have a laundry service, delivering and picking up bath towels that would have daily use when the pool remained opened.

Alex could sometimes be seen wearing his alma mater's faded green sweatshirt with Tennis Club, Dartmouth College, barely legible. Just months before his wife had died Alex and she were in the process of making arrangements to spend ten days in London in July specifically to attend their first tennis matches at the prestigious tennis lawn club, Wimbledon. Unfortunately the trip there never transpired. Caroline being diagnosed with leukemia was too ill to do any traveling, and her treatments prevented her from being too distant from the hospital in Boston where she became an outpatient.

After the initial shock wore off on seeing Alex, Sophie asked Markus, the older of the two brothers, to help Stefan pack a few clothes and to be sure to include shorts, tops, socks, and pajamas. And of course to take any other items he and his brother would need for the five days away from home.

"Markus, if you think of anything else just add it. I'm thinking toothbrushes, and throw your bathing suits, too, on top. Call me if you need me!"

The young boy, he was eleven years old, two years older then his younger brother, nodded in agreement and headed upstairs.

Sophie turned her attention to Alex not sure where to begin. He obviously was in no condition to be flying off to Denver the next day.

"Alex, I think you need a shower! Let's see if we can get you in a position, and with a lot of luck, so you will be able to catch your flight tomorrow. I'm not sure we can accomplish it; but I'm willing to try, but you have to do your part. Let's get going!"

"You are going to give me a shower!"

"No, but I'll help you into the shower."

She walked over to him almost afraid that he was incapable of standing on his own for much longer. She took his arm and led him to the bedroom where the shower adjoined the master suite. She instructed him to remove his clothes, and reassured him she would return to help him. Surprisingly he offered no resistance to the fact he was standing completely naked before her. It had been a long time since she saw a man naked. It upset her to think she couldn't remember if it were Viktor or Luke that was the last one to make love to her; and at this moment, she couldn't help but wonder if that part of her life would ever be returned to her.

"I'll bring you a towel as soon as you need it!" hoping he could hear her above the running water.

While he was taking a shower Sophie stripped the bed and changed the linens. She would later that evening repeat the process in the boy's bedrooms. Laundry was piled in all corners of their room. She would return in the morning; and with help from Maria, she would try to straighten up. She wondered what had happened to the cleaning crew that came every Thursday. It was obvious they had not been here for awhile.

"Alex, I am going to suggest you wait until morning to shave. I'm not so sure you are capable of holding a razor! Now let me get you into bed. It's early but you need to sleep if there is a remote chance you will make it to Denver. Your flight should be in the morning. Do you remember what time? And I'm going to make a suggestion that you give top priority to getting your life back together; if not for yourself, think of the two young boys who lost their mother and now are having a father that is not available for them. It's time to stop mourning for those no longer with us. I know you loved Caroline, I know, and I truly feel for you, but its time to move on."

"Caroline is not the issue, I'm afraid. Are you surprised? And yes my flight, it's at eight-twenty I think, somewhere around eight o'clock."

She couldn't possible guess what he was talking about. Maybe it was the liquor that was doing the talking.

"I'll set the alarm clock for five. That should give you enough time, do you think? And is Fred driving you to the airport?"

"Yes, he is, and yes to question number one."

"I'll go and get the boys. They are upstairs with Amber getting ready to leave. I want you to call me in the morning when you get up. If I don't get a call I will assume you cancelled or postponed the trip."

When she turned to leave she knew that he had already fallen asleep. She couldn't help but wonder if he would be in any condition to be up and out by early morning. The smell of alcohol still lingered throughout the entire house. She had assumed this recent episode was over the loss of Caroline, wife, mother of his two boys. After all it was only just over a year since she had died. It would be a few days before she and the family would be privileged to learn the truth that he had managed to conceal so well.

Sophie packed up the boys, and Amber and she headed home. The phone rang at five-thirty the next morning. He and Ben were headed for Denver. He thanked her for all she did the night before and reminded her they would be home late Friday. He was feeling better with the exception of a major headache. Sophie would later learn from Markus his father had been drinking heavily the past few weeks, maybe an explanation for the reason that he had avoided her since Sugar Hill, but it was only one-half of this puzzle. Markus would also inform her that his Aunt Susan had become a frequent visitor. The family would soon discover that not only was Susan a visitor but it was possible that she and Alex were having an affair. There was much more to this story as everyone would soon discover, Sophie included, but she was pleased that Alex had found someone even though it was Luke's wife. She couldn't help but wonder why he was in so much pain that he had to numb himself with alcohol.

Now that a year had passed since loosing Viktor and Luke, she for some unknown reason, felt less guilty about her affair with Luke. At least she had felt something, and the misery that Luke brought with it was better then feeling nothing at all. These days she went through the motions that felt like she was prompted by some unknown force eliminating all joy and purpose into her solitary life. And to add to her despair she hadn't received any correspondence from Mikael. She wrote to Erik who also had not heard from his brother in a long time. One letter had been returned to him, and he told Sophie that he was convinced it had been opened before it had been returned. He was constantly aware when writing to Mikael to stir away from any controversy concerning the politics of the country that now had occupied Lithuania since the end of the war. His letters were not frequent, brief, so to ensure that Mikael had a better chance of receiving them.

Sophie had made a decision to fly to England in the near future mainly to see Erik and Sara and the new baby. It would be the closest to Mikael she could have, and Amber would get to see her cousins. And this time of year they could all visit the horse farm that Sara's brother had recently purchased, and he had extended an open invitation to her and Amber the next time they came to London.

CHAPTER 62

It was just shy of four years since Sophie had been to Lithuania and seen Mikael. He was standing there waiting outside of the rectory smiling as she and Amber walked over to him. He was about to meet his daughter for the very first time. Sophie's tears were ones of joy something that was missing from her life for a long time. She had forgotten how incredibly handsome he was, tall, broad shoulders, and his smile, the one that she noticed for the first time the day she sat next to him on the train to Trakai. So much had changed since that first meeting, and a few things remained the same. She wondered how difficult it would be this time when she would have to leave him once again.

"Sophie!" he called to her his voice barely audible." You are more beautiful then ever! It is so good to see you, to have you here with me. There were so many times when I believed that I would never see you again."

"And, may I ask, who is this pretty young lady there with you?"

"I'm Amber, your daughter." She responded without a second's hesitation.

"Yes, I guess you are. I'm so glad to meet you, and I am so very glad you are my daughter. May I have a hug?"

"I would like that very much. May I call you Papa? I had another father but he died. I always called him daddy."

"Papa sounds just fine."

As the evening wore on father and daughter spend time getting to know each other, one question at a time. One of the first questions Amber asked,

"Do you have other children?"

"No, I just have you."

"Like my mom. She just has one, me! But I have Madeline. We are very close, as close as sisters."

Sophie could see Mikael watching her and a nice warm feeling engulfed her. This was the first time in a very long time she had any reason to be happy again; and if it lasted for only a short while, she would embrace it. She and Mikael would have only three days together, the number of days that the tour was scheduled to be here in Vilnius. Sophie was pleasantly surprised at how accommodating and understanding the tour company had been to her after she explained the purpose of her trip. On the morning of the fourth day the tour was scheduled to leave for Riga, Latvia, the second country on the itinerary. It would be difficult and painful leaving Mikael, but there was no recourse. Sophie knew that Lithuania, now under control of the Kremlin, had a secret police called the KGB with a reputation of ferretting out those they believed to be enemies of the State. She was aware of the terror that they were capable of instilling in the citizens of their satellite countries, Lithuanian being one of them. But for now, for the next three days, she would try to erase the possibility of any interference on her visit here. The days would evaporate quickly, but she felt the energy that was needed to organize just the three days and the trials attached to her stay were definitely worth it. The thought of never seeing Mikael again would periodically flash through her mind making her forget the risks involved in coming here. She would take it one minute, one hour at a time.

"Where is your television, Papa?" the young girl asked.

"I'm afraid I do not have a television."

"You must buy one. Everyone has to have a T.V."

"Are you absolutely sure? Then I shall definitely have to get one! The next time you come to visit, I promise I will have one."

"Promise?"

"Yes, I promise."

"Papa, do you live in this house all by yourself?"

"Yes, I am afraid I do.

"Do you ever get lonesome?"

"Sometimes I do."

"Do you want to stay with us at the Cape for awhile?"

"There's nothing in the whole wide world, Amber, that would please me more, but I am afraid it's not going to be in the near future. You see, Lithuania is now part of the Soviet Union; and they have a rule that forbids the people living here to leave the country. Someday I predict that will all change, and then I shall go to America and spend a long time with my favorite daughter. Can you wait awhile longer?"

"I'll be sad if it's a real long time, but I will wait for you. Yes, of course, I will!'

In the year 1990 Lithuania gained her independence, the very first country to break away from the Soviet Union followed by the two other Baltic States, Latvia and Estonia. Rules were relaxed and the citizens were allowed to travel outside their countries for the very first time since the Red Army marched into the Baltic States just a short time after the end of the Second World War. Mikael, however, his health declining left his country only on one occasion. He attended his brother's Bar Mitzvah in the new State of Israel. Amber and Sophie, after 1990, made two trips back to the country where Sophie was born to visit with Mikael and to spend time with her family. Her sister, the only remaining member of her family, on one visit accompanied Sophie back to the Cape where the two sisters reveled in the fact they were together after so many years, a lifetime.

"Amber, it's time you head to bed. Tomorrow we are going to have a long, busy day ahead of us. So say good-night to Papa."

"Good-night, Amber, I'll see you in the morning. It's going to be a busy day."

"Good-night, Papa!" She liked the sound of her new word!

Sophie after tucking her daughter in bed returned to the parlor where Mikael was seated.

"Sophie, come here and sit with me. I poured a glass of vodka for you, the only gift we ever got from the Russians!"

"You've done a great job, she's perfect. You have to be so proud of her. She's very bright and speaks perfect Lithuanian!"

Sophie glanced toward him, and it felt like all the years dispersed before her.

"Sometimes I wonder how our lives would have turned out if I didn't return here. Trust me, I thought about it often. You know that I have never stopped loving you, missing you, especially since Justas was taken away. It has become a lonely life. The nights are the most difficult for me, and I really dread the holidays even the most religious ones. I'm convinced that God intended us to share our lives with someone we loved, not to live out our lives alone. But the dye had been cast for me. I never doubted I would not return to the Church after the war had ended. And at that time what gave me strength and some joy was to know that you would be happy in England. The decision to leave here was the best one you could have made. We have become nothing but slaves under the dictatorship of Stalin, a monster probably worse than Hitler. At least Hitler didn't enslave or annihilate the entire German population. Just think what we have been forced to endure under the rule of the two worse mass murderers in the history of all mankind. And it amazes me that the Lithuanians never lost their faith! I have tried to analyze it but I came to the conclusion that there was no common denominator, no one answer, for myself included. Perhaps it was the only thing these predators could not completely steal from us, the glue that held us together to face each day when we were stripped of everything else. It seemed for me it was buried in my soul for as long as I could remember. Hitler, now Stalin, and the misery they have inflicted on us I never once questioned God. I never lost my faith. Why? I don't have an answer for it!"

"You are very special, you know, Mikael. You have always been special to me. You are ingrained in my soul, my being. I sometimes feel so cheated that God had won, and I had to make a life without you all these years. And there is Amber who now has to leave you after such a short time; but I am grateful that we have these few days together even though they will slip by quickly."

"I have never stopped loving you, Sophie, not for a day. I guess I just loved God a little more. If only there was a way I could have had both of you, but you know it was impossible. Sometimes I wake up in the middle of the night knowing you were in my dreams, and the dreams are always in Traskai, with no doubt were the happiest years of my life. In the morning I can't always remember the dream, usually in just bits and pieces."

Sophie sat quietly listening to all he had said, she not saying a word. She moved closer to him, reached over and touched his face, fighting back her tears. He pulled her closer to him, found her lips, and kissed her. For the priest and the young widow all of time diminished, and they were transported back to the island in Trakai beside the lake where they found love each for the first time.

"Mikael, are you sure you want to do this? Will you be capable of dealing with this when I have to leave?"

He did not answer her. He reached over and took her in his arms, and two lonely souls joined together once again discovering a passion that once existed between them.

When it was time for her to leave this place once again, sadness embraced her. And once again she would have to deal with something which she had no control.

Just hours before she and Amber were preparing to depart planning to join the tour company, Sophie took Mikael aside.

"I left a jacket in the closet upstairs. In the lining there is a small amount of money for you. Because, as you know, there is a restriction on the amount of currency allowed into the country I had no choice but to come up with a plan to smuggle it in to you."

"Sophie, you know what the consequences are if they discovered the money! You would have been arrested! You do know that, don't you! We are totally under the control of these monsters. The KGB is everywhere and nothing makes them any happier then to put you on trial and send you off to one of their infamous labor camps."

"Yes, I am well aware; but I knew there was less risk coming with a tour, and it turns out I was right. Of course you will have to be careful how and where you spend this money. My guess is that the Black Market would impose less risk to you and could provide pretty much anything you want or would need, but use your own judgment. Promise me you will be careful, Mikael. There will be some danger attached no matter what; but again, be very careful."

"So my dear Sophie you really are a wealthy widow after all!"

His intention was to make her smile, which she did. She never mentioned the amount, $5,000. American dollars, a small fortune in a Communist country, but he would have to draft a plan before he could spend it.

"And I want to thank you. There is a food shortage here, and it probably will not get any better soon. There are many farms in our country, but we are one of the suppliers to much of Russia. That leaves a shortage for us. And rumors filter in that Russia recently, too, is experiencing a wide-spread problem the same as we have here but actually even worse if that makes any sense. Moscow alone has a population of millions of people, and that is the problem. The winter will definitely take its toll. It will be beyond expectations, very sad. Just a few years back, during the war almost as many Russians staved to death as were killed by the Germans. That alone is a reason that war doesn't make any sense. There are no winners if you stop and think about it."

And as Sophie had predicted the time melted away and now the dreaded hour was here when they would have to say good-by again not knowing if or when they would ever be together once again. She would never forget the look of pain on his face as they gathered their things together not knowing if they would ever see one another again. But with a formula for determination and assistance from Agnes, Amber and her mother would return here.

"The bus will be here shortly. This is the most difficult thing I have ever had to do. Pray for me, Mikael. Amber, we have to leave shortly so give Papa a hug and say good-by to him."

"Listen to me for a minute, Amber. Even though you will be far away remember you will always be here in my heart. I want you to know how much I love you and how very proud I am to have you for my daughter. And I need you to promise me that you will take care of your mother for me."

"And I love you too! We will come back to see you, real soon, won't we mommy?"

And tears filling her eyes she said good-by as she nodded her answer to her father.

"One more thing, Sophie, I want you to find someone to be happy with, to share the rest of your life with. You are entitled to enjoy your life. You deserve to find happiness. You have paid your dues. And I know you do not need my permission, but I am giving it to you. If I know you are fine, then I will be the same. I will be fine too. Enjoy whatever years God has planned for you. I demand it!

CHAPTER 63

"Sophie, hello, it's Ben. We just landed a few minutes ago. Alex, I am afraid, has had a little too much to drink on the plane so I'm planning on dropping him off at home. Would you mind if the boys slept over for one more night?"

"No, of course not. They are actually in their pajamas getting ready for bed."

"And I have another request. I need to talk to you. Will you still be up around ten or so, it could possibly be a little later. I'd rather not wait until morning if I'm not imposing on you."

Sophie was a little curious and wondered what was so urgent that it couldn't wait until the next day.

"Ben, please stop by. I rarely go to bed before mid-night. I will leave the porch light on for you. Just ring the bell when you get here. I should see you soon."

She had an idea that the subject they would discuss when Ben would arrive was the topic of her other step-son, Alex. It became obvious to her and to his family that something was definitely wrong. It was so much out of character for him to be intoxicated every day, seemingly wallowing in self-pity. But whatever it was he was not sharing with anyone. But that was about to change.

Sophie always got along well with the Paleckis brothers but the one that reminded her most of Luke was Alex. They bore a strong resemblance to their father, all handsome young men; but unlike their father who was quite reserved his two sons had a presence of self-confidence at times bordering on arrogance. Ben was more like Viktor she had always thought.

Several hours passed. Markus and Stefan and Amber had been asleep now for some time. Sophie had picked up a copy of a book that she had almost finished reading; but could not concentrate, so she went and poured herself a glass of Scotch and turned on the television.

Another hour passed, it was now just after eleven o'clock when she heard the door bell knowing it had to be Ben. She opened the door and invited him to the parlor asking him if he would like anything to eat or drink.

"No, thank you, I'm fine; but if its o.k. with you, I'll take a minute and call Jean to let her know I'm here. I didn't have time to call her from Boston."

"Take as long as you need."

"I will be right back!"

In a few minutes he returned starting to speak before he even sat down.

"This is difficult for me. I'm not even sure I have the story right. You know, of course, that Alex has not been acting like himself for awhile now. The family is concerned. We knew he had been through so much more than the rest of us and until a few days ago we all had been thinking loosing Caroline had precipitated his excess drinking. He is really in a bad state. Prudence has invited him and the boys for dinner on several occasions; and he accepts her invitation, but then he doesn't show up. He never gives an excuse or an explanation. He does come into the office most days, functions as normal even with the problem drinking evident. We are really concerned for Markus and Stefan, and this is where you come to the table, Sophie. I know, we all know, it a great deal to ask of you; but we need to know if you would consider letting the boys stay here for awhile, hopefully it would not be too long."

"You need not ask, Ben. You know I adore them and I, too, am concerned about them."

"Adam and I are going to try to convince him to get some help; and until he sobers up there is no way Stefan and Markus can stay in that house. And you are aware Caroline's mother recently had surgery so will be in no condition to oversee the boys as she has the last few months. Part of this puzzle as Prudence recently told me he is having an affair with Susan. Alex did confide in me just recently, and I had made the decision to tell my brothers. At that time he didn't tell me the entire story. One night while we were having dinner while staying in Colorado, the end of a long exhausting day, he started to drink heavily even for him these days. It seems Susan is pregnant. She wants to terminate the pregnancy, go to Sweden with her two boys, stay a few weeks and return when the school year starts. She has a cousin that lives on the outskirts of Stockholm, and Alex somehow remembers that her cousin is an obstetrician. It seems she is determined to follow through on her plan, and nothing he says will change her mind. He told her they could get married, keep the baby, and plan a life together. And of course there would not be any financial issues for either of them. He suggested they sell both houses, build a new one. She wanted no part of it she told him, no marriage, no baby, no house. She admitted she was still grieving over Luke and could not at his time cope with a pregnancy nor a new baby. You could only imagine the nightmare my brother was experiencing, and it became evident that he was not going to be able to fix it. And, Sophie, he also confided in me that he wished you could have been a part of his life this last year, but he was convinced it just didn't seem logical knowing you were married to his father. He turned to Susan, as he told me, because he couldn't endure the loneliness. He admitted to me that they were not in love, just filling a gap that they had inherited at the same time in their lives. I somehow understand the need."

"My God, Ben! I feel so very sad. It's almost like a curse has been put on this family! I don't know what to say right now. It's hard to comprehend all at once. What's the next chapter, have you figured it out yet?"

"No, I like you am in shock. It's the abortion part that sickens me. And just think about it for a minute, there is no guarantee that the mother either will survive the ordeal. Dear Lord what is she thinking of! I know Alex is more upset over the baby then he is about the possibly that Susan will decide to get on with her life and not want him in it. He as much told me. If I were in his situation I would feel exactly the same way as he does. Leave me if you wish, go to the moon if that's what makes you happy but don't kill our baby! And that's the latest chapter in this saga! I felt you had a right to know. I'll see Alex tomorrow. He can decide for himself if he wants to tell you his story. With the boys staying here I have a feeling you will be seeing more of him than you did all winter. So I will be on my way. I had a good feeling you wouldn't mind if Stefan and Markus camped out here for a few weeks; but I needed to ask you personally, not on the phone. I know they are in good hands and staying here will not be too big an adjustment for them. Adam and I are just a phone call away if you need or want anything. And Sophie, please do not hesitate if for any reason you decide at any point that you are not up to this!"

"I will be fine, Ben. Please don't worry. I am so glad I can do a small part. It really is for the boys. They certainly have had enough disruptions in their young lives. And, Ben, do be careful driving home. The fog is like pea soup tonight."

The letter arrived the middle week of September. Alex read it for a second time before placing it back in the envelope and putting it down. It took a few minutes before the shock wore off.

Dear Alex,

This is very difficult for me. I am aware of all the pain and suffering I have inflicted on you and the hurt I have caused you. I would reverse all of it if it was possible to do so, but it is way too late. I am sorry. I am truly sorry. I do not expect you to forgive me, but I am hoping you might understand.

I am in Sweden staying with my cousin. She is a doctor on the staff of Lying-in-Woman's Hospital and she was instrumental in my decision not to terminate my pregnancy. The baby is due on or around the first of the year, and I am looking forward to his or her arrival. I have had time to reflect on why initially I did not want to have this baby, and the only explanation was I still was grieving after loosing Luke. There were so many dark days for me I honestly did not know how I would survive the lost of him and in such a tragic and sudden manner. Then you came into my life, quite unexpectedly, and for a short time I started to feel alive and happy again. Then another hurdle came my way when I discovered that I was pregnant. I knew I would not be able to cope with it. I am not sure if you can digest all of this, but I am hoping you understand and maybe forgive me.

The boys are adjusting well and indicated they are in no hurry to leave and return to the Cape. I have made a decision to stay here until after the baby is born. My cousin's address is listed below along with the telephone number.

Love, Susan

Just days after receiving the letter from Susan almost everything shifted back to where it once had been before Susan had announced there would be no baby. The drinking bouts ceased almost immediately; and he again became the father his boys needed, the father that had been missing from their lives during the last several months. Alex wasn't sure if he would write or make a phone call, but once the dust had settled he planned to make contact with the woman carrying his child. It was the right thing to do. He couldn't help but wonder if it was already too late for any kind of a commitment, but the baby would never lack for anything he vowed.

On January 4 a baby girl which was named Bridget Anderson Paleckis arrived. Tending her birth were Dr. Erickson and waiting outside the delivery room was her father and her four brothers!

CHAPTER 64

Winter roared on to the Cape with roads disappearing under drifts of snow. Sand dunes that dotted the shoreline appeared like a strange, lunar setting. The ocean shifted the sand covered by ice and snow. Record amounts of snow accumulated here in the eastern section of the state. Mother Nature, usually sparing the Cape most winters, decided to change course.

Sleds were extricated from cellars, sheds, garages, and runners waxed in preparation for the hours they would be used sliding down the hills. The Paleckis children were in their glory enjoying the time spent on their sleds. And it brought back so many happy memories for Sophie when as children she and her sister would spend the entire day on their sleds disappointed when nightfall would sneak up, and they would have to go home.

In the weeks ahead Alex, Susan, and the children arrived on the Cape from Sweden. The boys were enrolled in a private school just a short distance away, a nanny and a housekeeper had been hired, and Susan devoted herself to being a mother. A mutual decision had been made to sell both homes, and they focused on planning the new house for their blended family. Blueprints were drafted, the lots selected, and construction scheduled for the beginning of April. The house would be located on the edge of the ocean with panoramic views of the Atlantic. The ocean extended to the horizon in all directions. The sound emitted from the constant movement and churning of the water provided a peaceful, tranquil feeling. It was extremely difficult to imagine living in a different place far away from here with no ocean to sooth ones soul.

The plans for the new house included a special suite for Susan's parents who had become frequent visitors. The boys would each have their own bedrooms, and a nursery for Bridget would include stenciled walls of old Swedish nursery rhymes. When Bridget would outgrow her crib it would be disassembled, and she would transfer to the built-in bed complete with sloping roofs and a peaked trim that was surrounded by two trolls. A painting on the ceiling would depict boys and girls in full

Swedish costume dancing around the flagpole, an event that happened every year in Sweden to celebrate the coming of spring. The start of a small doll collection would eventually fill the shelves that had been drafted for her bedroom.

No plans for marriage had been announced, but the subject had been discussed on several occasions.

The wind finally calmed down, the sun immerged preparing itself for the melting assignment ahead, and Sophie glancing out the window felt like the entire landscape was transformed into a giant mural covered in white a complete change from the summer seascape to become a foreign" snowscape" a gigantic canvas that only nature could assemble.

Standing before the window she saw a car inch up the driveway. At first glance she thought it was Adam. He made an effort to visit at least a few times a month; but it soon became clear to her, it was not Adam as she originally thought, but it was Alex. She had received the news that he had returned to the Cape last month, but she had no contact with him. There was always some trepidation on seeing him. He reminded her of Luke. They not only looked alike, but Sophie always felt that their mannerisms were similar.

Sophie greeted him at the door and invited him in.

"Hello! What brings you out in this weather, Alex?"

"As you probably already have been informed; Susan and I got home a few weeks back, and I have wanted to stop by to see you. The office was closed today for obvious reasons so I decided to come by. And I was fairly sure you would be here!"

"It's so good to see you. Let me interrupt you for a second. I just put a pot of coffee on; and we can go sit by the fire, and I'll pour each of us a cup. And I made blueberry muffins this morning. We can have them with the jam that Prudence sent over a short while back. Just give me a minute or so, and I'll be right back. Make yourself comfortable."

They settled beside the fireplace, Alex reported on the time spent living in Sweden, getting organized now as much as possible before construction on the new house would start, and finally touched on the subject for wanting to be here.

"I'm somewhat afraid, Sophie, what I am planning to tell you may be upsetting. I hope you will understand and agree with me you would want the information I'm going to give to you, that you truly would want to know. I've spent the last few months trying to reach the right decision. I would never want to cause you any unnecessary pain or stress. You do know that don't you!"

Sophie held her breath not knowing what to expect.

"I was designated to arrange for Luke's boat to be hauled out of the water, stored for the winter along with my boat and sort out any of Luke's belonging that he may have had on the boat. Susan had indicated that she was not up to the task. I kept procrastinating; but then of course I knew it shouldn't be postponed, the sorting out part. As you know I was drinking heavily, completely out of touch with reality so it became months before I finally found the strength needed to go through his things. I knew it would be difficult for me. What I found shocked me. There were really no words to describe my initial reaction to what I discovered that day. It concerned you and him and what he was planning. I gathered the notes I found and have placed them in this envelope. When you feel you want to read them; or just toss in the fire, has to be your decision. There was also a great deal of money hidden with the notes. I placed all of it in a fund for the boys. I didn't tell Susan any of it. It would serve no purpose. The only thing it would have accomplished would be to cause sadness to her life. And nothing would have changed."

"My initial reaction to his notes was to destroy them. As you read them; if you do decide, you may now understand the circumstances leading to your accident. And I'm not sitting in judgment. God knows that I'm last on the list to be judgmental! And before you ask the question, Sophie, I knew. It was not for a long time. When I finally figured it all out, I became enraged. There were so many lives that would be destroyed, especially my father who was so completely in love with you. You had replaced the loneliness with a new zest for living for him. The Luke part I did understand. It took a little time, but I do admit I got it. I don't blame you. I just wish I could get my brother back."

Sophie could not move. She could not speak. She looked over at Alex. For a split second she saw Luke sitting there. Even before she would read the notes, she knew the accident was not an accident at all and was orchestrated by Luke long before that dreadful night. Though it brought back so many painful memories, she felt it brought some closure for her. There would no longer be the uncertainty of what really happened on the night she almost died. Luke had not taken this to his grave after all!

After Alex left that evening, Sophie read the notes that Luke had written and left behind. She re-read them for a second time, tore then into small pieces, and placed them in the fire that was still blazing. For so many years to come she wondered why Luke had not destroyed the papers himself. Could it really have been an accident? Did he somewhere in the time after he drafted the papers decide not to carry out his plan! Maybe there would never be an answer to the puzzle, but one thing was certain. Luke was dead as a result of his obsession over his father's wife.

CHAPTER 65

The Last Days

Mikael would live long enough to see the dissolution of the Soviet Union in 1990. Lithuania was the first country to declare its independence followed shortly by the other two Baltic States, Latvia and Estonia. Church bells once again peeled across the country, and the synagogues, too, slowly started to hold services and citizens of all ages flocked to their houses of worship joyous in their new found freedom denied them for so long.

Over the years Sophie, Amber, and eventually his grandchildren, would make several visits to Vilnius; and later near the Baltic Sea where Mikael would spend his remaining years living in a retirement home for members of Catholic religious orders.

On his dresser he kept three framed pictures. One of Sophie taken at Trakai, one of Sophie with Amber, and one of Erik and him taken together on Erik's first trip to Vilnius. Tucked on the side of the mirror frame attached to the bureau was a photograph of Justas and him on the day of their ordination so many years ago.

God took Mikael home twelve years before he came for Erik. As he had requested, he was buried in St. Jude's Cemetery beside the mother who died giving birth to him. He always felt that someday there would be a reunion for them in Heaven. With the exception of one trip to Israel to attend his brother's bar mitzvah, he never left Lithuania. To the very day that he died he often thought of Sophie, beautiful, free-spirited Sophie. Next to his God, it was Sophie he loved.

Erik
The Last Days

Erik lived the last fifteen years of his life in Tel Aviv, Israel, a city situated on the Mediterranean Sea. He loved Israel's pioneering spirit which he always felt was contagious, so completely foreign to anything he had experienced in Europe.

He immigrated to his new country a year after Sara had died. His children remained in England. They, after several unsuccessful attempts to persuade him to remain in the country where he had lived for over half of his life, soon became adjusted to the fact that he was determined to move to Israel. After coming to terms with their father's plan they did eventually visit him on several occasions and soon learned the reason their father came here. And on the day he made his bar mitzvah at fifty-eight years old at the Western Wall with his family, Mikael, Sophie, joining in the celebration, he would always refer to that day as the most important day of his life

Now that he was retired he put all his efforts into studying Judaism and learning to read and write in Hebrew. On Saturday he would attend services, walking to the synagogue which was a short distance from his apartment and obeying one of the commandments given to Moses by God.

One of his sons and three of his grandchildren would eventually immigrate to Israel and convert to Judaism. They would spend the rest of their lives in the country that had adopted their grandfather.

Erik passed away twelve years after Mikael had died. He never returned to Germany. He was buried in the land of his ancestors. On his headstone was written the name, Erik Diamond Mueller.

Sophie
The Last Days

Sophie died in 2009. She lived to be eighty-nine years old. She would return to the country where she was born several times, the second to introduce Mikael to his daughter. Before Sara passed away and before Erik immigrated to Israel Sophie would visit them in London. She stood beside Mikael when Erik made his bar mitzvah in Jerusalem.

In the last years of her life she rarely ventured from the Cape. Amber and her family lived a short distance from her and provided the luxury of enjoying her grandchildren and eventually great-grandchildren, including a set of twin boys.

Sophie would spend hours looking out over the ocean from the front porch, boats filling the harbor in the warm weather, anticipating the change of seasons, and be tuned into all the wonderful and magical combinations that made the Cape such a special place.

Her wish in the end was to be cremated, her ashes divided, half to be buried with Viktor, the remaining to be scattered in the lake at Trakai in Lithuania. Some of her happiest and fondest memories were those during the war years with Mikael. Maybe now she and Mikael could enjoy what had been denied them in this world.